Unmasked

Renold Elstrack. Frederick, Count Palatine, and Princess Elizabeth, standing full-length. c.1613. Engraving 1864,1210.490 © The Trustees of the British Museum.

Unmasked

*Lost Music for the
1613 Palatine Wedding Masques*

ROSS W. DUFFIN

OXFORD
UNIVERSITY PRESS

Oxford University Press is a department of the University of Oxford.
It furthers the University's objective of excellence in research, scholarship,
and education by publishing worldwide. Oxford is a registered trade mark of
Oxford University Press in the UK and certain other countries.

Published in the United States of America by Oxford University Press
198 Madison Avenue, New York, NY 10016, United States of America.

© Oxford University Press 2025

All rights reserved. No part of this publication may be reproduced, stored in a retrieval system, transmitted, used for text and data mining, or used for training artificial intelligence, in any form or by any means, without the prior permission in writing of Oxford University Press, or as expressly permitted by law, by license or under terms agreed with the appropriate reprographics rights organization. Inquiries concerning reproduction outside the scope of the above should be sent to the Rights Department, Oxford University Press, at the address above.

You must not circulate this work in any other form
and you must impose this same condition on any acquirer

CIP data is on file at the Library of Congress
ISBN 978-0-19-777148-8

DOI: 10.1093/oso/9780197771488.001.0001

Printed by Integrated Books International, United States of America

The publisher gratefully acknowledges support from
the Margarita M. Hanson Fund of the America Musicological Society

Contents

Acknowledgments	vii
Preface	ix
Part I: The Campion, Chapman, and Beaumont Masques	1
Introduction to Part I	3
The Lords' Masque, by Thomas Campion	11
Introduction	12
Table of Musical Contents	26
Masque: Speeches, Description, and Music	27
The Memorable Masque of the Middle Temple and Lincoln's Inn, by George Chapman	60
Introduction	61
Table of Musical Contents	72
Masque: Speeches, Description, and Music	73
The Masque of the Inner Temple and Gray's Inn, by Francis Beaumont	113
Introduction	114
Table of Musical Contents	123
Masque: Speeches, Description, and Music	124
Conclusion	152
Index to Song Sources for Part I	153
First Line Index to Masque Songs and Models in Part I	155
Part II: The Masque of Truth	157
The Masque of Truth	159
Introduction	159
Origins	162
Lyrics	164
Authorship	168
Dances	170
Resources	172
Performance	175
Table of Musical Contents	178
Masque: Description and Music	179
Notes on the Music	208
Appendix 1: Reports on The Masque of Truth	217
Appendix 2: Related Images	221
Bibliography	225
Index	231

Acknowledgments

My thanks to Peter Holman, Peter Walls, and John Cunningham for lending their expertise and offering insightful comments on a draft of this work. For help with various details of Part I, my thanks go to Kerry McCarthy, Herbert W. Myers, John Romey, Peter Kirwan, David Crystal, and Nicoline Winkler. For Part II, my thanks, first of all, to David Norbrook, who first drew attention to *The Masque of Truth*, and gave it its name. Tom Bishop, Nadine Akkerman, and Alana Mailes all offered valuable comments. Further help has come from Anthony Parr, Anne Daye, Line Cottegnies, Marie-Claude Canova-Green, Eileen A. Reeves, Joanna Seidenstein, Susanne Meurer, Benjamin Ravier-Mazzocco, Jim Doelman, Alisa James, Rebecca Harris-Warrick, and Amanda Eubanks Winkler. Thanks also to two anonymous reviewers for Oxford University Press for their helpful critiques. Last, my wife Beverly Simmons contributed her usual indispensable mix of musical comment, copyediting, and cheerleading.

Preface

I began working on Jacobean masques more than three decades ago in preparation for a performance of Ben Jonson's *Oberon, the Faery Prince*, in 1993.[1] Since that time I have worked extensively on play-songs in English drama of the sixteenth and seventeenth centuries, and in so doing have acquired experience in reconstructing lost music to lyrics in staged productions. In fact, all but one of the lyrics from the three well-known masques for the 1613 Palatine wedding survive without definitive musical direction, and although Thomas Campion's *The Lords' Masque* was issued in a performance score by Andrew Sabol in 1993,[2] the other two masques have languished without significant musical attention since the modern publication of their texts in 1828.[3] Upon further investigation, I noted many things about Sabol's reconstruction that I would have done differently, and that has led to this musical reconstruction of all of the song lyrics in the three famous Palatine wedding masques (Part I of this volume). Besides recovering period music for the lyrics, which is obviously of paramount importance, I also propose that the "songs" are almost entirely "partsongs," with multiple singers participating, rather than solo songs. This fundamentally alters our conception of the music for these important historical events and, ultimately, enables reconstructed performances which have not been possible heretofore.

Meanwhile, I was intrigued to find a reference to *The Masque of Truth* (Part II of this volume), a "lost" masque for the 1613 Palatine wedding—extant but apparently never performed. In 2019, I had a chance to discuss it at the Folger Library with David Norbrook, who first brought it to light in 1978. An earlier project had led me to discover a connection between chorus lyrics in early Elizabethan tragedy and the emerging repertoire of metrical psalmody;[4] in looking more closely at *The Masque of Truth*, I was struck

---

[1] A video of that Case Western Reserve University production, with an introduction and documentary following, may be found at https://youtu.be/rs0Z3jbPAPc.
[2] *A Score for The Lords' Masque by Thomas Campion*, ed. Andrew J. Sabol (Hanover, NH, 1993).
[3] John Nichols, *Progresses, Processions, and Magnificent Festivities of King James the First*, vol. 2 (London, 1828), 554–86 and 591–600.
[4] Ross W. Duffin, "Hidden Music in Early Elizabethan Tragedy," *Early Theatre* 24 (2021), 11–61, https://doi.org/10.12745/et.24.1.4162.

by the similarity of its communal song lyrics to metrical psalms. Although such usage would be unique—even revolutionary—in a Jacobean masque, further investigation strengthened that connection and led me to attempt this reconstruction. Masques were dominated by dancing, however, so in order to make the masque performable today, proposing music for the dance insertions also seems important. Conveniently, a group of dances published in 1612 seem appropriate for that use. Finally, there are three sources with images related to elements in *The Masque of Truth* that conjure an impression of how it might have appeared to spectators if it had been performed. First, the masque revolves around the various continents of the globe (the eastern hemisphere, at least), so I have included maps from Abraham Ortelius, *Theatrum Orbis Terrarum* (1608), that might have come to mind as these various continents, countries, and rivers were named, and that may have inspired the masque's set and its machinery as originally conceived. Second, each of the three continents introduced in the masque is represented by a queen, and it happens that artwork in a seventeenth-century Central European manuscript, preserved at the Huntington Library, provides a colorful model for how they might have been depicted in the masque.[5] Last, representations of masquers and musicians from a contemporary book of festive processions resemble several of those described in *The Masque of Truth*.[6]

Thus, while they are both focused entirely on masques for the 1613 Palatine wedding, the two parts of this book are not congruent: the Campion, Chapman, and Beaumont masques are already well known, but extensive discussion of the evidence for newly reconstructing their individual song settings is necessary, and inserting their presumed dances among the speeches and descriptions is useful, bringing the primary musical events of

---

[5] Huntington Library, MS HM 1016. Nothing in the manuscript dates it precisely, but the German text identifies the region. The red and white striped flag and double-headed eagle standard on the left of the Europa image (Color Plate 4) may indicate an origin in Nuremberg, but this is not clear. That same image, at bottom right, seems to be signed "M J From:"—otherwise unknown. The images in the manuscript gain further relevance to the 1613 masques since the Inigo Jones watercolor of an American Indian torchbearer for the *Memorable Masque* (Color Plate 1) closely resembles the Huntington manuscript's painting of "Queen" America (Color Plate 10). Both costumes may be based on the "Indo Africano" in Cesare Vecellio's *De gli Habiti Antichi, et Moderni* (Venice, 1590), fol. 494r. The composition of the HM 1016 America painting, however, is clearly taken from Albrecht Dürer's engraving, *The Virgin and Child with a Monkey*, executed in Nuremberg ca.1498. For the Vecellio and Dürer images, see App. 2.1 and 2.2.

[6] Balthasar Küchler, *Repraesentatio der Fürstlichen Auffzug vnd Ritterspil* (Stuttgart, [1611]).

those major entertainments together for the first time and placing them in context.[7] *The Masque of Truth*, on the other hand, requires an exploration of how and why it might have been created, excluded from performance, and all but forgotten, as well as a complete reconstruction of its songs and dances, and a translation from its French original.

---

[7] Besides the sources noted above, all of the dances have been edited in Andrew Sabol, *Four Hundred Songs and Dances from the Stuart Masque* (Hanover, NH, 1982), nos. 78, 90–2, 263–8.

PART I
THE CAMPION, CHAPMAN, AND BEAUMONT MASQUES

PART 2

Introduction to Part I

When the sixteen-year-old Princess Elizabeth, only daughter of King James I of Great Britain, married the sixteen-year-old Frederick, Count Palatine, on Valentine's Day 1613, there was much rejoicing.[1] In part, the festivities were a welcome release after the unexpected death in November of her older brother, Prince Henry, heir to the throne, and the period of national mourning that ensued. The wedding was lavishly celebrated with banquets, tournaments, a mock sea battle, fireworks, and most notably, with masques—extravagant entertainments with elaborate sets, lavish costumes, much dancing, and songs.[2] Three masques have long been associated with the wedding, *The Lords' Masque*, by Thomas Campion, *The Memorable Masque of the Middle Temple and Lincoln's Inn*, by George Chapman, and *The Masque of the Inner Temple and Gray's Inn*, by Francis Beaumont. Campion's masque was presented at the Whitehall Banqueting House on the evening of the wedding day, a Sunday;[3] Chapman's took place in the Hall of the same Palace on the Monday evening following; Beaumont's was scheduled for Tuesday but was put off until Saturday at the request of King James.[4] The three masques were each printed in quarto in 1613,[5] with descriptions of the action, dialogue,

---

[1] Elizabeth Stuart is not so well known today, although a recent major biography has begun to raise her profile. See Nadine Akkerman, *Elizabeth Stuart, Queen of Hearts* (Oxford, 2022), https://doi.org/10.1093/oso/9780199668304.001.0001.

[2] Inter alia, on Stuart masque sets and costumes, see Stephen Orgel and Roy Strong, *Inigo Jones: The Theatre of the Stuart Court*, vol. 1 (Berkeley, 1973), and Barbara Ravelhofer, "Visual Effects in the Wedding Masques of 1613," in *Churfürstlicher Hochzeitlicher Heimführungs Triumph: Inszenierung und Wirkung der Hochzeit Kurfürst Friedrichs V. mit Elisabeth Stuart (1613)*, ed. Nichola Hayton, Hanns Hubach, and Marco Neumaier (Ubstadt-Weiher, 2020), 277–90; on music, see Peter Walls, *Music in the English Courtly Masque, 1604–1640* (Oxford, 1996); on dance, see Barbara Ravelhofer, *The Early Stuart Masque: Dance, Costume, and Music* (Oxford, 2006).

[3] This was not the existing Banqueting House designed by Inigo Jones in 1619, but its wooden predecessor, built in 1607.

[4] Though it was apparently never performed, a description survives of a fourth wedding masque, in French, dubbed *The Masque of Truth*. See Part II of this volume.

[5] *A Relation of the late Royal Entertainment.... Whereunto is annexed the Description, Speeches, and Songs of the Lords Maske* (1613; STC: 4545); *The Memorable Maske of the two Honorable Houses or Inns of Court; the Middle Temple, and Lyncolns Inne* (1613; STC: 4981); *The Masque of the Inner Temple and Grayes Inne* (1613; STC: 1663 and 1664). Additionally, Chapman's masque was issued a second time, probably in 1614 (STC: 4982), without substantial variants, although the title was given as *The Memorable Masque*, used here for consistency with the other masques. Again "for George Norton," the printer of this second quarto was "F. K."—presumably Felix Kingston (or Kyngston)—instead of G[eorge] Eld, who had printed the first quarto. STC, which appears often in the footnotes,

indications for dancing, and lyrics for songs, and they have long been known in modern times since they were printed in 1828.[6]

We know a fair amount about the performances because of accounts for expenditures at court, for *The Lords' Masque*, and at the Inns of Court for *The Memorable Masque*, in addition to costume and set designs preserved in drawings by Inigo Jones.[7] Unfortunately, we have less information about the music used. Some pieces can be identified from titles in manuscript and printed collections, most notably the dances of the Inns of Court, in British Library, Add. MSS 10444/5 (hereafter BL 10444/5),[8] and concordances in the collections of five-part dances in the expatriate English violinist William Brade's *Newe Ausserlesene liebliche Branden, Intraden, Mascharaden, Balletten*, published in Hamburg in 1617,[9] and in *Courtly Masquing Ayres* (1621) by the recorder and cornetto player John Adson who, in 1613, had recently returned from France.[10] From what we know of musical resources for masque performances, it seems likely that these five-part scores represent something close to the original ensemble versions for the 1613 masques.[11] From those sources, we have candidates for the three main dances for each masque, as well as a number of "antimasque" dances that can tentatively be connected to these events. The main masque dances, or "measures,"[12] would

is the abbreviation of "Short Title Catalogue," a numbering of all printed materials in England up to 1640. Most of the items in the catalogue are available on the Early English Books Online (EEBO) website that contains facsimiles of these materials.

[6] John Nichols, *Progresses, Processions, and Magnificent Festivities of King James the First*, vol. 2 (London, 1828), 554–86 and 591–600.

[7] For Jones's designs for those two masques, see Orgel and Strong, *Inigo Jones*, 240–63.

[8] These are treble and bass partbooks containing dances for the Inns of Court, with the treble partbook apparently copied ca.1620 by Sir Nicolas L'Estrange. See Pamela Willetts, "Sir Nicholas Le Strange's Collection of Masque Music," *British Museum Quarterly* 29 (1965), 79–81, https://doi.org/10.2307/4422895; and Peter Walls, *Music in the English Courtly Masque, 1604–1640* (Oxford, 1996), 29–30.

[9] On Brade's career as a violinist in Germany, see Arne Spohr, "From 'Seiten-Kunst' to 'Fursten Gunst': The Careers of the Anglo-German Musicians William, Christian, and Steffen Brade in the Context of the Thirty Years War," *Journal of Seventeenth-Century Music* 26, no. 1 (2020), par. 2.1–10, https://sscm-jscm.org/jscm-issues/volume-26-no-1/spohr-anglo-german-musicians-brade/.

[10] STC: 153: *Courtly Masquing Ayres, Composed to 5. and 6. Parts, for Violins, Consorts, and Cornets*. On Adson, see Andrew Ashbee and David Lasocki, eds., *A Biographical Dictionary of English Court Musicians, 1485–1714* (Aldershot, 1998), vol. 2, 7–10.

[11] Peter Walls, *Music in the English Courtly Masque*; and Peter Holman, *Four and Twenty Fiddlers: The Violin at the English Court, 1540–1690* (Oxford, 1993).

[12] These are sometimes referred to as Entry, Main, and Exit dances, although that is modern terminology. The number of such dances could vary, furthermore, though all three of these 1613 masques have three numbered masque dances in BL 10444/5. Peter Walls traces the emerging use of "entry" to the influence of the "entrée" in the French *ballet de cour*. See Walls, *Music in the English Courtly Masque*, 231. See also John M. Ward, "Newly Devis'd Measures for Jacobean Masques," *Acta Musicologica* 60 (1988), 111–42, https://doi.org/10.2307/932788.

have been danced by courtiers or gentlemen in the cast of the masque, while the antimasque dances, such as the *Baboons Dance* from Chapman's masque, would normally be danced by professionals.[13] All of these extant pieces were collected by Andrew Sabol in his monumental *Four Hundred Songs and Dances from the Stuart Masque.*[14]

Unfortunately, the situation for the songs is far less favorable than for the dances. In the three masques combined, Sabol is able to point to only one song specifically preserved and labeled as used in one of the masques: Campion's *Wooe her and win her*. It was printed, not in the quarto for *The Lords' Masque*, but as an afterthought in the 1614 quarto of the so-called *Somerset Masque* (also called the *Squires' Masque*) for the wedding of the Earl of Somerset and Frances Howard: "A Song, made by Th. Campion, and sung in the Lords Maske at the Count Palatine's Marriage, we haue here added, to fill vp these emptie Pages."[15] As Frederick Sternfeld wrote of the other songs in the masque: "Unhappily, whatever strains were employed in the *Lord's* [sic] *Maske* to charm and heal, to symbolize the lofty power of kingship, are lost to posterity."[16] That may be overstated, as we shall see.

The survival of the fifth song in *The Lords' Masque* is definitive, but the music to the first song has also been identified, not because of any label, but because of the close similarity of its lyric to *Come away, arm'd with loues*

---

[13] In addition to dances as part of the show, each masque also had a section of "revels," where the masquers broke character and took members of the audience to the floor for social dances, like galliards, corantos, and branles. These revels were an essential part of the Jacobean masque, and could last quite a long time before the masquers were recalled to their roles, and the masque was brought to a close.

[14] (Hanover, NH, 1982). In assembling literally hundreds of musical items that are (or seem to be) connected to the Jacobean masque, this is a valuable repository, although the connections between the music and various masques are often more speculative than readers are led to believe.

[15] Thomas Campion, *The Description of a Maske Presented . . . At the Mariage of the Right Honorable the Earle of Somerset and the Right Noble, the Lady Frances Howard* (1614; STC: 4539), sigs. D1v–D2r. See Frederick W. Sternfeld, "A Song for Campion's Lord's Masque," *Journal of the Warburg and Courtauld Institutes* 20 (1957), 373–35, https://doi.org/10.2307/750790. For a discussion of the songs in *The Lords' Masque* among Campion's other masques, see Christopher R. Wilson, "Some Musico-Poetic Aspects of Campion's Masques," in *The Well Enchanting Skill: Music, Poetry and Drama in the Culture of the Renaissance: Essays in Honour of F. W. Sternfeld*, ed. John Caldwell, Edward Olleson, and Susan Wollenberg (Oxford, 1990), 91–105, at 100–103. Sources in the footnotes of this book that begin with "sig." or "sigs." are references to "signatures" within the print, typically used to specify location where there are no page or folio numbers.

[16] See Sternfeld, "A Song for Campion's Lord's Masque," 374–35.

delights from Campion's own *Second Booke of Ayres*.[17] Here are the first stanzas of each lyric in parallel:

Lords' Masque	Campion: *Second Booke of Ayres* (1613)
Come away; bring thy golden theft,	Come away, arm'd with loues delights,
Bring bright *Prometheus* all thy lights,	Thy sprightfull graces bring with thee,
Thy fires from Heau'n bereft	When loue and longing sights,
Shew now to humane sights.	They must the sticklers be.
Come quickly come; thy stars to our stars straight present,	Come quickly, come the promis'd houre is wel-nye spent,
For pleasure being too much defer'd, loseth her best content,	And pleasure being too much deferr'd looseth her best content.
What fair dames wish, should swift as their own thoughts appeare,	
To louing & to longing harts euery houre seemes a yeare.	

There is no doubt that the music to the lutesong was used for the lyric in the masque as well: Both songs begin with "Come away"; "lights" and "sights" occur as rhymes in the first quatrains; the fifth lines begin "Come quickly come"; and the sixth line—the final line of the lutesong lyric's stanza—is almost identical in the two versions. They were both printed in 1613, but there is nothing to suggest which came first—ayre or masque song. Some significant things can be noted, however. One song is definitely a *contrafactum* of the other: Campion wrote a song, then repurposed it, either taking the masque song and making a generalized version for his lutesong collection, or taking his existing lutesong, and repurposing it for the masque.

Creating masque songs as *contrafacta* of existing songs makes perfect sense. Masques almost never have multiple performances,[18] so composing

---

[17] Printed as part of *Two Bookes of Ayres* (1613; STC: 4547), no. 17, sig. M1v. The first person to remark on the similarity seems to be Percival Vivian, who noted the correspondence of ll. 5–6 in his edition, *Poetical Works, in English, of Thomas Campion* (London, 1907), 268. The evident musical connection seems first to have been pointed out in *The Works of Thomas Campion*, ed. Walter R. Davis (London, 1969), 233. Christopher Wilson also refers to these two poems in his study of Campion's poetry, *Words and Notes Coupled Lovingly Together: Thomas Campion, a Critical Study* (New York, 1989), 359–60.

[18] On one masque from the period that made the rounds of aristocratic houses, see James Knowles, "The 'Running Masque' Recovered: A Masque for the Marquess of Buckingham (c.1619–20)," *English Manuscript Studies* 8 (2000), 79–135.

a new song that will be used for only a single performance could be seen as wasted effort. In fact, *Come away; bring thy golden theft* is not the only instance of this process for masques in general and for Campion in particular. Campion's song *Moue now with measurd sound* from *Lord Hay's Masque* of 1607,[19] reappears in his 1613 song collection as *The peacefull westerne winde*.[20] In that case, the 1613 lutesong lyric has an eight-line cross-rhymed stanza of 33334343, repeating the music for the trimeter couplet, while the 1607 masque song has a twelve-line stanza where both trimeter couplet and ballad-meter quatrain sections of the music are repeated. A later example occurs with Nicholas Lanier's song, *Bring away this sacred Tree*, printed in Campion's *Somerset Masque* quarto of 1614,[21] which appears in three later song manuscripts with the lyric *Weep no more my wearied eyes* (in one of those wrongly attributed to Henry Lawes).[22]

In the process of modifying and reusing his own material, Campion showed a certain amount of flexibility. The lutesong setting, for example, repeats the opening two words, "Come away," even though doing so breaks the metrical pattern of the lyric, and such repetition would have been required in performance of the masque song as well. Similarly, both lyrics begin with a cross-rhymed quatrain of tetrameters and trimeters (abab 4433), followed by a rhyming couplet with lines of greater length (cc 67). The rarity of this versification confirms that one song is a *contrafactum* of the other, but the masque song has a second 67 couplet to complete the stanza, whereas the lutesong does not. Even with the same music used for both songs, however, there are obvious variants from the masque quarto's text to the text set to music in the song book, and differences in form, with the repetition of musical strains as necessary to accommodate the different lyrics.

This process of flexible contrafaction, combined with a close reading of payment records, makes it possible to plausibly reconstruct all of the songs in Campion's *Lords' Masque*, and by extension, the songs in the other Palatine wedding masques. I am not the first to attempt this. Andrew J. Sabol, whose

---

[19] This was printed in the quarto for the masque, *The Discription of a Maske* (1607; STC: 4538), sigs. D3v–D4r.
[20] *The Second Booke of Ayres* (1613; STC: 4547), no. 12, sig. L1r
[21] Sigs. C1v–C2r.
[22] New York Public Library, MS Drexel 4257, no. 168 (attr. H. L.), and Cambridge, Fitzwilliam Museum, Mu MS 782, fol. 99r. An ornamented version of the cantus part is also found in Dublin, Trinity College, MS 412 (Quintus partbook of the Wode Psalter), fols. 58r–58v.

Four Hundred Songs and Dances from the Stuart Masque is a standard reference for the field, later published a complete performance score of *The Lords' Masque*.[23] It is an ambitious reconstruction, with 129 musical items, including dances and incidental music, as well as contrafact versions of the songs. So far as I am aware, no comparable performance edition has been published of the other two wedding masques. In a 2011 performance of *The Memorable Masque* at the Shakespeare Institute, the song lyrics were spoken, not sung.[24]

Everyone involved in producing early modern theater—scholars, actors, choreographers, designers, directors—is aware that the text of any masque production is only a ghost of what was actually seen onstage, although the modern impulse to have it come alive—to reenact—is what led the Shakespeare Institute to mount a production in the first place. As Anna Pakes says concerning historical dance reconstruction, however, "invention is part and parcel of reconstruction because the archive is 'gappy.'"[25] The archive is especially "gappy" for music, which is why some kind of invention is always necessary for performance, whether by composing music anew or repurposing music from the period. Being unwilling or unable to "invent" the music required means leaving the song lyrics as spoken poetry, which is not a convincing way to reenact a genre that depends so heavily on music for its effect.

Of course, however much we lament the loss of musical settings for these masque songs, making a historical reconstruction—repurposing music from the period—is fraught with potential peril,[26] leaving an editor open to accusations of "make believe" or, at least, "wishful thinking." As Peter Holman says, "Songs have to be found that fit the metre and phrase structure of the missing songs, choruses have to be composed (none survive for any Jacobean

---

[23] Andrew J. Sabol, ed., *A Score for The Lords' Masque by Thomas Campion* (Hanover, NH, 1993). Sabol makes the astonishing claim (p. 22) that twenty-five of his reconstruction choices are "incontestable." In addition to Sabol's reconstruction, some differently reconstructed songs from *The Lords' Masque* appear on the CD, *Fly Cheerful Voices: Die Hochzeit Friedrich V und Elizabeth Stuart*, Ensemble i Ciarlatani (Christophorus Chr 77214, 1998). These selections, reconstructed by Klaus Winkler, were used as part of a staged performance of the three wedding masques combined, *Die Hochzeit zwischen Rhein und Themse*, at Amberg in 2003.

[24] See Peter Kirwan's blog review: https://blogs.warwick.ac.uk/pkirwan/entry/the_memorable_masque/.

[25] Anna Pakes, "Reenactment, Dance Identity, and Historical Fictions," in *The Oxford Handbook of Dance and Reenactment*, ed. Mark Franko (Oxford, 2017), 79–100, at 88.

[26] On the complications of using historical music in new productions of early modern plays, see Amanda Eubanks Winkler, "A Tale of *Twelfth Night*: Music, Performance, and the Pursuit of Authenticity," *Shakespeare Bulletin* 36 (2018), 251–70, http://doi.org/10.1353/shb.2018.0023.

court masque)." He notes also the necessity to "choose music that comes from the right time and place,"[27] while avoiding, as Peter Walls admonishes, choices that are based entirely on "making connections (which might charitably be called circumstantial)."[28] Those are the challenges for anyone making a reconstruction, and I have done my best to answer those caveats here, using songs that match the versification of the masque lyrics in a demonstrable way, and that come from collections that are somehow connected to the masque or its musical personnel.

Indeed, only one of Sabol's contrafact choices overlaps what I propose here, while his others are problematic, in my opinion. Three decades on, a reassessment of those contrafact choices seems justified, and I believe my work in period lyrics and music during the intervening time has prepared me to attempt it for *The Lords' Masque,* and the other two Palatine wedding masques as well.[29] All three masques are given in full below, along with plausible dances,[30] and the new song reconstructions. The songs are unquestionably the most important part of these new masque editions. As Peter Walls says:

> On the whole, masque dances are so weakly differentiated from each other that it is difficult to argue for any profound dramatic significance in being able to link a particular dance to a specific production. It is for this reason that, in attempting a musical reconstruction of a masque, priority must be given to the vocal music. It hardly matters which set of dances are chosen.[31]

New song reconstructions based on period song models are, thus, the heart of this book. At the same time, it is useful to have all of these musical pieces assembled in one place. The measures and antimasque dances are charming,

---

[27] Peter Holman, review of Sabol's *A Score for The Lords' Masque, Musical Times* 135 (1994), 765, https://doi.org/10.2307/1003356.

[28] Peter Walls, review of Sabol's *A Score for The Lords' Masque, Music & Letters* 76 (1995), 467–70, at 467, http://www.jstor.org/stable/737179.

[29] My work in this area began with reconstructing the songs for a 1993 production of Ben Jonson's masque *Oberon, the Faery Prince* (1611) at Case Western Reserve University in Cleveland, still available on video at https://youtu.be/rs0Z3jbPAPc. Projects in print include *Shakespeare's Songbook* (New York, 2004), *Some Other Note: The Lost Songs of English Renaissance Comedy* (Oxford, 2018), and numerous articles and editions.

[30] Not included here are the social dances, the "Revels," where the gentlemen masquers took the ladies in the audience out on the floor to dance. Potential branles, galliards, corantos, etc. for use in the revels are superabundant, and it is difficult or impossible to match any of them to particular masques.

[31] Walls, review of *A Score*, 467.

furthermore, in spite of their "remarkable sameness of style" (to use John Ward's characterization),[32] and help to give a fuller picture of the masques as entertainments.

The scoring of the new song settings for four voices is not an arbitrary choice. We do not always know how many voices sang these lyrics, or in what ranges, but since the vast majority of the lyrics labeled "Song" in these masques were sung by multiple voices, and since some of the models survive with four voices in their printed sources, it seems worth standardizing arrangements with that number. Pieces with sections for solo voice give the three lower voices as consort-song accompaniments for melodic instruments, using one or more of the three court instrumental ensembles that we know from payment records took part in masque performances: lutes, violins, and winds. For convenience, the songs have also been adapted to work entirely by themselves, without the accompaniment of lute or other chordal instruments.[33] Voices added editorially can be distinguished throughout by reduced size in the score. The masque text follows the sources, including original spelling and punctuation.[34] Obscure words are glossed in footnotes.

---

[32] Ward, "Newly Devis'd Measures," 121.
[33] In the original performances, the songs certainly were accompanied by lutes and possibly other instruments. The editorial purpose here is to make arrangements that are workable even when no such instruments are available, or when only melodic instruments accompany the singing. In rare instances, therefore, even in extant vocal parts, notes have been adjusted to fill out the harmony.
[34] Spelling exceptions include "Joue" and "Juno" for "Ioue" and "Iuno." Instances of "loue" near "Ioue" made the former change advisable.

The Lords' Masque

Thomas Campion

Plate 1.1 Thomas Campion, *The Lords' Masque*, Title Page (1613) Courtesy of the Huntington Library.

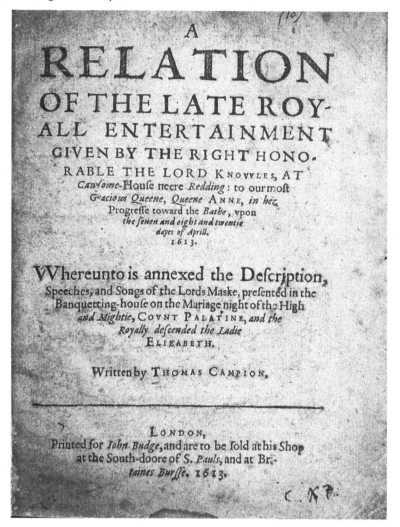

Introduction

We know from payment records that Thomas Campion was paid more than anyone else for *The Lords' Masque*.[1] He received £66 13s 4d, which looks like a completely arbitrary amount but turns out to be exactly two-thirds of £100. Inigo Jones received £50 for his set and costume designs, and various dancing masters received the next highest amounts: Jerome Herne (£40), Jacques Bochan (£40), Nicolas Confesse (£30), and Thomas Giles, the only Briton (£30).[2] Among other things, this combined expense for the dancing masters—£140—demonstrates how important dance was in these productions. Musicians were paid less, but there were a lot of them: More than fifty instrumentalists were paid about £1 each, including "10 of the Kinges violins," perhaps supporting the idea that two five-part violin bands participated, as suggested by Campion's description of the opening of the masque, with "the sound of a double consort, exprest by seuerall instruments, plac't on either side of the roome."[3] Also of musical interest are payments to Robert Johnson, lutenist and composer (£10), Thomas Lupo, violinist and composer (£10), and John Coprario, viol player and composer (£20).

Some of these same people were listed in accounts for Ben Jonson's masque, *Love Freed from Ignorance and Folly* (1611), with more information about their roles: Confesse was paid "for teaching all the dances"; Bochan "for teaching the ladies the footing of 2 dances"; Johnson "for setting the songes to the lutes"; and Lupo "for setting the dances to the violins."[4] In that case also, Alfonso Ferrabosco Jr. was paid "for making the songes," an expression that is used below for *The Memorable Masque*.[5] Coprario was a household musician for Prince Henry, and then for Prince Charles, and had an association with Campion because he contributed three songs to Campion's *Somerset Masque*

---

[1] Kew, National Archives, E.403/2372, fol. 183v. I have used the accounts in Andrew Ashbee, *Records of English Court Music*, vol. 4, 1603–25 (Snodland, 1991), 234, which vary in some details from those printed in Orgel and Strong. See also I. A. Shapiro's edition of *The Lords' Masque* in *A Book of Masques*, ed. Gerald Eades Bentley (Cambridge, 1967), 97–123.

[2] Evidence suggests that Herne specialized in choreographing the comic antimasques, Bochan the ladies' dances, Confesse the dances of boys and youths, and Giles the gentlemen's measures. See Anne Daye, "'Graced with Measures': Dance as an International Language in the Masques of 1613," in *The Palatine Wedding of 1613: Protestant Alliance and Court Festival*, ed. Sara Smart and Mara R. Wade (Wiesbaden, 2013), 289–318, at 292.

[3] Sig. C1r. "Double consort" could also refer to dual ensembles of strings, winds, or lutes.

[4] Kew, National Archives, E407/57/1.

[5] This term remains slightly ambiguous. In the 1614 *Somerset Masque* quarto, for example, one song was "made and exprest by Mr. Nicholas Laneir," one was "made by Th. Campion," and a set of three songs were "composed by Mr. Coprario."

at the end of 1613.[6] He also accompanied the wedding couple to Heidelberg after the wedding,[7] underscoring his prominence at court at precisely this time. Sabol attributes the three masque dances in *The Lords' Masque* to Coprario,[8] which is possible, but there is no evidence from the musical sources, nor from the masque itself, that they are his, except the higher fee he received.

We can be more confident that the original songs were composed by Campion, since he was paid such an enormous fee and because no one else is listed as contributing to the vocal settings, either composing or arranging, though it is possible that Johnson or Lupo (or Coprario) arranged the songs as a way of earning their fee. Campion was notoriously lax about publishing his own songs, but it is striking that *Come away; bring thy golden theft* is a contrafact of a song from one of Campion's song collections from 1613, the same year as the masque. Between 1613 and 1617, moreover, Campion published four books of songs in two prints,[9] in addition to *A Description of a Maske* (1614) which contains the one extant song setting, and in spite of the complicated versifications of some of the lyrics in *The Lords' Masque*, seven of its ten songs can plausibly be set to music from those books, and an eighth from an earlier Campion book. This versification analysis is at odds with the one made by Andrew Sabol, who concluded that seven of the masque lyrics "are cast in metrical patterns for which there are no complements among the remaining dozens of settings in the Campion canon."[10]

Only two lyrics in this new reconstruction are set to models by a different composer (Robert Jones in both instances), but their versification does not match any extant song by Campion, from any of his song books. Still, the effect of using so many Campion songs from 1613–17 as models is to create an approximate unity of musical style, appropriate to the time and the event. We are, indeed, fortunate, to have so many musical options, and the fact that one of the masque songs is definitely related to a song from one of these

---

[6] Campion, *The Description of a Maske*, sigs. C2v–D1r. *Somerset Masque* is the modern epithet for the masque described in this print.

[7] See Thurston Dart, "Two English Musicians at Heidelberg in 1613," *Musical Times* 111 (1970), 29, 31–32, https://doi.org/10.2307/952296. Just a few months later, despite this foreign journey, Coprario contributed three songs to Campion's masque for the Earl of Somerset's wedding. During his 1613 trip, Coprario is possibly responsible for carrying the Palatine wedding masque dances to Germany, where Brade gathered and printed them four years later, though with alternative titles that suggest ongoing use and re-use of the music. On Coprario as a possible music courier, see Arne Spohr, "English Masque Dances as Tournament Music?," in *The Palatine Wedding of 1613*, 546–65, at 552–53.

[8] Sabol, *Four Hundred Songs and Dances*, Nos. 73–5, 257–60.

[9] Campion, *Two Bockes of Ayres* (1613; STC 4547) for Books 1 and 2; and *The Third and Fourth Booke of Ayres* (1617; STC: 4548).

[10] Sabol, *A Score for The Lords' Masque*, 16.

songbook collections, leads to the possibility, if not probability, that other *contrafacta* exist there too, even if their text connections are not so obvious as for the first song.[11]

Numerous opportunities exist for incidental music in all of these masques, whether brief flourishes or something more substantial, and not all of them will be given here, especially in the absence of evidence as to the original music. Music is definitely needed at the beginning of *The Lords' Masque*, however, where the opening scene was "discovered" and Orpheus entered "vpon the sound of a double consort, exprest by seuerall instruments, plac't on either side of the roome." Whatever it was, Orpheus calls for it to sound again, and the consorts on both sides comply while gently calling forth Mania from her cave. The music needs to be noble, since Orpheus refers to it as "*Phoebus* sounds," but it must also be capable of being performed gently. It also needs to be brief since it is played and repeated soon afterward. One conjectural piece that fits those criteria is *The second [of my Lord of Essex]* (no. 1.1), a masque dance in BL 10444/5 (no. 94), which also appears in John Adson's 1621 *Courtly Masquing Ayres* (no. 6).[12] Adson was a wind player, and that supports a performance with combined forces of strings and winds as part of the "double consort," especially because Mania afterward describes the sound as a "powerfull noise."

The next musical item is an antimasque dance (no. 1.2), performed by twelve "Frantickes": a "madde measure, fitted to a loud phantasticke tune," which then softens toward the end. No dance survives labeled as "First antimasque of the Lords" or anything like that, but one dance in BL 10444/5 (no. 72), is entitled *The Furies*, and it has lots of stopping and starting, with fermatas that would have allowed for fanciful improvisation of both music and movement. Unlike most of the BL 10444/5 dances from these masques, this one does not survive in either Brade's 1617 collection nor Adson's 1621 collection, so its treble and bass parts have been augmented with three editorial inner parts to make up the expected complement of five.[13]

The first song is *Come away; bring thy golden theft* (no. 1.3), set to *Come away, arm'd with loues delights*, from Campion's *Second Booke of Ayres*. As printed there, the song has three texted voices, Cantus, Altus, and Bassus,

---

[11] See also above for a discussion of *Moue now with measurd sound*, a 1607 Campion masque song with a *contrafactum* in one of his 1613 songbooks.

[12] Like some other dances in Adson's collection, this one does not indicate a repeat of the final section, though it is repeated in BL 10444/5.

[13] It should be noted that the first bass note of *The Furies* in BL 10444/5 has been emended from E-flat to G, to match bar 5; the treble notes in bar 12 have been reversed to avoid parallel fifths with the bass; and the bass rhythms in bars 25–26 have been changed to avoid several dissonances with the treble.

along with a lute part which has been omitted here. I have also added a fourth vocal part, nominally a Tenor, but because of the ranges of the existing parts, placed between the Cantus and Altus.

These Campion songs are often performed today as solo ayres, with one voice accompanied by lute, and that reflects Campion's own rubric: "These Ayres were for the most part framed at first for one voyce with the Lute or Violl, but vpon occasion, they haue since beene filled with more parts, which who so please may vse, who like not may leaue."[14] Sometimes today called "partsongs,"[15] these lutesongs with *si placet* parts, still self-advertised as "songs," are scattered throughout the lutesong repertoire, beginning with John Dowland's pioneering *First Booke of Songes or Ayres*, in 1597. In this case, Orpheus introduces *Come away; bring thy golden theft* in the masque by referring to multiple voices: "Flie cheerfull voices, through the ayre," which itself might be taken as punning on the word "ayre" as a song. It is, indeed, labeled "A Song," but it is a song for multiple voices, not a solo song.

The second song, *Aduance your Chorall motions now* (no. 1.4), is described in the text as a "chorall dance." It consists of three eight-line stanzas of cross-rhymed ballad meter, a versification that it shares with the one extant song from the masque, *Wooe her and win her*. In this case, the best choice for a model seems to be *Where shee her sacred bowre adornes*, from Campion's *Second Booke of Ayres*.[16] This is the same model chosen by Andrew Sabol for his reconstructed edition.[17] Here are the two first stanzas in parallel:

Lords' Masque	Campion: *Second Booke of Ayres* (1613)
Aduance your Chorall motions now	Where shee her sacred bowre adornes
You musick-louing lights,	The Riuers clearely flow;
This night concludes the nuptiall vow,	The groues and medowes swell with flowres,
Make this the best of nights,	The windes all gently blow.
So brauely Crowne it with your beames,	Her Sunne-like beauty shines so fayre
That it may liue in fame,	Her Spring can neuer fade:
As long as *Rhenus* or the *Thames*	Who then can blame the life that striues
Are knowne by either name.	To harbour in her shade?

---

[14] Campion, *Two Bookes of Ayres* (1613; STC: 4547), "To the Reader," sig. A2v.
[15] See, for example, *Collected English Lutenist Partsongs*, ed. David Greer, Musica Britannica 53–54 (London, 1987–89).
[16] No. 5, sig. 11v.
[17] Sabol, *A Score for The Lords' Masque*, 16, 140. Klaus Winkler set this song to a portion of the Second Lord's Dance. See Winkler, *Fly, Cheerful Voices*.

An eight-line stanza in ballad meter is not uncommon, though it is significant that the model occurs in a 1613 Campion print. The second stanza of the masque lyric, furthermore, includes the word "Bowres," and the third stanza includes "Flowres," revealing an affinity of pastoral spirit beyond the mechanical match of versification. Once again, the Cantus, Altus, and Bassus of Campion's original have been augmented by an added voice part.

After that song comes a second antimasque dance (no. 1.5), performed by "Sixteene Pages like fierie spirits" bearing torches of Virginia wax.[18] Once again, there is no extant antimasque labeled specifically as used in this situation, but BL 10444/5 does include a dance entitled *The Pages Masque* (no. 58). Anne Daye considers that the connection to the torchbearing pages is enough to confirm this music "with reasonable certainty" as the dance used.[19] Since the pages seem to be youths rather than professional antimasque dancers, this dance is less chaotic than the first, and in fact, it is described in the text as "a likely measure"—measures being also the almains that form the main dances of the gentlemen masquers. Daye, indeed, considers the torchbearer dances of the Campion and Chapman masques as "a serious prelude to the main entry rather than a comic or grotesque counterpoint."[20] Like the first antimasque, this one survives with only treble and bass parts, so the three inner parts have been reconstructed.

Svpported now by Clouds descend (no. 1.6), the third song in *The Lords' Masque*, is introduced as "A full Song," meaning one in which all parts are sung. Defining the term in that way is an assumption, though one for which there is solid evidence. For one thing, the term "full anthem" means that voices sing all of the parts, as opposed to "verse anthem" where instruments accompany solo voices and alternate with chorus. The Chapel Royal Cheque Book's entry for the Palatine wedding, for example, relates that once everyone was in their places for the ceremony, then "began the Gentlemen of the Chappell to singe a full Anthem."[21] "Full song" also occurs as a term in Ben Jonson's *Masque of Blackness* and *Masque of Beauty*, printed together in

---

[18] "Virginia" figures prominently in *The Memorable Masque* (see below), and was understood to mean the entire Atlantic coast north of Florida. For Inigo Jones's watercolor of a torchbearing fiery spirit, see the cover image of this book.

[19] See Anne Daye, "Torchbearers in the English Masque," *Early Music* 26 (1998), 246–62, at 259, https://www.jstor.org/stable/3128624.

[20] Daye, "Torchbearers in the English Masque," 261.

[21] London, St. James's Palace, Old Cheque Book of the Chapel Royal, fol. 77v.

1608. In the former, the closing "full song" is contrasted with others "sung by a *tenor* voice," or "a *tenor* and two *trebles*," or "a *Song* of two *Trebles*."[22] In the *Masque of Beauty*, similarly, songs are sung by "a loud *Tenor*," by two trebles and a tenor in succession, then by "the first *Tenor*" again.[23] Framing those songs in *The Masque of Beauty* are two "full Songs." In the first instance, "the *Musitians*, which were placed in the *Arbors*, came forth ... singing this full *Song*."[24] Clearly, several musicians—instrumentalists—were singing together on the lyric. The final song from the *Masque of Beauty* is also described as a "full *Song*," and it includes a chorus, so there are definitely multiple singers, although not all of the lyric is assigned to the full group. In Chapman's *Memorable Masque*, the first lyric is sung by a group of lute-playing priests: "the Phoebades (or Priests of the Sunne) appear'd first with sixe Lutes, and sixe voices, and sung ... this ful Song." The final lyric in that masque is described as "sung full," and also as "A Hymn," with language that suggests collective singing. I think all of this confirms that "full song" was generally used to describe a lyric sung by voices on all parts together, and that is how I interpret it here.[25]

Svpported now by Clouds descend consists of ten lines with an unusual aabbcccdcd rhyme scheme and a versification of 4444444343. Thus, the first six lines are in tetrameter rhyming couplets and the last quatrain in cross-rhymed ballad meter. Andrew Sabol viewed *Aduance your Chorall motions now* as "the only one that finds an appropriate tune in Campion's canon";[26] this third song falls outside that group. True, there is no song in Campion's 1613 and 1617 prints that comes close to this versification, but there are some similarities to Campion's song, *Mistris since you so much desire*, from Rosseter's 1601 *A Booke of Ayres*,[27] though that song has only eight lines. The

---

[22] *The Characters of Two Royall Masques* (1608; STC:14761), sigs. C1v, B4v, A4v, C1r.
[23] *The Characters of Two Royall Masques* (1608), sigs. E1r–E2r.
[24] *The Characters of Two Royall Masques* (1608), sig. D4r.
[25] This is consistent with the usage in Walls, *Music in the English Courtly Masque*, 26, 36.
[26] For setting this lyric, Sabol uses a solo dance for lute, *Ballet angloys*, from a manuscript copied in 1611 by Victor de Montbuysson, Kassel, Landesbibliothek MS 4° Mus. 108.1, fol. 70r. See Sabol, *A Score for The Lords' Masque*, 156–57. 339. It is unclear why Sabol felt the need to go so far afield for a setting, especially when the versification of the second half of the lyric is not well served by that music.
[27] No. 16, sig. F1r. This collection, ostensibly setting lyrics entirely by Campion, is half composed by Philip Rosseter and half by Campion himself. For a counter-argument that Campion is not the author of the lyrics in Rosseter's portion of the collection, see Ralph W. Berringer, "Thomas Campion's Share in *A Booke of Ayres*," *PMLA* 58 (1943), 938–48, https://doi:10.2307/458919. The two seem to have been close friends as well as colleagues: Rosseter was Campion's sole heir at his death in 1620. See E. A. J. Honigman and Susan Brock, *Playhouse Wills, 1558–1643* (Manchester, 1993), 119.

ayre calls for a reprise of the last couplet, allowing the music to accommodate the complete lyric from the masque. Here are the two in parallel:

Lords' Masque	Campion/Rosseter: *A Booke of Ayres* (1601)
Svpported now by Clouds descend,	Mistris since you so much desire,
Diuine *Prometheus, Hymens* friend,	to know the place of Cupids fire,
Leade downe the new transformed fires,	in your faire shrine that flame doth rest,
And fill their breasts with loues desires:	yet neuer harbourd in your brest,
That they may reuell with delight,	it bides not in your lips so sweete
And celebrate this nuptiall night,	nowhere the rose and lillies meete,
So celebrate this nuptiall night,	But a little higher, but a little higher,
That all which see may stay.	There there, O there lies Cupids fire.
They neuer viewed so faire a sight,	
Euen on the cleerest day.	

Parallels between the lyrics—divine "fire," "desire," and "breasts"—set an appropriate tone for the masque's epithalamium. The original song repeats "but a little higher" several times, which obscures the versification but works well as a repetition in the masque song, with "So celebrate." It is also worth noting that, although the song was published in 1601, Campion seems to have kept it in mind all through this period since he published a new version as *Beauty since you so much desire*, in his *Fourth Booke of Ayres*, of 1617.[28] Both versions survive with a texted Cantus part and untexted Bassus, so the inner parts and the texting of the Bassus are editorial.

The fourth song, *Powerfull Joue, that of bright starres* (no. 1.7), is an invocation to Jove in the form of another "full Song," which Prometheus introduces as a "Hymne." After the fifth song, which follows this, a "second Invocation to the tune of the first" appears, so *Powerfull Joue* is really a strophic setting, with the two stanzas separated by dialogue and a different song. Each stanza consists of a quatrain of tetrameter rhyming couplets, a versification that actually works with two of Campion's 1613 songs, though they are both cross-rhymed tetrameters rather than couplets.[29] The model used here is *View me Lord a worke of thine*,

---

[28] No. 22, sig. L1v. Christopher Wilson discusses the versification of Campion's pair of poems in *Words and Notes*, 241–42.

[29] Finding no suitable model among Campion's songs, Sabol sets this lyric to a short work for two virginals by Giles Farnaby in the Fitzwilliam Virginal Book (Cambridge, Fitzwilliam Museum Mu MS 168), fol. 101. See Sabol, *A Score for the Lords' Masque*, 162–63, 339. Sabol describes it (p. 20) as "a capital setting—a perfect fit" for the lyric, but since the Farnaby piece would seem most suitable for an eight-line tetrameter stanza, Sabol omits the repeats of its two strains, and also ignores the description of the masque lyric as a full song, setting it instead as an accompanied vocal solo.

which suits the situation well for its hymn-like quality, with four texted voices addressing a powerful deity. Here are the two first stanzas in parallel:

Lords' Masque	Campion: *First Booke of Ayres* (1613)
Powerfull *Joue*, that of bright starres,	View mee Lord, a worke of thine;
Now hast made men fit for warres;	Shall I then lye drown'd in night?
Thy power in these Statues proue,	Might thy grace in mee but shine,
And make them women fit for loue.	I should seem made all of light.

The fifth song—the one that separates the two stanzas of the fourth song—is *Wooe her and win her* (no. 1.8), the only song from the three wedding masques to have a musical setting preserved and labeled as coming from the masque. As noted above, it was printed as an afterthought in the quarto of the 1614 *Somerset Masque* (or *Squires' Masque*) for the wedding of the Earl of Somerset and Frances Howard at the end of 1613: "A Song, made by *Th. Campion*, and sung in the Lords Maske at the *Count Palatine's* Marriage, we haue here added, to fill vp these emptie Pages" (Plate 1.2).[30]

Plate 1.2 Thomas Campion, *Wooe her and win her*, from *The Description of a Maske* (1614), sigs. D1v–D2r. Courtesy of the Huntington Library.

[30] Campion, *The Description of a Maske*, sigs. D1v–D2r.

Wooe her and win her also survives as a continuo song in Tenbury MS 1018 (ca.1615–25), which transcribes the print quite closely, using the vocal part with the "Basso" as a shorthand for the accompaniment (Plate 1.3).

Plate 1.3 Thomas Campion, *Wooe her and win her*, from Bodleian Library, MS Tenbury 1018, fol. 46r. Courtesy of the Bodleian Library.

The voice part with accompaniment found in both of these sources has been expanded to four voices in the musical reconstruction below. This is because of introductory dialogue that indicates the participation of multiple singers: "Goe new-borne men, and entertaine with loue, These new-borne women, though your number yet Exceedes their's double." With four statues newly reconstituted as women, this suggests eight men singing, fulfilling the song's second line, "Each woman hath two louers."[31]

After that song comes "the first new entring dance" (no. 1.9)—not really an entry dance since the masquers have been onstage for some time, participating in the pageantry and singing. In this case, we have a dance in BL 10444/5 that is entitled *The first of the Lords* (no. 22), which seems to be the music used at this point—or, part of it, at least. The music also survives in Brade's 1617 *Newe Ausserlesene liebliche Branden* (no. 19) and it contains an opening section that survives without title in BL 10444/5 as the very last dance in the manuscript (no. 138), so we are able to put the two parts together to make the complete dance. As with all of Brade's concordances, however, his titles bear little or no relation to the original context in the English masques. There, it is entitled simply *Ballet*—intriguingly, the general term for dances in the *ballet de cour*, the closest French counterpart to the English masque. Brade's five-part arrangements seem to match the expected format for the violin band at the English court, so the piece is presented as given there.[32]

---

[31] Sabol chooses to ignore this indication for multiple singers, giving instead the accompanied solo of the 1614 print, though with an elaborate accompaniment added. See Sabol, *A Score for The Lords' Masque*, 169–70, 339.

[32] Brade tends not to use key signatures, instead applying accidentals where needed; the versions here conform more closely to modern practice.

The next lyric, *Breath[e] you now, while Io Hymen* (no. 1.10), is described as a "dialogue song," though the division of the dialogue is not clear. There is certainly a "Chorus" of everyone singing together at the end, so perhaps there were two groups of singers alternating couplets. Two stanzas appear in the text, separated by "The Maskers second dance." The versification of each stanza is unusual, with an abcb quatrain followed by eight lines in rhyming couplets in a unique 4343443445-55 versification, with the final pentameter couplet comprising the chorus. This is extremely unusual and matches nothing in the repertoire, although a setting can be made with Campion's *Harden now thy tired heart*, from his *Second Booke of Ayres*, of 1613.[33] Here are the first stanzas in parallel:

Lords' Masque	Campion: *First Booke of Ayres* (1613)
Breathe you now, while Io Hymen	Harden now thy tyred hart,
To the Bride we sing:	with more then flinty rage;
O how many ioyes, and honors,	Ne're let her false teares hence forth
From this match will spring?	thy constant griefe asswage.
Euer firme the league will proue,	Once true happy daies thou saw'st,
Where only goodnesse causeth loue.	when shee stood firme & kinde:
Some for profit seeke	Both as one then liu'd and held
What their fancies most disleeke,	one eare, one tongue, one minde.
These loue for vertues sake alone:	
Beautie and youth vnite them both in one.	But now those bright hours be fled,
Cho: Liue with thy Bridegroome happy,	and neuer may returne,
sacred Bride;	What then remaynes, but her vntruths to
How blest is he, that is for loue enui'd.	mourne.

The versification match is not precise, but using the second strain (corresponding to "But now those bright hours" to the end), for the final two couplets of the masque song works well, including the setting of the chorus couplet. *Harden now* is printed with three vocal parts, Cantus, Bassus, and Contratenor, here augmented with a fourth.

---

[33] No. 3, sig. H2v. Sabol sets this lyric to *Why dost thou turne away faire mayde*, a dialogue song from Giles Earle's Song Book (BL 24665) of 1615 (fols. 68v–69r). The dialogue and date are right, but its eight-line stanzas of iambic ballad meter (with an additional echo after the fourth line) are not a good match for the masque lyric. Sabol, in fact, omits the echo and fashions a repeat of the final strain in order to accommodate the lyric. See Sabol, *A Score for The Lords' Masque*, 196–97, 341.

As with *Powerfull Joue*, this song has two stanzas separated by a different musical event—in this case, "The Maskers second dance" (no. 1.11). Like the first measure, BL 10444/5 labels a dance *The second of the Lords* (no. 23), which gives us a clue to the appropriate music. The dance is included in Brade's collection (no. 7) with an unrelated title: *Der Königinnen Intrada*.[34] After that dance, the second stanza of *Breathe you now* is sung.

Next come the revels, where the masquers take members of the audience, including the bride and bridegroom, out onto the floor to dance several dances. Such dances probably included various branles (line and circle dances), as well as couple dances, like the galliard (sometimes called "cinquepace" because of the five movements in each step-unit), coranto (a skipping dance), and passamezzo or "passing measures" (a kind of pavan at a faster pace). Numerous examples of these dances are preserved in period musical sources, though none can be connected specifically to any of the Palatine wedding masques.[35] These revels "continued a long space, but in the end were broken off with this short Song." The song given, *Cease, cease you Reuels, rest a space* (no. 1.12), is very short, consisting of only three tetrameter lines, all with the same rhyme. This versification is called a triplet, and the only tetrameter triplet with a musical setting from this entire period is *She whose matchles beauty stayneth*, from the *The First Booke of Songes & Ayres* (1600), by Robert Jones,[36] a circumstance that amply justifies the use of a model outside the Campion canon. Here is the masque lyric in parallel with the first stanza of Jones's song:

Lords' Masque	Jones: *First Booke of Songes & Ayres* (1600)
Cease, cease you Reuels, rest a space,	She whose matchles beauty stayneth,
New pleasures presse into this place,	what best iudgment fairst maintaineth,
Full of beautie and of grace.	shee O shee my loue disdaineth.

Jones printed his song with four texted voices, providing all the parts of the setting given for the masque song in the musical reconstruction below. The last line may be reprised from the sign of congruence.

---

[34] In this case, Brade's slower meter for the triple section is preferred.
[35] Modern performers are thus free to choose any they like for presentation.
[36] STC: 14732: no. 3, sigs. B5v–B6r. Sabol sets this song to a short anonymous keyboard solo from Paris, Conservatoire, MS Rés. 1186 (1630s), fol. 21r. Unfortunately, that piece seems more suited to a six-line tetrameter stanza of aabcbc and, in fact, because it provides too much music, Sabol neither repeats the second strain nor sets any text at all to the first musical phrase. See Sabol, *A Score for The Lords' Masque*, 284–85, 344.

The next lyric, *Come triumphing, come with state* (no. 1.13), is described as "A Song," which often implies a solo song but, again, we know it was not. Entheus introduces it, saying, "Raise high your voices now, like Trumpets fill, / The roome with sounds of Triumph, sweete and shrill." The lyric consists of six lines of ababcc in a unique 444344 versification. A close match is found in Campion's *Leaue prolonging thy distress* from his *Fourth Booke of Ayres*, of 1617,[37] which features a slightly variant abcbdd rhyme scheme and a versification of 444334. Nothing else in the repertoire comes close. The lyrics are shown in parallel here:

Lords' Masque	Campion: *Fourth Booke of Ayres* (1617)
Come triumphing, come with state,	Leaue prolonging, thy distresse,
Old *Sibilla*, reuerend Dame,	All delayes afflict the dying.
Thou keep'st the secret key of fate,	Many lost sighes long I spent,
Preuenting swiftest fame.	To her for mercy crying:
This night breathe onely words of ioy,	But now vaine mourning cease;
And speake them plaine, now be not coy,	Ile dye and mine owne griefes release

Campion's ayre is for voice with lute and untexted Bassus, so the inner parts and the texting of the Bassus are editorial. The last strain may be reprised from the sign of congruence.

The ninth song (no. 1.14) is "A Song and dance triumphant of the Maskers." In other words, *Dance, dance and visit now the shadowes of our ioy* seems to be dance music with lyrics—sung and danced at the same time. It consists of two eight-line stanzas in rhyming couplets, but the versification—confirmed in the second stanza—is very unusual, with 67756666. The best match I could find is *Will saide to his mammy that hee woulde goe woo*, from *A Musicall Dreame, or the Fourth Booke of Ayres* (1609) by Robert Jones.[38] That may seem an incongruous choice since there are no obvious text connections between the lyrics. A light-hearted wooing song about "a wife in my bed" would

---

[37] No. 1, sig. G1v. Sabol sets this lyric to another anonymous keyboard piece from Paris, Rés. 1186 (1630s), fol. 52r, which he had earlier used as an instrumental prelude, and which looks more like a setting for a poulter's measure lyric (typically abcb 3343).

[38] STC: 14734: no. 4, sigs. C2v–C3r. Once again sourcing anonymous music from Paris, MS Rés. 1186, Sabol uses "three slightly differing keyboard settings of an item that are here conflated to serve as a contrafactum for an orphaned lyric of no little complexity because of its irregularity." See Sabol, *A Score for The Lords' Masque*, 344. The lyric is complex, but combining three different untexted keyboard pieces to create a song setting seems extreme.

certainly have been humorously ironic, however, and somehow apt for an epithalamium. Here are the first stanzas of the two lyrics in parallel:

Lords' Masque	Jones: *Fourth* Booke *of Ayres* (1609)
Dance, dance, and visit now the shadowes of our ioy,	Will saide to his mammy that hee would goe woo,
All in height, and pleasing state, your changed formes imploy.	Faine would he wed but he wot not who.
And as the bird of *Ioue* salutes, with loftie wing, the morn;	Soft a while my lammy stay, and yet abide,
So mount, so flie, these Trophees to adorne.	Hee like a foole as he was replide,
Grace them with all the sounds and motions of delight,	In faith chil haue a wife, a wife, a wife,
Since all the earth cannot expresse a louelier sight,	O what a life do I lead for a wife in my bed I may not tell you,
View them with triumph, and in shades the truth adore,	O there to haue a wife, a wife, a wife,
No pompe or sacrifice can please *Ioues* greatnesse more.	O tis a smart to my hart, tis a racke to my backe And to my belly.

One complication of the setting is that apparently repeated sections of the masque lyric have different numbers of syllables, requiring different note divisions or syllable extensions on repeat. Jones's ayre is set for texted Cantus and Altus with lute and untexted Bassus, so the Tenor part and the texting of the Bassus here are editorial.

The tenth and final song (no. 1.15), *No longer wrong the night*, is also possibly meant to be both sung and danced, given that the final line is "Dance then and goe," and Orpheus introduces the song, saying "Then singing the last dance induce." That could also be interpreted as meaning that the song precedes the last dance, however, especially because the lyric is immediately followed by an indication for "*The last new Dance of the Maskers.*" The best match for a song model is Campion's *Now let her change and spare not*, from his *Third Booke of Ayres* (1617).[39] This is a lyric by Campion that was previously set to music by both Robert Jones and Francis Pilkington in 1605,[40] so

---

[39] No. 2, sig. B1r. Sabol chooses music from yet another anonymous and untitled keyboard piece from Paris, MS Rés. 1186 (1630s), fol. 46r. It bears no text but would seem to be designed for an eight-line stanza of 44434443, which does not match this lyric well. See Sabol, *A Score for The Lords' Masque*, 344.

[40] Robert Jones, *Ultimum Vale* (1605; STC: 14738), no. 17, sigs. K1v–K2r; Francis Pilkington, *The First Booke of Songs or Ayres* (1605; STC: 19922), no. 8, sigs. E2v–F1r.

Campion's setting was almost certainly written by 1613 in spite of its 1617 publication. *No longer wrong the night* has a single six-line stanza in rhyming couplets, with an unusual 334432 versification. *Now let her change* also has rhyming couplets, but with a versification of 334443—close enough to set the masque lyric well. Certainly, it is the only six-line lyric in the entire lutesong repertoire to begin 3344, so it seems a clear choice. Here is the masque lyric in parallel with the first stanza of the lutesong.

Lords' Masque	Campion: *Third* Booke *of Ayres* (1617)
No longer wrong the night,	Now let her change and spare not,
Of her *Hymenaean* right,	Since she proues strange I care not:
A thousand *Cupids* call away,	Fain'd loue charm'd so my delight,
Fearing the approching day,	That still I doted on her sight.
The Cocks alreadie crow,	But she is gone new ioies imbracing
Dance then and goe.	And my desires disgracing.

Campion's 1617 setting is for voice and lute with untexted Bassus, so the two inner parts and the texting of the Bassus are editorial,[41] though the song may be sung by the texted top line alone, with instruments below. The last strain may be reprised from the sign of congruence.

After that song, the masquers exit to the third and final measure (no. 1.16), "which concludes all with a liuely straine at their going out." Once again, BL 10444/5 has a dance that seems to be the one called for: *The third of the Lords* (no. 24). The version preserved there is shorter, however, and seems to be incomplete. Fortunately, the concordance in Brade's collection, *Des jungen Prinsen Intrada* (no. 8), contains the opening section that is missing in BL 10444/5; both sources include a triple-meter section which would seem to be the "liuelie straine" for getting the masquers off the stage and sending everyone on their way.

---

[41] Pilkington's setting of the lyric is in four voices, while Jones's is for two texted Cantus parts and lute.

Table of Musical Contents for
The Lords' Masque

Song / Dance	Model	Source
1.1. Entry – Orpheus	*The second [of my Lord of Essex]*	BL10444:94; Adson (1621), no. 6
1.2. Antimasque – Franticks	*The Furies*	BL10444:72
1.3. *Come away, bring thy golden theft*	*Come away, arm'd with loues delights*	Campion: *Second Booke of Ayres* (1613)
1.4. *Aduance your Chorall motions now*	*Where she her sacred bowre adornes*	Campion: *Second Booke of Ayres* (1613)
1.5. Antimasque – Torchbearers	*The Pages Masque*	BL10444:58
1.6. *Svpported now by Clouds descend*	*Mistris since you so much desire*	Campion: *A Booke of Ayres* (1601)
1.7. *Powerfull Joue, that of bright starres*	*View mee Lord, a worke of thine*	Campion: *First Booke of Ayres* (1613)
1.8. *Wooe her and win her*	[extant]	Campion: *Description of a Maske* (1614)
1.9. First Measure	*The first of the Lords*	BL10444:138, 22; Brade (1617), no. 19
1.10. *Breath[e] you now while Io Hymen*	*Harden now thy tired heart*	Campion: *Second Booke of Ayres* (1613)
1.11. Second Measure	*The second of the Lords*	BL10444:23; Brade (1617), no. 7
Revels		
1.12. *Cease, cease you revels, rest a space*	*She whose matchles beauty stayneth*	Jones: *First Booke of Songes* (1600)
1.13. *Come triumphing, come with state*	*Leaue prolonging, thy distresse*	Campion: *Fourth Booke of Ayres* (1617)
1.14. *Dance and visit now the shadowes*	*Will saide to his mammy*	Jones: *Fourth Booke of Ayres* (1609)
1.15. *No longer wrong the night*	*Now let her change and spare not*	Campion: *Third Booke of Ayres* (1617)
1.16. Third Measure	*The third of the Lords*	BL10444:24; Brade (1617), no. 8

A RELATION
OF THE LATE
ROYALL ENTERTAINMENT GIVEN BY THE RIGHT
HONORABLE THE LORD Knowles, AT
Cawsome-House neere *Redding*: to our most
Gracious Queene, Queene Anne, *in her*
Progresse toward the *Bathe*, vpon
the seuen and eight and twentie
dayes of Aprill.
1613.
Whereunto is annexed the Description,
Speeches, and Songs of the Lords Maske, presented in the
Banquetting-house on the Mariage night of the High
and Mightie, Covnt Palatine, *and the*
Royally descended the Ladie
Elizabeth.

Written by Thomas Campian.

London,
Printed [by William Stansby] for *Iohn Budge*, and are to be sold at his Shop
at the South-doore of S. *Pauls*, and at
Britaines Bursse. 1613.

...

THE DESCRIPTION,
SPEECHES, AND SONGS, OF
The Lords Maske, Presented In
the Banquetting-house on the mariage night
of the high and mightie Count Palatine,
and the royally descended the Ladie
Elisabeth.
(*⁎*)

I haue now taken occasion to satisfie many, who long since were desirous that the Lords maske should be published, which (but for some priuate lets), had in due time come forth. The Scene was diuided into two parts from the roofe to the floore, the lower part being first discouered (vpon the sound of a double consort, exprest by seuerall instruments, plac't on either side of the roome) there appeared a Wood in prospectiue, the innermost part being of releaue, or whole round, the rest painted. On the left hand from the seate was a Caue, and on the right a thicket, out of which came Orpheus, *who was attired after the old Greeke manner, his haire curled, and long; a lawrell wreath on his head; and in his hand hee bare a siluer bird, about him tamely placed seuerall wild beasts,* …

Example 1.1 Entry—Orpheus: *The second [of my Lord of Essex]*: BL 10444/5, no. 94; Adson's *Courtly Masquing Ayres* (1621), no. 6.

… and vpon the ceasing of the Consort Orpheus *spake.*

ORPHEVS. Agen, agen, fresh kindle *Phœbus* sounds,
T'exhale *Mania* from her earthie den;
Allay the furie that her sense confounds,
And call her gently forth, sound, sound, agen. [repeat 1.1]

The Consorts both sound againe, and Mania *the Goddesse of madnesse appeares wildly out of her caue. Her habit was confused and strange; but yet gracefull, shee as one amazed speaks.*

Mania. What powerfull noise is this importunes me,
T'abandon darkenesse which my humour fits?
Joues hand in it I feele, and euer he
Must be obai'd eu'n of the franticst wits.

Orpheus. Mania?

Mania. Hah.

Orpheus. Braine-sick, why start'st thou so?
Approch yet nearer, and thou then shalt know
The will of *Joue*, which he will breath from me,

Mania. Who art thou? if my dazeled eyes can see,
Thou art the sweet Enchanter heau'nly *Orpheus*.

Orpheus. The same *Mania*, and *Joue* greets thee thus,
Though seuerall power to thee, and charge he gaue,
T'enclose in thy Dominions such as raue
Through blouds distemper, how durst thou attempt
T'imprison *Entheus*, whose rage is exempt
From vulgar censure? it is all diuine
Full of celestiall rapture, that can shine
Through darkest shadowes, therefore *Joue* by me
Commands thy power strait to set *Entheus* free.

Mania. How can I? Franticks, with him many more
In one caue are lockt vp, ope once the dore,
All will flie out, and through the world disturbe,
The peace of *Joue*; for, what power then can curbe
Their rainelesse[42] furie? —

---

[42] reinless, unbridled.

Orpheus. —Let not feare in vaine
Trouble thy crazed fancie, all againe
Saue *Entheus* to thy safeguard shall retire,
For *Joue* into our musick will inspire
The power of passion, that their thoughts shall bend
To any forme or motion we intend:
Obey *Joues* willing then, go, set *Entheus* free.

Mania. I willing go, so *Joue* obey'd must bee.

Orph. Let Musicke put on *Protean* changes now,
Wilde beasts it once tam'd, now let Franticks bow.

At the sound of a strange musicke twelue Franticks enter, six men, and six women, all presented in sundry habits and humours: there was the Louer, the Selfe-louer, the melancholicke-man full of feare, the Schoole-man ouer-come with phantasie, the ouer-watched Vsurer,[43] with others that made an absolute medly of madnesse, in middest of whom Entheus (or Poeticke furie) was hurried forth, and tost vp and downe, till by vertue of a new change in the musicke, the Lunatickes fell into a madde measure, fitted to a loud phantasticke tune, but in the end thereof the musick changed into a very solemne ayre, which they softly played, while Orpheus spake.

Example 1.2 Antimasque—Franticks: *The Furies*: BL 10444/5, no. 72.

[43] exhausted miser.

THE LORDS' MASQUE 31

Example 1.2 Continued

Orph. Through these soft and calme sounds *Mania* passe
With thy Phantasticks hence; heere is no place
Longer for them or thee; *Entheus* alone
Must do *Joues* bidding now, all else be gone.

During this speech, Mania *with her Franticks depart, leauing* Entheus *behind them, who was attired in a close Curace*[44] *of the Anticke fashion, Bases with labels, a Roabe fastned to his shoulders, and hanging downe behind; on his head a wreath of Lawrell, out of which grew a paire of wings, in the one hand he held a booke, and in the other a pen.*

Enth. Diuinest *Orpheus*, ô how all from thee
Proceed with wondrous sweetnesse, am I free?
Is my affliction vanish't?

Orph.   —Too too long
Alas, good *Entheus*, hast thou brook't this wrong;
What? number thee with madmen? ô mad age,
Sencelesse of thee, and thy celestiall rage.
For thy excelling rapture, eu'n through things
That seems most light, is borne with sacred wings:
Nor are these Musicks, Showes, or Reuels vaine,
When thou adorn'st them with thy *Phoebean* braine;
Th'are pallate sicke of much more vanitie,
That cannot taste them in their dignitie.
Joue therefore lets thy prison'd spright obtaine
Her libertie and fiery scope againe:
And heere by me commands thee to create
Inuentions rare, this night to celebrate,
Such as become a nuptiall by his will
Begun and ended, —

Enth.   —*Joue* I honor still,
And must obey, *Orpheus* I feele the fires
Are reddy in my braine, which *Joue* enspires,

---

[44] Curace = cuirass

THE LORDS' MASQUE   33

Loe, through that vaile, I see *Prometheus* stand
Before those glorious lights, which his false hand
Stole out of heau'n, the dull earth to enflame
With the affects of Loue, and honor'd Fame,
I view them plaine in pompe and maiestie,
Such as being seene might hold riualitie,
With the best triumphes; *Orpheus* giue a call
With thy charm'd musicke, and discouer all.
Orph. Flie cheerfull voices, through the ayre, and clear
These clouds, that yon hid beautie may appeare.

A Song.

Example 1.3 *Come away; bring thy golden theft*, set to *Come away, arm'd with loues delights*, from Campion's *Second Booke of Ayres* (1613).

Example 1.3 Continued

1. Come away; bring thy golden theft,
   Bring bright *Prometheus* all thy lights,
Thy fires from Heau'n bereft
   Shew now to humane sights.
Come quickly come; thy stars to our
   stars straight present,
For pleasure being too much defer'd,
   loseth her best content,
What fair dames wish, should swift as
   their own thoughts appeare,
To louing & to longing harts euery
   houre seemes a yeare.

2. See how faire; O how faire they shine,
   What yeelds more pompe beneath the skies?
Their birth is yet diuine,
   And such their forme implies.
Large grow their beames, their nere approch
   afford them so
By nature sights that pleasing are, cannot
   too amply show,
O might these flames in humane shapes descend this place,
How louely would their presence be, how
   full of grace!

THE LORDS' MASQUE 35

In the end of the first part of this Song, the vpper part of the Scene was discouered by the sodaine fall of a curtaine, then in clowdes of seuerall colours (the vpper part of them being fierie, and the middle heightned with siluer) appeared eight Starres of extraordinarie bignesse, which so were placed, as that they seemed to be fixed betweene the Firmament and the Earth; in the front of the Scene stood Prometheus, *attyred as one of the ancient Heroes.*

Enth. Patron of mankinde, powerfull and bounteous,
Rich in thy flames, reuerend *Prometheus*,
In *Hymens* place aide vs to solempnize
These royall Nuptials, fill the lookers eyes
With admiration of thy fire and light,
And from thy hand let wonders flow to night.

Prom. Entheus and *Orpheus* names both deare to me,
In equall ballance I your Third will be
In this nights honour, view these heau'n borne Starres,
Who by my stealth are become Sublunars.
How well their natiue beauties fit this place,
Which with a chorall dance they first shall grace,
Then shall their formes to humane figures turne,
And these bright fires within their bosomes burne.
Orpheus apply thy musick for it well
Helps to induce a Courtly miracle.

Orp. Sound best of Musicks, raise yet higher our sprights,
While we admire *Prometheus* dancing lights.

A Song

Example 1.4 *Aduance your Chorall motions now*, set to *Where shee her sacred bowre adornes*, from Campion's *Second Booke of Ayres* (1613).

Example 1.4 Continued

1. Aduance your Chorall motions now
    You musick-louing lights,
This night concludes the nuptiall vow,
    Make this the best of nights,
So brauely Crowne it with your beames,
    That it may liue in fame,
As long as *Rhenus* or the *Thames*
    Are knowne by either name.

2. Once moue againe, yet nearer moue
    Your formes at willing view,
Such faire effects of ioy and loue,
    None can expresse but you,

Then reuell midst your ayrie Bowres
    Till all the clouds doe sweat,
That pleasure may be powr'd in showres
    On this triumphant Seat.

3. Long since hath louely *Flora* throwne
    Her Flowers and Garlands here,
Rich *Ceres* all her wealth hath showne,
    Prowde of her daintie cheare.
Chang'd then to humane shape descend,
    Glad in familiar weede.
That euery eye may here commend
    The kinde delights you breede.

  According to the humour of this Song, the Starres mooued in an exceeding strange and delightfull maner, and I suppose fewe haue euer seene more neate artifice, then Master *Innigoe Iones shewed in contriuing their Motion, who in all the rest of the workmanship which belong'd to the whole inuention, shewed extraordinarie industrie and skill, which if it be not as liuely exprest in writing as it appeared in view, robbe not him of his due, but lay the blame on my want of right apprehending his instructions for the adoring of his Arte. But to returne to our purpose; about the end of this Song, the Starres suddainely vanished, as if they had beene drowned amongst the Cloudes, and the eight Maskers appeared in their habits, which were infinitly rich, befitting States (such as indeede they all were) as also a time so farre heightned the day before, with all the richest shew of solemnitie that could be inuented. The ground of their attires was massie Cloth of Siluer, embossed with flames of Embroidery, on their heads, they had Crownes, Flames made all of Gold-plate Enameled, and on the top a Feather of Silke, representing a cloude of smoake. Vpon their new transformation, the whole Scaene being Cloudes dispersed, and there appeared an Element of artificiall fires, with seuerall circles of lights, in continuall motion, representing the house of Prometheus, who then thus applies his speech to the Maskers.

They are transformed.
Prometh. So, pause awhile, and come yee fierie spirits,
Breake forth the earth-like sparks t'attend these Knights.

Sixteene Pages like fierie spirits, all their attires bing alike composed of flames, with fierie Wings and Bases, bearing in either hand a Torch of Virgine Waxe, come forth below dauncing a likely measure, and the Daunce being ended, Prometheus *speakes to them from aboue.*

The Torch-bearers Daunce

Example 1.5 Antimasque—Torchbearers: *The Pages Masque*: BL 10444/5, no. 58.

Example 1.5 Continued

Example 1.5 Continued

    Pro. Wait spirits wait, while through the clouds we pace,
    And by descending gaine a hier place.

The Pages returne toward the Scaene, to giue their attendance to the Maskers with their lights: from the side of the Scaene appeared a bright and transparant cloud, which reached from the top of the heauens to the earth: on this cloud the Maskers led by Prometheus, *descended with the musicke of a full song; and at the end of their descent, the cloud brake in twaine, and one part of it (as with a winde) was blowne ouerthwart the Scaene.*

While this cloud was vanishing, the wood being the vnder-part of the Scaene, was insensibly changed, and in place thereof appeared foure Noble women-statues of siluer, standing in seuerall nices, accompanied with ornaments of Architecture, which filled all the end of the house, and seemed to be all of gold-smithes work. The first order consisted of Pillasters all of gold, set with Rubies,

Saphyrs, Emeralds, Opals, and such like. The Capitels were composed, and of a new inuention. Ouer this was a bastard order with Cartouses reuersed,[45] *comming from the Capitels of euery Pillaster, which made the vpper part rich and full of ornament. Ouer euery statue was placed a history in gold, which seemed to be of base releaue; the conceits which were figured in them were these. In the first was* Prometheus, *embossing in clay the figure of a woman, in the second he was represented stealing fire from the chariot-wheele of the Sunne: in the third, he is exprest putting life with this fire into his figure of clay; and in the fourth square,* Jupiter *enraged, turnes these new made women into statues. Aboue all, for finishing, ran a Cornish,*[46] *which returned ouer euery Pillaster, seeming all of gold and richly carued.*

A full Song.

Example 1.6 Svpported now by Clouds descend, set to *Mistris since you so much desire*, from Campion's *A Booke of Ayres* (1601/1617).

[45] Cartouses reuersed = reversed scrollwork (cartouches)
[46] Cornish = cornice

Example 1.6 Continued

Svpported now by Clouds descend,
Diuine *Prometheus*, *Hymens* friend,
Leade downe the new transformed fires,
And fill their breasts with loues desires:
That they may reuell with delight,

And celebrate this nuptiall night,
So celebrate this nuptiall night,
  That all which see may stay.
They neuer viewed so faire a sight,
  Euen on the cleerest day.

While this Song is sung, and the Maskers court the fowre new transformed Ladies, foure other Statues appeare in their places.

Entheus. See, see *Prometheus*, foure of these first dames
Which thou long since out of thy purchac't flames,
Did'st forge with heau'nly fire, as they were then,
By *Joue* transformed to Statues, so agen,
They suddenly appeare by his command
At thy arriuall, Loe how fixt they stand,
So did *Joues* wrath too long, but now at last,
It by degrees relents, and he hath plac't
These Statues, that we might his ayde implore,
First for the life of these, and then for more.

Prom. Entheus, Thy councels are diuine and iust,
Let *Orpheus* decke thy Hymne, since pray we must.

The first Inuocation in a full Song.

Example 1.7 *Powerfull Joue, that of bright starres*, set to *View mee Lord, a worke of thine*, from Campion's *First Booke of Ayres* (1613).

Example 1.7 Continued

Powerfull *Joue*, that of bright starres,
Now hast made men fit for warres;   [Second stanza below]
Thy power in these Statues proue,
And make them women fit for loue.

Orpheus. See *Joue* is pleas'd, Statues haue life & moue,
Goe new-borne men, and entertaine with loue,
These new-borne women, though your number yet
Exceedes their's double, they are arm'd with wit,
To beare your best encounters, Court them faire:
When words and Musicke speake, let none despaire.

The Song.

Example 1.8 *Wooe her and win her*, from Campion's *Description of a Maske* (1614).

Example 1.8 Continued

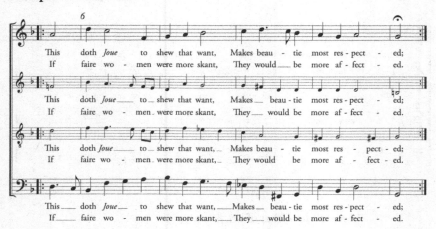

1. Wooe her, and win her, he that can,
   Each woman hath two louers,
So shee must take and leaue a man,
   Till time more grace discouers;
This doth *Joue* to shew that want,
   Makes beautie most respected;
If faire women were more skant,
   They would be more affected.

2. Courtship and Musicke, suite with loue,
   They both are workes of passion,
Happie is he whose words can moue,
   Yet sweete notes helpe perswasion.
Mix your words with Musicke then,
   That they the more may enter;
Bold assaults are fit for men,
   That on strange beauties venture.

> *Promet.* Cease, cease your woing strife, see *Joue* intends,
>   To fill your number vp, and make all friends,
> *Orpheus*, and *Entheus*, ioyne your skils once more,
>   And with a Hymne the Dietie implore.

The second Inuocation to the tune of the first [no. 1.7].

2. Powerfull *Joue*, that hast giuen fower,
   Raise this number but once more,
That complete, their numerous feet
   May aptly in iust measures meet.

The other foure statues are transformed into women, in the time of this inuocation.

> *Enth.* The number's now complete, thankes be to *Joue*,
>   No man needs feare a Riuall in his loue;
> For, all are sped, and now begins delight,
>   To fill with glorie, this triumphant night.

*The Maskers hauing euery one entertained his
Lady, begin their first new entring dance:*

Example 1.9 The First Measure: *The first of the Lords*: BL 10444/5, nos. 138 and 22; William Brade's *Newe Ausserlesene liebliche Branden* (1617), no. 19, *Ballet.*

THE CAMPION, CHAPMAN, AND BEAUMONT MASQUES

Example 1.9 Continued

after it, while they breath, the time is entertained with a dialogue song.

Example 1.10 *Breath[e] you now, while Io Hymen*, set to *Harden now thy tired heart*, from Campion's *Second Booke of Ayres* (1613).

Example 1.10 Continued

1. Breathe you now, while Io Hymen
    To the Bride we sing:
 O how many ioyes, and honors,
    From this match will spring?
 Euer firme the league will proue,
 Where only goodnesse causeth loue.
 Some for profit seeke
 What their fancies most disleeke,

These loue for vertues sake alone:
Beautie and youth vnite them both in one.
   CHORVS.
Liue with thy Bridegroome happy, sacred Bride;
How blest is he, that is for loue enui'd.

[Second stanza below]

The Maskers second dance

Example 1.11 Second Measure: *The second of the Lords*: BL 10444/5, no. 23; Brade's *Newe Ausserlesene liebliche Branden* (1617), no. 7, *Der Königinnen Intrada*.

Example 1.11 Continued

[Second stanza of no. 1.10]

2. Breathe againe, while we with musicke
   Fill the emptie space:
O but do not in your dances,
   Your selues only grace.
Eu'ry one fetch out your *Pheare*,
Whom chiefely you will honor heere,
Sights most pleasure breed,

When their numbers most exceed:
Chuse then, for choice to all is free,
Taken or left, none discontent must bee.
                  Chorvs.
Now in thy Reuels frolicke-faire delight,
To heape Ioy on this euer honored night.

    The Maskers during this Dialogue take out others to daunce with them, men women, and women men, and first of all the Princely Bridegroome and Bride were drawne into these solemne Reuels, which continued a long space,...

[Revels]
    ... but in the end were broken off with this short Song.

A Song.

Example 1.12 *Cease, cease you Reuels, rest a space*, set to *She whose matchles beauty stayneth*, from the *The First Booke of Songes & Ayres* (1600), by Robert Jones.

Cease, cease you Reuels, rest a space;
    New pleasures presse into this place,
Full of beautie and of grace.

The whole scaene was now againe changed, and became a prospectiue with Porticoes on each side, which seemed to go in a great way, in the middle was erected an Obeliske, all of siluer, and in it lights of seuerall colours, on the side of this Obeliske, standing on Pedestals, were the statues of the Bridegroome and Bride, all of gold in gratious postures. This Obeliske was of that height, that the toppe thereof touched the highest cloudes, and yet Sybilla did draw it forth with a threed of gold. The graue Sage was in a Roabe of gold tuckt vp before to her girdle, a Kirtle gathered full, and of siluer; with a vaile on her head, being bare neckt, and bearing in her hand a scrole of Parchment.

> *Entheus.* Make cleare the passage to *Sibilla's* sight,
> Who with her Trophee comes, to crowne this night,
> And as her selfe with Musicke shall be led,
> So shall shee pull on with a golden thread.
> A high vast *Obeliske*, dedicate to fame,
> Which immortalitie it selfe did frame.
> Raise high your voices now, like Trumpets fill,
> The roome with sounds of Triumph, sweete and shrill.

A Song.

Example 1.13 *Come triumphing, come with state*, set to *Leaue prolonging, thy distresse*, from Campion's *Fourth Booke of Ayres* (1617).

Example 1.13 Continued

Come triumphing, come with state,
   Old *Sibilla*, reuerend Dame,
Thou keep'st the secret key of fate,
   Preuenting swiftest fame.
This night breathe onely words of ioy,
And speake them plaine, now be not coy,

Sib.

Debetur alto iure, Principium Ioui,	The beginning is rightly due to lofty Jove,
Votis det ipse vim meis, dictis fidem.	Let him give strength to my vows, my words of faith.
Vtrin{que} decoris splendet egregium Iubar,	On each side shines forth the light of glory,
Medio triumphus mole stat dignus sua,	In the midst stands the worthy triumphal obelisk,
Coelum{que} summo Capite dilectum petit;	And it seeks the delight of Heaven, with its peak;
Quam pulchra pulchro sponsa respondet viro!	How the fair bride responds to her fair husband!
Quam plena numinis? Patrem vultu exprimit,	How full of power? She expresses her Father in her face,
Parens futura masculae prolis, Parens	The future parent of male offspring, Parent
Regum, imperatorum: Additur Germaniae	Of Kings, of emperors: Added to German is
Robur Britannicum. ecquid esse par potest?	British strength. Can anything equal that?
Vtram{que} iunget vna mens gentem, fides,	And one mind unites both nations: faith,
Dei{que} Cultus vnus, & simplex amor.	And one worship of God, and simple love.
Idem erit vtri{que} hostis, sodalis idem, idem	Both will have the same enemy, the same ally,
Votum periclitantium, at{que} eadem manus.	The same prayer for those in danger, and the same valor.
Fauebit illis Pax, fauebit bellica	Peace will favor them, warlike Fortuna will favor them,
Fortuna, semper aderit Adiutor Deus.	God will always be nigh as their helper.
Sic, sic Sibilla; vocibus nec his deest	Thus, thus Sibyl; nor are these words wanting
Pondus, nec hoc inane monumentum trahit.	Weight, nor does she tow this monument empty.
Et aureum est, & quale nec flammas timet,	For it is golden, and as such fears no flames,
Nec fulgura, ipsi quippe sacratur Ioui.	Nor lightning, since it is sacred to Jove himself.

  Pro. The good old *Sage* is silenc't, her free tongue
  That made such melodie, is now vnstrung:
  Then grace her Trophee with a dance triumphant,
  Where *Orpheus* is none can fit musick want.

54 THE CAMPION, CHAPMAN, AND BEAUMONT MASQUES

A Song and dance triumphant of the Maskers.

Example 1.14 *Dance, dance and visit now the shadowes of our ioy*, set to *Will saide to his mammy that hee woulde goe woo*, from Jones's *Fourth Booke of Ayres* (1609).

Example 1.14 Continued

1. Dance, dance, and visit now the shadowes of our ioy,
All in height, and pleasing state, your changed formes imploy.
And as the bird of *Joue* salutes, with loftie wing, the morn;
So mount, so flie, these Trophees to adorne.
Grace them with all the sounds and motions of delight,
Since all the earth cannot expresse a louelier sight,
View them with triumph, and in shades the truth adore,
No pompe or sacrifice can please *Joues* greatnesse more.

2. Turne, turne, and honor now the life, these figures beare,
Loe, how heau'nly natures farre aboue all art appeare,
Let their aspects reuiue in you, the fire that shin'd so late,
Still mount and still retaine, your heauenly state.
Gods were with dance, and with musick seru'd of old,
Those happie daies deriu'd their glorious stile from gold:
This pair by *Hymen* ioyn'd, grace you with measures then,
Since they are both diuine, and you are more then men.

Orph. Let here *Sybilla's* Trophee stand,
Leade her now by either hand,
That shee may approch yet nearer,
And the Bride and Bridegroome heare her
Blesse them in her natiue tongue,
Wherein old prophesies shee sung,
Which time to light hath brought:
Shee speakes that which *Joue* hath taught.
Well may he inspire her now,
To make a ioyfull and true vow.

Syb. Sponsam sponse toro tene pudicam,	Hold the chaste bride by the bride-bed, O bridegroom,
Sponsum sponsa tene toro pudicum.	Hold the chaste bridegroom by the bride-bed, O bride.
Non haec vnica nox datur beatis,	This is not the only night given to the blessed,
At vos perpetuò haec beabit vna	But this one will bless you forever
Prole multiplici, pari{que} amore.	With many offspring, and with equal love.
Laeta, ac vera refert Sybilla, ab alto	Happily and truthfully, Sybilla reports; from on high
Ipse Juppiter annuit loquenti.	Jupiter himself approves her prophecy.

Pro. So be it euer, ioy and peace,
And mutuall loue giue you increase,
That your posteritie may grow
In fame, as long as Seas doe flow.

Enth. Liue you long to see your ioyes,
In faire Nymphs and Princely Boyes:
Breeding like the Garden flowers,
 Which kinde heau'n drawes with her warme showers.

Orph. Enough of blessing, though too much
Neuer can be said to such;
But night doth wast, and *Hymen* chides,
Kinde to Bridegroomes and to Brides,
Then singing the last dance induce,
So let good night preuent excuse.

THE LORDS' MASQUE 57

The Song.

Example 1.15 *No longer wrong the night*, set to *Now let her change and spare not*, from Campion's *Third Booke of Ayres* (1617).

No longer wrong the night,   Fearing the approching day,
Of her *Hymenaean* right,   The Cocks alreadie crow,
A thousand *Cupids* call away,   Dance then and goe.

58 THE CAMPION, CHAPMAN, AND BEAUMONT MASQUES

*The last new Dance of the Maskers, which concludes
all with a liuely straine at their going out.*

Example 1.16 Third Measure: *The third of the Lords*: BL 10444/5, no. 24; Brade's *Newe Ausserlesene liebliche Branden* (1617), no. 8, *Des jungen Prinsen Intrada*.

Example 1.16 Continued

The Memorable Masque of the Middle Temple and Lincoln's Inn

George Chapman

Plate 2.1 George Chapman, *The Memorable Masque*, Title Page (1613) Courtesy of the Huntington Library.

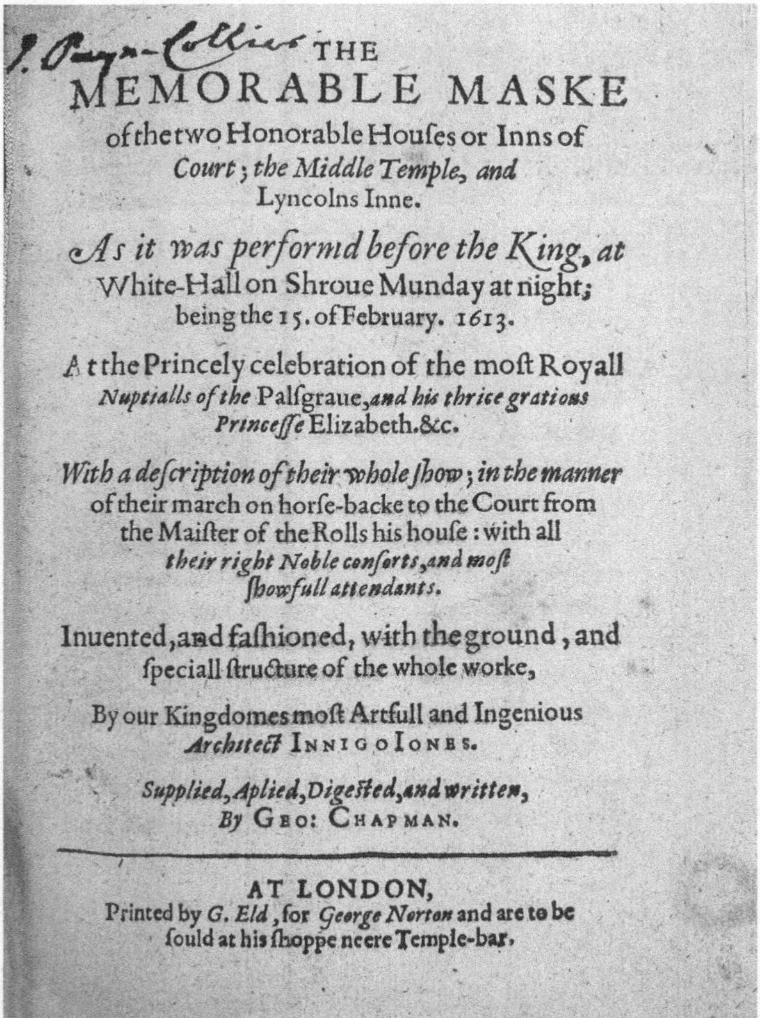

THE
MEMORABLE MASKE
of the two Honorable Houſes or Inns of
Court; the Middle Temple, and
Lyncolns Inne.

As it was performd before the King, at
White-Hall on Shroue Munday at night;
being the 15. of February. 1613.

At the Princely celebration of the moſt Royall
Nuptialls of the Palſgraue, *and his thrice gratious*
Princeſſe Elizabeth.&c.

With a deſcription of their whole ſhow; in the manner
of their march on horſe-backe to the Court from
the Maiſter of the Rolls his houſe: with all
their right Noble conſorts, and moſt
ſhowfull attendants.

Inuented, and faſhioned, with the ground, and
ſpeciall ſtructure of the whole worke,

By our Kingdomes moſt Artfull and Ingenious
Architect INNIGO IONES.

Supplied, Aplied, Digeſted, and written,
By GEO: CHAPMAN.

AT LONDON,
Printed by *G. Eld*, for *George Norton* and are to be
ſould at his ſhoppe neere Temple-bar.

Unmasked, Ross W. Duffin, Oxford University Press. © Oxford University Press 2025.
DOI: 10.1093/oso/9780197771488.003.0002

Introduction

Financial accounts for this masque[1] survive in the so-called Black Books of Lincoln's Inn, and give some useful details about the artists involved.[2] Besides £100 to Inigo Jones, Robert Johnson was paid £45 "for musicke and songes"; Thomas Cutting, John Dowland, and Philip Rosseter each received £2 10s, and John Sturt, Robert Taylor, Robert Dowland (John's son), and Thomas Davies each received £2 "for playing of Lutes"; Mathias Johnson received £2 "for singing," and "7 singing men"—including one boy "Querester"—were paid lesser amounts.[3] In addition, Thomas Ford received £2 10s "for playing of Lute," just like his famous colleagues, but a further £5 "for setting songes used at the Maske." Oddly, George Chapman is not listed as receiving payment, though we know from the title page of the quartos that the masque was "*Supplied, Aplied, Digested, and written,* By GEO: CHAPMAN."[4]

As with *The Lords' Masque,* the three masque dances survive in the dance music manuscript associated with the Inns of Court, BL 10444/5, and also in five-part arrangements in Brade's 1617 collection. Also preserved in both of those sources is the antimasque, *The Babboons Dance.*[5] None of this dance music bears a composer ascription in any of the sources, but all of it has been attributed to Robert Johnson. This makes sense, as he was paid £20 specifically "for making the Daunces" for Prince Henry's masque of *Oberon, the Faery Prince,* in 1611.[6] No song settings survive for Chapman's masque, however. As John F. Cutts, Robert Johnson's modern champion, lamented: "I cannot trace Robert Johnson's settings of any of the songs."[7]

---

[1] The 1614? quarto uses "Masque," rather than "Maske" and that has been preferred here.
[2] These were first published in W. P. Baildon, ed., *The Records of the Honorable Society of Lincoln's Inn: The Black Books,* vol. 2 (London, 1898), 154–57. For a recent edition, see *Records of Early English Drama: Inns of Court,* ed. Alan H. Nelson and John R. Elliott, vol. 1 (2010), 155–58. The payment lists are in Lincoln's Inn Archive, A1a6 (Black Book 6), fols. 526–27.
[3] Among these singing men was composer Walter Porter.
[4] John Ward speculates that Chapman and the dancing masters were not paid by the Middle Temple, but by Lincoln's Inn, whose payment records for the event do not survive. See Ward, "Newly Devis'd Measures," 131, n. 49. Chapman's masque was edited by Blakemore Evans in *The Plays of George Chapman* (Urbana, 1970), 557–94, and in *Court Masques: Jacobean and Caroline Entertainments, 1605–1640,* ed. David Lindley (Oxford, 1995), 74–91.
[5] See Sabol, *Four Hundred Songs and Dances,* Nos. 78, 90–92, 263–68. The Sabol edition includes two settings from *Taffel Consort* (Hamburg, 1621) by Thomas Simpson, another expatriate English violinist, on whom, see Peter Holman, "An Englishman Abroad: Thomas Simpson Revisited," *Viola da Gamba Society Journal* 18 (2024), 18–51.
[6] Kew, National Archives, E403/2730, fol. 181v.
[7] Cutts, "Robert Johnson and the Court Masque," 123.

Indeed, not only do musical settings of the masque lyrics not survive, but it is difficult to see how any of them might be set as *contrafacta* by versification match to any of Johnson's extant songs. That difficulty is compounded by the fact that Johnson did not publish any of his song settings, and virtually all of those that do survive are in manuscripts compiled after his death in 1633.[8] In February 1611, Johnson was paid £5 for setting Ferrabosco's songs 'to the lutes,'[9] apparently for the Jonsonian masque, *Love freed from ignorance and folly*. That seems clearly to be arranging, rather than composing, so what must be considered is that Johnson did not compose the music for the songs in Chapman's *Memorable Masque*, as has been generally assumed, but was paid for composing the dances and arranging the songs that were made by someone else. One likely candidate for "making" some of the songs—specifically, for repurposing them from his own earlier compositions—is Thomas Ford, who, as already noted, was paid £5 "for setting songes used at the Maske." That entry has been overshadowed by the amount paid to Johnson "for musicke and songes," but it might hold a key to recovering some of the songs in this masque.

One observer who provides intriguing details about this masque is the inveterate letter-writer John Chamberlain, who describes the gallant procession and shares hearsay about the performance in a letter to Alice Carleton on 18 February 1613, three days after the event. This is mostly peripheral to the performance, but we learn that there were trumpeters in the company, that boys played the antimasque of the baboons, and that the musicians were sufficiently esteemed that they got to ride with the actors in four-horse chariots.

> On monday night was the middle Temple and Lincolns ynne maske presented in the hall at court, whereas the Lords was in the banketting roome, yet went from the Rolles all up fleetstreet and the Strand, and made such a gallant and glorious shew that yt is highly commended. They had forty gentlemen of best choise out of both houses rode before them in thayre best array vpon the k[ing]s horses, and the twelve maskers wth

---

[8] For a summary of the attribution situation in Johnson's songs, see Ross W. Duffin, "Thomas Morley, Robert Johnson, and Songs for the Shakespearean Stage," in *The Oxford Handbook of Shakespeare and Music*, ed. Mervyn Cooke and Christopher R. Wilson (Oxford, 2022), 356–86, https://doi.org/10.1093/oxfordhb/9780190945145.013.12.

[9] National Archives, E407/57/1, cited in *RECM* 4 (1603–1625), 31.

thayre torchbearers and pages rode likewise vpon horses excedingly well trapped and furnished, besides a dousen litle boyes drest like babones that serued for an antimaske; (and they say performed yt exceedingly well when they came to yt), and three open shariots drawne wth fowre horses apeece that caried theyre musicians and other personages that had parts to speake; all wch together wth theyre trumpetters and other attendants were so well set out, that it is generally held for the best shew that hath ben seen many a day. The king stoode in the gallerie to behold them and made them ride about the tiltyard, and then were receued into James parke and went all along the galleries (into) the hall, where themselves and theyre deuises (wch say were excellent) made such a glittering shew that the king and all the companie were exceedingly pleased, and specially wth theyre dauncing, wch was beyond all that hath ben yet. The king made the maskers kisse his hand at parting and gaue them many thankes, saying he neuer saw so many proper men together.[10]

Chapman's masque begins with copious "speeches and narrations," whose duration, in the quartos, he felt obliged to defend against "certaine insolent obiections." The dialogue is between the god Plutus (or Riches) and the capricious Capriccio, "a man of wit." After several minutes, their exchange ends with a call for the "Antemasque," whereupon a troop of baboons enters and performs a dance, both "Anticke, and delightful" (no. 2.1).[11] Their dance can be identified in BL 10444/5 as *The Babboons Dance* (no. 27)—especially fortunate because the concordance in Brade's collection is entitled *Intrada der Jungen Princessinnen* (no. 9), which has no connection to baboons. The five-part version in Brade is probably close to what was performed, but its final triple section is in 3, whereas the same section in BL 10444/5 is in 3 I,[12] a faster meter that Brade sometimes notates as 6/4. The faster tempo seems

---

[10] Kew, National Archives, SP 14/72, fols. 46v–47r.

[11] The 1614? quarto has "Anti-masque," rather than "Antemasque." Concerning onstage baboons, see Holly Dugan, "'To Bark with Judgment': Playing Baboon in Early Modern London," *Shakespeare Studies* 41 (2013), 77–93 https://hcommons.org/deposits/item/hc:19691. See also James Knowles, "'Can Ye Not Tell a Man from a Marmoset?': Apes and Others on the Early Modern Stage," in *Renaissance Beasts: Of Animals, Humans, and Other Wonderful Creatures*, ed. Erica Fudge (Urbana, 2004), 138–63.

[12] From a proportional standpoint, 3 would normally represent ₃, meaning three notes in the time of two previously, but 3 I would seem to indicate double that speed, with three notes in the time of one previously. The proportional system of mensuration was breaking down at this time, but clearly, a faster tempo was implied, whether or not it is taken to be twice as fast.

more appropriate to the antics of the baboons (and antimasques in general), so it has been preferred.

The next musical item is introduced simply as "Loud Musick, and Honor appears." This could have been a simple fanfare from the "trumpetters," but the text then refers to "The Musique ceasing," so that suggests it was an actual piece, corresponding to another antimasque. In this case, from BL 10444/5 I have chosen a dance with a fanfare-like opening: *The second [of the Temple Anticke]* (it follows *The first of the Temple Anticke*, so the continuation of the title is assumed). This dance does not appear in Brade, but it is among the five-part pieces in John Adson's 1621 *Courtly Masquing Ayres* (no. 8). Adson was a wind player, so a setting from his collection seems especially well suited to "Loude Musick," and the connection to The Temple is felicitous even though the use of this music is conjectural.

Ope Earth thy womb of golde (no. 2.3), the first song in *The Memorable Masque*, reveals the masquers' earnest hope that Virginia would soon yield quantities of gold, as the Spanish colonies had done. In fact, the colony's treasure was to be tobacco, the first fruits of which came to Britain in 1614.[13] The song is not set here with music by Thomas Ford, though it could be by one of the other performers. With six lines of ababcc and a versification of 333344, it matches two songs by Thomas Campion and one by John Dowland.[14] Campion's masque was performed on the previous evening, but Dowland was playing lute in Chapman's masque, so one of his songs might have appeared suitable as a model. The one used here, *What poore Astronomers are they*,[15] is not a perfect match in versification: the rhyme scheme is identical, but the versification is 434344, instead of 333344. It matches in other ways, however. Here are the masque lyric and the first stanza of Dowland's song in parallel:

---

[13] See Wesley Frank Craven, *The Virginia Company of London, 1606–1624* (Williamsburg, 1957), 30. On the Virginia connections to Chapman's masque, along with the significance of the baboons, see Patricia Crouch, "Patronage and Competing Visions of Virginia in George Chapman's 'The Memorable Masque' (1613)," *English Literary Renaissance* 40 (2010), 393–426, http://www.jstor.org/stable/43740814.

[14] *Giue beauty all her right* (1613), and *Her fair inflaming eyes* (1617) by Campion, and *Flow not so fast yee fountaines* (1603) by Dowland.

[15] John Dowland, *The Third and Last Book of Songs or Aires* (1603; STC: 7096), no. 20, sigs. L2v–M1r.

Memorable Masque	Dowland: *Third Booke of Songs* (1603)
Ope Earth thy wombe of golde,	What poore Astronomers are they,
Shew Heauen thy cope of starres.	Take womens eies for stars
All glad Aspects vnfolde,	And set their thoughts in battell ray
Shine out, and cleere our Cares:	To fight such idle warres,
Kisse Heauen and Earth, and so combine	When in the end they shall approue,
In all mixt ioy our Nuptiall Twine.	Tis but a iest drawne out of loue.

Besides using the imagery of "Heauen" and "Earth" in a nuptial song opposite the "Astronomers" of Dowland's love song, the word "stars" occurs in an identical and prominent phrase-ending position in each lyric. The masque song is introduced as follows: "the Phoebades (or Priests of the Sunne) appear'd first with sixe Lutes, and six voices, and sung ... this ful Song." As noted above, a "full song" is one where all of the parts are sung, which works well here because Dowland's original has four texted voices in addition to the lute accompaniment. Since Dowland was one of the seven named lutenists in the Black Book accounts, he was almost certainly one of the six lutenists for this piece as well. The final phrase of the song may be reprised from the sign of congruence.

The second song in Chapman's masque, *Descend (faire Sun) and sweetly rest* (no. 2.4), has no single model that stands out above all others, and several pieces could work. Again, the Sun's Priests, the Phoebades, sing this lyric, "in an Hymne addresse to *Phoebus* setting" (i.e., a hymn at sunset), so a full song is once more expected. The stanza, or "Stance," as it is called,[16] is divided into three cross-rhymed tetrameter quatrains. The first is sung by "One alone," the second by "Another alone," and the third quatrain is assigned to the Chorus. Since each of these seems to be discrete, it is tempting to use a model that has tetrameter quatrain stanzas, and one that works well is Thomas Ford's *There is a lady sweet and kind*, from *Musicke of Sundrie Kindes*, of 1607 (no. 2.4a).[17] The first two quatrains would be sung as solos by the top part accompanied by instruments (so the lyrics in the lower parts would be unnecessary), and the other voices would join the instruments for the chorus on the third quatrain.

Another possibility, especially since the song is described as a "Hymne," is Campion's *As by the streames of Babilon* (no. 2.4b), a setting of Psalm 137,

---

[16] "Stance" is emended to "Stanze" in the 1614? quarto.
[17] No. 9, sigs. E2v–F1r.

even though it comes from his *First Booke of Ayres* (1613).[18] In spite of its source, this has a definite hymn-like quality, and it was published the same year as the masque. Again, the first two quatrains would be sung as solos by the top part accompanied by instruments, as described above, and the other voices would join the instruments for the chorus.

A third quatrain setting for this song can be made to *Sweet Cupid, ripen her desire*, from *Ayres to Sing and Play to the Lvte and Basse Violl* (1610) by viol player and composer William Corkine.[19] It hardly seems necessary to offer a third quatrain setting, although it would allow the two soloists and the chorus to use different music for each of the three quatrains within each larger stanza as a highly unusual but distinctive means of differentiating their singing. There is, moreover, a contemporary connection between the composer and the Middle Temple: William Corkine was not listed as performing in *The Memorable Masque*, but on 2 February 1613, John Dowland signed a receipt for payment of himself and Corkine for a "consorte" at Middle Temple on that day (Candlemas Day).[20] That was surely during the time that the masque was being prepared, involving Dowland himself, and less than two weeks before the wedding day and the masque performance. Combined with the sentiment of the model, appropriate for an epithalamium, it seems worth offering this setting by Corkine as another alternative (no. 2.4c). A texted Cantus with tablature and untexted Bassus are given in Corkine's print, so the inner parts and the texting of the Bassus are editorial. As with the other quatrain settings, the first two quatrains would be sung as solos by the top part accompanied by instruments, as above, and the other voices would join in on the chorus. As noted above, an alternative would be to use the three quatrain settings given here for the three distinct sections within each stanza.

One problem with using a quatrain setting is that it creates a lot of repetition, with four "Stances" of the song in the masque, each having three quatrains. That raises the possibility that it was intended to be set to a song that had stanzas consisting of twelve cross-rhymed tetrameter lines, divided into three sections that could accommodate the sections for the two soloists and chorus. In fact, only one lutesong from the period fits that description: *Now O now I needs must part* (no. 2.4d), from John Dowland's *First*

---

[18] No. 14, sig. E2v–F1r.
[19] STC: 5768: no. 7, sigs. C1v. In all, there are nine cross-rhymed tetrameter songs in the lutesong repertoire through Campion's 1617 print, so further possibilities exist, though the best matches are given here.
[20] Middle Temple, Archive, MT.7/GDE/3. Another player paid by this receipt was Richard Goosey, who is otherwise unknown. See Elliott, "Invisible Evidence," 54.

Booke of Songes or Ayres, of 1597.[21] There are no obvious verbal parallels to support that choice, though the final rhymes of the first stanza, "discends–attends," do recall the "sends–offends" rhymes of Dowland's first stanza.

One odd aspect of the four twelve-line stanzas of *Descend (faire Sun)* is that the last two are both apparently headed "third stance." The fourth stanza is clearly the last because it is introduced with "Againe our Musique and conclude this Song."[22] The second and fourth stanzas also have similar but confusing headings: "Other Musique, and voyces; and this second Stance was sung," and "The other voyces sung to other Musike the third [i.e., fourth?] stance." What this means is unclear. It seems most likely that "other music and voices" indicate two groups of singers and instruments that alternated in performing the four stanzas, the first and third by group 1 and the second and fourth by group 2. An alternative is that the first and last stanzas were performed by group 1, and the second and third by group 2, with the stage direction correctly referring to "the third stance" in spite of its position before the fourth.

After that song, the priestess Eunomia pleads with the sun-worshipping Virginian Princes—apparently resembling North American Indians in Inigo Jones's watercolor (Color Plate 1)—to renounce their superstitions for Christian devotion.[23] This is followed by another "Antemaske" with torchbearers, this time "with torches lighted at both ends." The conjectural choice here is a dance in BL 10444/5 entitled *Essex Anticke Masque* (no. 92), which has no apparent connection to Chapman's masque but which seems to fit the musical requirements well. Again, it is not in Brade's collection, but it is in Adson (no. 4). Unusually, it begins with a section in ϕ, which implies a faster duple tempo than music in $\mathbb{C}$.

The torchbearers having completed their dance, the gentlemen masquers immediately begin their first two measures in short succession. These can be identified as *The first of the Temple* (no. 2.6 [sic]) and *The second of the Temple* (no. 2.7 [sic]), dance titles from BL 10444/5, where they also appear consecutively (nos. 39 and 40). Their five-part versions in Brade, on the other hand, are

---

[21] STC: 7091: no. 6, sigs C2v–D1r.
[22] The text had previously said that "the *Phoebades* sung the third Stance," so this confirms that singers then perform the fourth (mislabeled) stanza, not the third.
[23] At the time of the masque, the Virginia Company of London was emphasizing the missionary aspect of their efforts to develop the fledgling colony. See Craven, *The Virginia Company of London*, 38. Jones's Virginian torchbearer may be derived from Vecellio's "Indo Africano" (see App. 2.1) and also has many features that resemble "America" from Huntington MS HM1016 (see Color Plate 10), like a long cape, feathered headdress, and feathers surrounding the waist and lower leg.

not consecutive and, once again, the titles there bear no apparent relation to this masque: *Auffzug der Kauffleute* (no. 21) and *Der Irlender Tantz* (no. 26). The two measures are followed by the first of two Revels, where the masquers take members of the audience out on the floor for a series of social dances.[24]

Finally, after all this dancing, comes the third song of Chapman's masque, *Bright Panthaea borne to Pan* (no. 2.8). The lyric has three six-line tetrameter stanzas, each followed by a tetrameter couplet for the chorus. One of the best matches for that versification is *Now I see thy lookes were fained*, from Thomas Ford's *Musicke of Sundrie Kindes*, of 1607.[25] Here are the first stanzas of the two songs in parallel:

Memorable Masque	Ford: *Musicke of Sundrie Kindes* (1607)
Bright *Panthaea* borne to Pan,	Now I see thy lookes were fained,
Of the Noblest Race of Man,	Quickly lost and quickly gained,
Her white hand to *Eros* giuing,	Soft thy skin like wooll of wethers,
With a kisse, ioin'd Heauen to Earth	Hart vnconstant light as feathers,
And begot so faire a birth,	Tongue vntrusty subtle sighted,
As yet neuer grac't the liuing.	Wanton will with change delighted,
CHO: A Twinne that all worlds did adorne,	Syren pleasant foe to reason,
For so were *Loue* and *Bewty* borne.	Cupid plague thee for thy treason.

Conveniently, Ford's song has a closing couplet refrain that matches the masque song's chorus, and it is set in four voices. The opening is labeled as "sung; single," however, which probably means that the stanza was sung by an accompanied soloist, with the chorus joining for the final couplet.[26] The last strain—the chorus—may be repeated from the sign of congruence. "This sung, the Maskers danc't againe with the Ladies," which means that following this song was a second episode of Revels, with social dancing involving members of the audience. Having a second revels—or having the revels interrupted by speaking and singing before resuming—was highly unusual (if not unique) in a Jacobean masque.[27]

The fourth and final song, described as "A Hymn to Sleep," is introduced with the rubric, "the last Song was sung full." *Now sleepe, binde fast, the*

---

[24] See further description in the Revels for *The Lords' Masque* earlier in the book.
[25] No. 4, sigs. C1v–C2r.
[26] See the third song in Beaumont's masque, below, where "Single" and "All" are more explicit.
[27] See William Dean, "Masques and like Devices in Chapman's Plays: Towards *The Memorable Maske*," *Parergon* 9 (1991), 31–43, at 32, https://doi.org/10.1353/pgn.1991.0042.

flood of Ayre consists of a single stanza of ten lines, with two cross-rhymed quatrains and a closing couplet. The versification is unusual, however, with ballad meter for the first quatrain, trimeters for the second quatrain, and tetrameters for the final couplet: 4343333344. There is no song in the lutesong repertoire with a versification to match that, but a good setting (no. 2.9a) can be made with *Unto the temple of thy beauty*, from Ford's *Musicke of Sundrie Kindes* (1607).[28] That song has only eight lines, but with a judicious repeat, the music accommodates the complete lyric from the masque.[29] In addition, the final strain from the sign of congruence could still be reprised, words and music together.

An alternative setting of this lyric (no. 2.9b) can be made with Campion's *Your faire lookes enflame my desire* from *A Booke of Ayres* (1601).[30] It has an eight-line stanza that matches the versification fairly well as far as it goes (43433343), with a poulter's-measure quatrain instead of trimeter quatrain for the second half. Accommodating the final tetrameter couplet of the masque lyric is not so straightforward, but it can work with a reprise of the last part of the song.[31] The original setting is for solo voice with lute and untexted Bassus, so the inner parts here are editorial, along with the texting of the Bassus.

The Memorable Masque concludes "with a dance, that brought them off," namely, the third measure (no. 2.10). In BL 10444/5, *The third of the Temple* follows directly after the first two (no. 41), so the evidence is strong for these three dances together. This third main dance also appears in Brade, as *Auffzug vor Grienwitsch* (no. 22)—again a title that is not apparently related to the masque, although it has a London (Greenwich) connection at least.

After the masque in the quartos, a long epithalamium is printed: *A Hymne to Hymen for the most time*-fitted Nuptialls of our thrice *gracious Princesse Elizabeth, &c*. With eighty-four pentameter lines in rhyming couplets, unbroken into stanzas, it does not look like something that might be sung and, indeed, no one to my knowledge has previously suggested that possibility. It begins, "Singe, singe," however, so that does seem to invite music, and there

---

[28] STC: 11166: no. 3, s.gs. B2v–C1r.
[29] Since a sign of congruence calls for a repeat of the final strain, it would be possible to repeat that, rather than the middle strain, but this solution preserves parallel rhymes in the music from couplet to couplet. One odd contrapuntal feature is an instance of parallel fifths between the Cantus and Tenor at the anticipation in the penultimate measure. It may be that its short duration rendered it insignificant, and that, though avoided throughout this edition, equivalent instances in reconstructed parts here could use a similar passing tone leading to the third of the final chord.
[30] STC: 21332: no. 17.
[31] In fact, the reprise indicated in the original is from bar 5, so this is a modification.

is much musical imagery throughout. Eighty-four divides evenly into twelve, so a song with a twelve-line stanza of pentameters in rhyming couplets seems like it would work best. Only one such song exists in the lutesong repertoire: *Away, away, call backe what you haue said*, from William Corkine's *The Second Booke of Ayres* (1612),[32] so that initially appears to be the prime candidate to set twelve-line stanzas in the epithalamium. Corkine's lyric, in fact, has many resonances with the masque, including Hymen and dancing Apes, but the setting is long and has enjambments and repetitions that complicate and extend what is already a long song.

As printed, the *Hymne* has some puzzling marginal notes, moreover, that point to a different and, perhaps, stronger possibility: at the ninth line in each quarto (and at odd places thereafter) appears the annotation "Simil." (*Similiter*, or Similarly), meaning something should happen at the ninth line to repeat what happened for the first eight. This could be interpreted as calling for an eight-line stanza, even though eighty-four does not divide evenly into eight. The only eight-line pentameter song in rhyming couplets preserved from the first half of the seventeenth century is, once again, by Corkine, from that same 1612 collection: *My deerest Mistrisse, let vs liue and loue* (no. 2.11)—a sentiment that also seems appropriate for an epithalamium.[33] Here is Corkine's stanza in parallel with the first eight lines of Chapman's poem.

Memorable Masque Epithalamium	Corkine: *Second Booke of Ayres* (1612)
Singe, Singe a Rapture to all Nuptial eares,	My deerest Mistrisse, let vs liue and loue,
Bright *Hymens* torches, drunke vp *Parcaes* tears:	And care not what old doting fooles reproue,
Sweete *Hymen*; *Hymen*, Mightiest of Gods,	Let vs not feare their sensures, nor esteeme,
Attoning of all-taming blood the odds;	What they of vs and of our loues shall deeme,
Two into One, contracting; One to Two Dilating, which no other God can doe.	Old ages critticke and sensorious brow, Cannot of youthfull dalliance alow,
Mak'st sure, with change, and lett'st the married try,	Nor neuer could endure that wee should tast,
Of Man and woman, the Variety.	Of those delights which they themselues are past.

---

[32] STC: 5769: no. 14, sig. E1v.
[33] No. 11, sig. D2r. Echoing the sentiment of Christopher Marlowe's "Come liue with me and be my loue" (though in pentameter verse), Corkine's lyric has just this single stanza. The setting below is transposed down a step from Corkine's original, and the fourth note of bar 16 has been raised a step to maintain the melodic pattern.

The final quatrain of the eighty-four lines would need to be sung to the second half of the music, from the editorial sign of congruence in bar 12, but with that adjustment, it works well. The last couplet echoing the first, with "Sing, sing," furthermore, seems to reinforce the possibility of a musical setting, and Corkine being paid for making music at Middle Temple just days before the wedding makes the choice of a recently published model by him all the more justified.

Table of Musical Contents for *The Memorable Masque*

Song / Dance		Model	Source
2.1.	Antimasque – Baboons	*The Babboons Dance*	BL10444:27; Brade (1617), no. 9
2.2.	Antimasque – Loud Music	*The second [of the Temple Anticke]*	BL10444:123; Adson (1621), no. 8
2.3.	*Ope Earth thy womb of golde*	*What poore Astronomers are they*	Dowland: *Third Booke of Songs* (1603)
2.4.	*Descend (faire Sun) and sweetly rest*	*There is a lady sweet and kind*	Ford: *Musicke of Sundrie Kindes* (1607)
		As by the streames of Babilon	Campion: *First Booke of Ayres* (1613)
		Sweet Cupid, ripen her desire	Corkine: *Ayres to Sing and Play* (1610)
		Now O now I needs must part	Dowland: *First Booke of Songes* (1597)
2.5.	Antimasque – Torchbearers	*Essex Anticke Masque*	BL10444:92; Adson (1621), no. 4
2.6.	First Measure	*The first of the Temple*	BL10444:39; Brade (1617), no. 21
2.7.	Second Measure	*The second of the Temple*	BL10444:40; Brade (1617), no. 26
Revels 1			
2.8.	*Bright Panthaea borne to Pan*	*Now I see thy lookes were fained*	Ford: *Musicke of Sundrie Kindes* (1607)
Revels 2			
2.9.	*Now sleepe binde fast the floode*	*Unto the temple of thy beauty*	Ford: *Musicke of Sundrie Kindes* (1607)
		Your faire lookes enflame my desire	Campion: *A Booke of Ayres* (1601)
2.10.	Third Measure	*The third of the Temple*	BL10444:41; Brade (1617), no. 22
2.11.	*Singe, Singe a Rapture to all Nuptiall eares*	*My deerest Mistrisse, let vs liue and loue*	Corkine: *Second Booke of Ayres* (1612)

THE MEMORABLE MASKE
of the two Honorable Houses or Inns of
Court; the Middle Temple, and
Lyncolns Inne.

As it was performd before the King, at
White-Hall on Shroue Munday at night;
being the 15. of February. 1613.

At the Princely celebration of the most Royall
Nuptialls of the Palsgraue, *and his thrice gratious*
Princesse Elizabeth. &c.

With a description of their whole show; in the manner
of their march on horse-backe to the Court from
the Maister of the Rolls his house: with all
their right Noble consorts, and most
showfull attendants.

Inuented, and fashioned, with the ground, and
speciall structure of the whole worke,

By our Kingdomes most Artfull and Ingenious
Architect INNIGO IONES.
Supplied, Aplied, Digested, and written,
By GEO: CHAPMAN.
AT LONDON,

Printed by G. *Eld*, for *George Norton* and are to be
sould at his shoppe neere Temple-bar.

TO THE MOST
Noble, and constant Combiner of Honor,
and Vertue, Sir EDWARD PHILIPS,
Knight, Mr. of the Rolls.

This Noble and Magnificent performance, renewing the ancient spirit, and
Honor of the Innes of Court; being especially furthered and followed by your

most laborious and honored endeuors, (for his Maiesties seruice; and honour of the all-grace-deseruing Nuptialls, of the thrice gracious Princesse Elizabeth, *his Highness daughter) deserues especially to be in this sort consecrate, to your worthy memory and honor. Honor, hauing neuer her faire hand more freely and nobly giuen to Riches (being a fit particle of this Inuention) then by yours, at this Nuptiall solemnity. To which assisted, and memorable ceremony; the ioin'd hand and industry, of the worthely honour'd Knight, Sir* H. Hubberd, *his Maiesties Atturny generall, deseruing, in good part, a ioint memory with yours; I have submitted it freely to his noble acceptance. The poore paines I added to this Royall seruice, being wholly chosen, and commanded by your most constant, and free fauour; I hope will now appeare nothing neglectiue of their expected duties. Hearty wil, and care enough, I am assured was employ'd in me; and the onely ingenuous will, being first and principall step to vertue; I beseech you let it stand for the performing vertue itselfe. In which addition of your euer-honour'd fauours, you shall euer binde all my future seruice to your most wished Commandement.*

God send you long health, and your Vertues will endue you with honor enough,

By your free merits euer vow'd honorer,
and most vnfainedly affectionate
Obseruant.
GEO. CHAPMAN.

THE MASKE OF THE
Gentlemen of the two combin'd houses,
or Inns of Court, the Middle-Temple,
and Lincolns Inne.

At the house of the most worthely honour'd preferrer and gracer of all honorable Actions, and vertues, (Sir *Edward Philips* Knight, Master of the Rolls) al the Performers and their Assistents made their *Rendes vous*, prepar'd to their performance, and thus set forth.

Fiftie Gentlemen, richly attirde, and as gallantly mounted, with Footmen perticularly attending, made the noble vant-guarde of these Nuptiall forces. Next (a fit distance obseru'd betweene them) marcht a mock-Maske of Baboons, attir'd like fantasticall Trauailers, in Neapolitane sutes, and great ruffes, all horst with Asses; and dwarfe Palfries, with yellow foot-cloathes, and casting Cockle-demois about, in courtesie, by way of lardges;

Torches boarn on either hand of them; lighting their state as ridiculously, as the rest Nobly. After them were sorted two Carrs Triumphall, adornd with great Maske heads, Festones, scroules, and antick leaues, euery part inricht with siluer and golde. These were through-varied with different inuention, and in them aduanc't, the choice Musitions of our Kingdome, sixe in each; attir'd like Virginean Priests, by whom the Sun is there ador'd; and therfore called the Phoebades. Their Robes were tuckt vp before; strange Hoods of feathers, and scallops about their neckes, and on their heads turbants, stucke with seuerall colour'd feathers, spotted with wings of Flies, of extraordinary bignesse; like those of their countrie: And about them march't two ranks of Torches. Then rode the chiefe Maskers, in Indian habits, all of a resemblance: the ground cloath of siluer, richly embroidered, with golden Sunns, and about euery Sunne, ran a traile of gold, imitating Indian worke,: their bases of the same stuffe and work, but betwixt euery pane of embroidery, went a rowe of white Estridge feathers, mingled with sprigs of golde plate; vnder their breasts, they woare bawdricks of golde, embroidered high with purle, and about their neckes, Ruffes of feathers, spangled with pearle and siluer. On their heads high sprig'd-feathers, compast in Coronets, like the Virginian Princes they presented. Betwixt euery set of feathers, and about their browes, in the vnder-part of their Coronets, shin'd Sunnes of golde plate, sprinkled with pearle; from whence sprung rayes of the like plate, that mixing with the motion of the feathers, shew'd exceedingly delightfull, and gracious. Their legges were adorn'd, with close long white silke-stockings: curiously embroidered with golde to the Midde-legge.

And ouer these (being on horse backe) they drew greaues or buskins embrodered with gould, & enterlac't with rewes of fethers; Altogether estrangfull, and *Indian* like.

In their Hands (set in seueral postures as they rode) they brandisht cane darts of the finest gould. Their vizerds of blue collour; but pleasingly visag'd: their hayre, blacke and lardge, wauing downe to their shoulders.

Their Horse, for rich show, equalld the Maskers them-selues; all their caparisons being enchac't with sunnes of Gould and Ornamentall Iewells. To euery one of which, was tackt a Scarffing of Siluer; that ran sinnuously in workes ouer the whole caparison, euen to the daseling of the admiring spectators.

Their heads, no lesse gracefully and properly deckt with the like light skarffing that hung about their eares wantonly dangling.

Euery one of these horse, had two Moores, attir'd like *Indian* slaues, that for state sided them; with swelling wreaths of gould, and watshed on their heads, which arose in all to the number of a hundred.

The Torch-bearers habits were likewise of the *Indian* garb, but more strauagant then those of the Maskers; all showfully garnisht with seueral-hewd fethers. The humble variety whereof, stucke off the more amplie, the Maskers high beauties, shining in the habits of themselues; and reflected in their kinde, a new and delightfully-varied radiance on the beholders.

All these sustaind torches of *Virgine* wax, whose staues were great canes al ouer gilded; And these (as the rest) had euery Man his Moore, attending his horse.

The Maskers, riding single; had euery Masker, his Torch-bearer mounted before him.

The last Charriot, which was most of all adornd; had his whole frame fill'd with moulded worke; mixt all with paintings, and glittering scarffings of siluer; ouer which was cast a Canopie of golde, boarne vp with antick figures, and all compos'd *a la Grotesea*. Before this in the seate of it, as the Chariotere; was aduanc't a strange person, and as strangely habited, half French, halfe Swizz; his name *Capriccio*; wearing on his head a paire of golden Bellowes, a guilt spurre in one hand, and with the other mannaging the reignes of the fowre Horses that drewe it:

On a seate of the same Chariot, a little more eleuate, sate *Eunomia*, the Virgine Priest of the Goddesse *Honor*, together with *Phemis*, her Herald: The habite of her Priest, was a Robe of white silke, gathered about the necke; a pentacle of siluered stuffe about her shoulders, hanging foldedly downe, both before and behind.

A vestall vaile on her head of Tiffany, strip't with siluer, hanging with a trayne, to the earth.

The Herrald was attyr'd in an Antique Curace[34] of siluer stuffe, with labells at the wings and basses; a short gowne of gould stuffe; with wide sleeues, cut in panes: A wreath of gould on his head, and a Rod of gould in his hand.

Highest of all in the most eminent seate of the Tryumphall sat, side to side, the coelestiall Goddesse, *Honour*; and the earthy Deity, *Plutus*; or Riches. His attire; a short robe of gould, frindg'd; his wide sleeues turn'd vp, and out-showd his naked armes: his Head and Beard sprinckl'd with showrs of

---

[34] Curace = cuirass

gould: his Buskins, clinckant, as his other attire. The Ornaments of Honor were these: a rich full robe of blew silke girt about her, a mantle of siluer worne ouer-thwart, ful gathered, and descending in folds behind: a vaile of net lawne, enbrodered with Oos and Spangl'd;[35] her tresses in tucks, braided with siluer: The hinder part shadowing in waues her shoulders.

These, thus perticularly, and with proprietie adorn'd, were strongly attended with a full Guard of two hundred Halbardiers: two Marshals (being choice Gentlemen, of either house) Commaunder-like attir'd, to and fro coursing, to keepe all in their orders.

A showe at all parts so nouell, conceit full and glorious, as hath not in this land, (to the proper vse and obiect it had purpos'd) beene euer before beheld. Nor did those honorable Inns of Court, at any time in that kinde, such acceptable seruice to the sacred Maiesty of this kingdome, nor were return'd by many degrees, with so thrice gratious, and royall entertainment and honor. But, (as aboue sayd) all these so marching to the Court at White Hall, the King, Bride, & Bridegroom, with all the Lords of the most honord priuy Councel, and our chief Nobility, stood in the Gallery before the Tilt-yeard, to behold their arriuall; who, for the more ful satisfaction of his Maiesties view, made one turn about the yeard, and dismounted: being then honorably attended through the Gallery to a Chamber appointed, where they were to make ready for their performance in the Hall, &c.

The King beeing come forth, the Maskers ascended vnseene to their scoene. Then for the works.

First there appear'd at the lower end of the Hall, an Artificiall Rock, whose top was neere as high as the hall it selfe. This Rock, was in the vndermost part craggy, and full of hollow places, in whose concaues were contriv'd, two winding paire of staires, by whose greeces the Persons aboue might make their descents, and all the way be seene: all this Rocke grew by degrees vp into a gold-colour; and was run quite through, with veines of golde: On the one side whereof, eminently raised on a faire hill, was erected a siluer Temple of an octangle figure, whose Pillars were of a compos'd order, and bore vp an Architraue, Freese, and Cornish: Ouer which stood a continued Plinthe; whereon were aduaunc't Statues of siluer: Aboue this, was placed a bastarde Order of Architecture, wherein were keru'd Compartements: In one of which

---

[35] "Oos" are metal eyelets used for decoration. Ben Jonson used the same term in *Hymenaei*, presented in 1606 but not printed until his *Workes* (1616; STC:14752), 926.

was written in great golde Capitalls, HONORIS FANVM:[36] Aboue all, was a *Coupolo*, or Type, which seem'd to be scal'd with siluer Plates.

For finishing, of all, vpon a Pedistall, was fixt a round stone of siluer, from which grew a paire of golden wings, both faign'd to bee Fortunes: the round stone (when her feet trod it) euer affirm'd to be rouling; figuring her inconstancy: the golden wings, denoting those nimble Powres, that pompously beare her about the world; On that Temple (erected to her daughter, *Honor*; and figuring this kingdome) put off by her, and fixt, for assured signes he would neuer forsake it.

About this Temple, hung Festones wreath'd with siluer from one Pillars head to another. Besides, the Freese was enricht with keruings, all shewing Greatnes and Magnificence.

On the other side of the Rocke, grewe a Groue, in whose vtmost part appear'd a vast, wither'd, and hollow Tree, being the bare receptacle of the Baboonerie.

These following should in duty haue had their proper places, after euery fitted speech of the Actors; but being preuented by the vnexpected haste of the Printer, which he neuer let me know, and neuer sending me a proofe, till he had past those speeches; I had no reason to imagine hee could haue been so forward. His fault is therfore to be supplied by the obseruation, and reference of the Reader, who will easily perceiue, where they were to bee inserted.

After the speech of *Plutus* (who as you may see after, first entred) the middle part of the Rocke began to moue, and being come some fiue paces vp towards the King, it split in peeces with a great crack; and out brake *Capriccio*, as before described. The peeces of the Rocke vanisht and he spake as in his place.

At the singing of the first Song, full, which was sung by the Virginian Priests; called the Phoebades, to sixe Lutes (being vsed as an Orphean vertue, for the state of the Mines opening): the vpper part of the Rock was sodainly turn'd to a Cloude, discouering a rich and refulgent Mine of golde; in which the twelue Maskers were triumphantly seated: their Torch-bearers attending before them. All the lights beeing so ordred, that though none were seen, yet had their lustre such vertue, that by it, the least spangle or spark of the Maskers rich habites, might with ease and cleerenesse be discerned as far off as the seate.

Ouer this golden Mine, in an Euening sky, the ruddy Sunne was seen ready to be set; and behind the tops of certaine white Cliffes, by degrees descended, casting

---

[36] Honoris Fanvm = Temple of Honor

vp a banke of Cloudes; in which, a while hee was hidden: but then gloriously shining, gaue that vsually-obseru'd good Omen, of succeeding faire weather.

Before he was fully set, the Phoebades (shewing the custome of the Indians to adore the Sunne setting) began their obseruance with the Song, to whose place, wee must referre you for the manner and words; All the time they were singing; the Torch-bearers holding vp their Torches to the Sun; to whome the Priests themselues, and the rest, did as they sung obeisance: Which was answred by other Musique and voices, at the commandement of *Honor,* withal' obseruances vs'd to the King &c. As in the following places.

To answer certaine insolent obiections made against the length of my speeches, and narrations; being (for the probability of all accidents, rising from the inuention of this Maske; and their aplication, to the persons, and places: for whome, and by whome it was presented) not conuenient, but necessary; I am enforct to affirme this; That: as there is no Poem nor Oration so generall; but hath his one perticular proposition; Nor no riuer so extrauagantly ample, but hath his neuer-so-narrow fountaine, worthy to be namd; so all these courtly, and honoring inuentions (hauing Poesie, and Oration in them, and a fountaine, to be exprest, from whence their Riuers flow) should expressiuely-arise; out of the places, and persons for; and by whome they are presented; without which limits, they are luxurious, and paine. But what rules soeuer are set downe, to any Art, or Act (though, without their obseruation; No Art, nor Act, is true, and worthy) yet are they nothing the more followd; or those few that follow them credited. Euery vulgarly-esteemd vpstart; dares breake the dreadfull dignity of antient and autenticall Poesie: and presume Luciforously, to proclame in place thereof, repugnant precepts of their owne spaune. Truth, and Worth, haue no faces, to enamour the Lycentious, but vaine-glory, and humor. The same body: the same beauty, a thousand men seeing: Onely the man whose bloud is fitted, hath that which hee calls his soule, enamourd. And this, out of infallible cause; for, men vnderstand not these of Maenander—

———est morbus oportunitas
Animae, quod ictus, vulnus accipit graue.[37]
[There is a maladie of the minde,
That it surpriseth fatally:
Who smitten is therewith, doth finde
Himselfe sore wounded inwardly.][38]

[37] Plutarch, *Amatorius,* 763, b.
[38] Plutarch, *The Morals,* quoting Menander, tr. Philemon Holland (1603; STC: 20063), 1148. The reference is to the god of Love.

But the cause of all Mens being enamourd with Truth. And of her slight respect, in others; is the diuine Freedom; one touching with his aprehensiue finger, the other, passing. The Hill of the Muses (which all men must clime in the regular way, to Truth) is said of ould, to be forcked. And the two points of it, parting at the Top; are Insania, *and,* diuinus furor. Insania, *is that which euery Ranck-brainde writer; and iudge of Poeticall writing, is rapt withal; when hee presumes either to write or censure the height of Poesie; and that transports him with humor, vaine-glory and pride, most prophane and sacrilegious: when* diuinus furor; *makes gentle, and noble, the neuer so truly inspired writer—*

Emollit mores nec sinit esse feros.[39]
[{Studying the Liberal Arts} doth make the maners or behauiour
of men to be ciuill, and suffereth them not to be rude or barbarous.][40]

And the mild beames of the most holy inflamer; easely, and sweetly enter, with all vnderstanding sharpenesse, the soft, and sincerely humane; but with no Time; No Study; No meanes vnder heauen: any arrogant, all-occupation deuourer (that will Chandler-like set vp with all wares; selling, Poesies Nectar and Ambrosia; as wel as musterd, and vineagar.) The chast and restraind beames of humble truth will euer enter; but onely grase, and glaunce at them: and the further fly them.

The aplicable argument of the Maske.

Honor, is so much respected, and ador'd; that shee hath a Temple erected to her, like a Goddesse; a Virgine Priest consecrated to her (which is *Eunomia*, or Lawe; since none should dare accesse to Honor, but by Vertue; of which Lawe being the rule, must needes be a chiefe) and a Herrald (call'd *Phemis*, or Fame) to proclame her institutions, and commandements. To amplefie yet more the diuine graces of this Goddesse; *Plutus*, (or Riches) being by *Aristophanes, Lucian. &c.* presented naturally blind, deformd, and dull witted; is here by his loue of Honor, made see, made sightly, made ingenious; made liberall: And all this conuerted and consecrate to the most worthy

---

[39] Ovid, Epistles from Pontus, 2.9.48.
[40] John Stockwood, *A Plaine and Easie Laying Open of the Meaning and Vnderstanding of the Rules of Construction in the English Accidence* (1590; STC: 23280), 14. Stockwood's translation is fairly literal, but as part of an exegesis likely known to Chapman, Francis Bacon amplifies this to: "It taketh away the wildnesse and barbarisme and fiercenesse of mens minds." See *The Proficience and Aduancement of Learning, Diuine, and Humane* (1605: STC: 1164), 41.

celebration of these sacred Nuptialls; all issuing (to conclude the necessary application) from an honorable Temple. &c.

> Non est certa fides, quam non Iniuria versat.[41]
> ——Fallit portus & ipse fidem.[42]
> [No faith is certain that cannot be provoked to quarrel.
> ——Even the haven betrays its trust.]

THE NAMES OF THE SPEAKERS.

Honour, a Goddesse.
Plutus, (or Riches) a God.
Eunomia (or law) Priest of honor.
Phemis, Honors Herrald.
Capriccio, a man of wit, &c.

THE PRESENTMENT.

Plutus *appear'd suruaying the worke with this speech.*

PLVTVS. Rockes? Nothing but Rockes in these masking deuices? Is Inuention so poore shee must needes euer dwell amongst Rocks? But it may worthily haue chaunc'd (being so often presented) that their vaine Custome is now become the necessarie hand of heauen, transforming into Rocks, some stonie hearted Ladies, courted in former masks; for whose loues, some of their repulst seruants haue perisht: or perhaps some of my flintie-hearted Vsurers haue beene heere metamorphosed; betwixt whom and Ladies, there is resemblance enough: Ladies vsing to take interest, besides their principall, as much as Vsurers. See, it is so; and now is the time of restoring them to their naturall shapes: It moues, opens, excellent! This metamorphosis I intend to ouer-heare.

> A ROCK, MOOVING
> and breaking with a cracke about
> Capriccio, *he enters with a payre of Bellows on
> his head, a spur in one hand, and a peece of
> golde Ore in the other, &c.*
>
> *He speakes, vt sequitur. [as follows]*

---

[41] Sextus Propertius, Elegy III 8. The classical elegiac poet Propertius is a character in Ben Jonson's *Poetaster,* acted in 1601 by the Children of the Chapel, and printed in 1602.
[42] Sextus Propertius, Elegy III 7.

CAPRICCIO: How hard this world is to a man of wit? hee must eate through maine Rockes for his food, or fast; a restles and tormenting stone, his wit is to him: the very stone of *Sisyphus* in hell; nay, the Philosophers stone, makes not a man more wretched: A man must be a second *Proteus*, and turne himselfe into all shapes (like *Vlisses*) to winde through the straites of this pinching vale of miserie; I haue turn'd my selfe into a Tailor, a Man, a Gentleman, a Nobleman, a Worthy man; but had neuer the witte to turne my selfe into an Alder-man. There are manie shapes to perish in, but one to liue in, and tha's an Aldermans: Tis not for a man of wit to take any rich Figure vpon him: your bould, proud, ignorant, that's braue and clinkant,[43] that findes crownes put into his shooes euery morning by the Fayries and will neuer tell; whose Wit is humor, whose Iudgement is fashion, whose Pride is emptinesse, Birth his full man, that is in all things something, in Sum totall, nothing. He shall liue in the land of *Spruce*,[44] milke and hony flowing into his mouth sleeping.

PLVTVS. This is no transformation, but an intrusion into my golden mines: I will heare him-further.

CAPRIC. This breach of Rockes I haue made, in needy pursuite of the blind Deity, Riches: who is myraculously ariued here. For (according to our rare men of wit) heauen standing, and earth mouing, her motion (being circular) hath brought one of the most remote parts of the world, to touch at this all-exceeding Iland: which a man of wit would imagine must needs moue circularly with the rest of the world, and so euer maintaine an equal distance. But, Poets (our chiefe men of wit) answere that point directly; most ingeniously affirming: That this Ile is (for the excellency of it) diuided from the world (*diuisus ab orbe Britannus*)[45] and that though the whole World besides moues; yet this Ile stands fixt on her owne feete, and defies the Worlds mutability, which this rare accident of the arriuall of Riches, in one of his furthest-off-scituate dominions, most demonstratiuely proues.

PLVTVS. This is a man of wit indeede, and knows of all our arriuals.

CAPRIC. With this dull Deity Riches, a rich Iland lying in the South-sea, called *Poeana*, (of the *Poeans* (or songs) sung to the Sun, whom they there adore (being for strength and riches, called the Nauill of that South-sea) is by earths round motion mou'd neere this Brittan Shore. In which

---

[43] clinkant = glittering
[44] Spruce = Prussia (cf. Sprucia)
[45] See a related usage in *The Masque of Truth*, below.

Island (beeing yet in command of the Virginian continent.) A troupe of the noblest Virginians inhabiting; attended hether the God of Riches, all triumphantly shyning in a Mine of gould. For hearing of the most royal solemnity, of these sacred Nuptialls; they crost the Ocean in their honor, and are here arriu'd. A poore snatch at some of the goulden Ore, that the feete of riches haue turnd vp as he trod here, my poore hand hath purchast; and hope the Remainder of a greater worke, wilbe shortly extant.

PLVT. You Sir, that are miching about my goulden Mines here.[46]

CAPR. What, can you see Sir? you haue heretofore beene presented blinde: like your Mother Fortune; and your Brother Loue.

PLVT. But now Sir, you see I see.

CAPR. By what good meanes, I beseech you Sir.

PLVT. That meanes, I may vouchsafe you hereafter; meane space, what are you?

CAPR. I am Sir a kinde of Man; A Man of wit: with whom your worship has nothing to do I thinke.

PLVT. No Sir, nor will haue any thing to doe with him: A Man of wit? whats that? A Begger.

CAPR. And yet no Diuell Sir.

PLV. As I am, you meane.

CAPR. Indeede sir your Kingdome is vnder the Earth.

PLVT. That's true; for Riches is the *Atlas* that holdes it vp, it would sinke else.

CAPR. Tis rather a wonder, it sinks not with you Sir, y'are so sinfully, and damnably heauy.

PLVT. Sinfull? and damnable? what a Puritane? These Bellowes you weare on your head, shew with what matter your braine is pufft vp Sir: A Religion-forger I see you are, and presume of inspiration from these Bellowes; with which yee study to blow vp the setled gouernments of kingdomes.

CAPR. Your worship knockes at a wrong dore Sir, I dwell farre from the person you speak of.

PLVT. What may you be then, beeing a man of wit? a Buffon, a Iester. Before I would take vpon mee the title of a man of wit, and bee baffl'd by euery man of wisedome for a Buffon; I would turne Banckrout,[47] or let vp a Tobacco shop, change clokes with an Alchemist, or serue an Vsurer, bee a watering post for euery Groome; stand the push of euery rascall wit; enter lifts of iests with trencher-fooles, and bee foold downe by them, or (which

---

[46] miching = skulking. lurking. The word was previously used by John Lyly, Thomas Dekker, Thomas Heywood, and Shakespeare.

[47] banckrout = bankrupt

is worse) put them downe in fooling: are these the qualities a man of wit should run proud of?

CAPR. Your worship I see has obtaind wit, with sight, which I hope yet my poor wit wil well be able to answer; for touching my iesting, I haue heard of some Courtiers, that haue run themselues out of their states with Iusting;[48] and why may not I then raise my selfe in the State with iesting? An honest Shoomaker, (in a liberall Kings time) was knighted for making a cleane boote, and is it impossible, that I for breaking a cleane Iest, should bee aduaunc't in Court, or Counsaile? or at least, serued out for an Ambassador to a dull Climate? Iests, and Merriments are but wild weedes in a rank soile, which being well manured, yield the wholesom crop of wisdome and discretion at time a th'yeare.

PLV. Nay, nay, I commend thy iudgement for cutting thy cote so iust to the bredth of thy shoulders; he that cannot be a courser in the field, let him learne to play the Iack-an-Apes in the Chamber, hee that cannot personate the wise-man well amongst wisards, let him learne to play the foole well amongst dizzards.

CAPR. Tis passing miraculous, that your dul and blind worship should so sodainly turne both sightfull, and witfull.

PLVT. The Riddle of that myracle, I may chance dissolue to you in sequell; meanetime, what name sustain'st thou? and what toies are these thou bear'st so phantastically about thee?

CAPR. These, toies Sir, are the Ensignes that discouer my name and qualitie: my name being *Capriccio*, and I weare these Bellowes on my head, to shew I can puffe vp with glory all those that affect mee: and besides, beare this spurre, to shew I can spur gall, euen the best that contemne me.

PLVT. A dangerous fellowe, But what makest thou (poore man of wit) at these pompous Nuptials;

CAPRIC. Sir, I come hether with a charge; To doe these Nuptialls, I hope, very acceptable seruice; And my charge is; A company of accomplisht Trauailers; that are excellent at Antemaskes; and will tender a tast of their quallity, if your worship please.

PLVT. Excellent well pleasd; of what vertue are they besides.

CAPR. Passing graue Sir, yet exceeding acute: witty, yet not ridiculous; neuer laugh at their owne iests: laborious yet not base, hauing

---

[48] Iusting = jousting

cutout the skirts of the whole world, in amorous quest of your gould and siluer.
PLVT. They shal haue enough; cal them: I beseech thee call them: how farre hence abide they?
CAPR. Sir (being by another eminent qualitie the admired souldiers of the world) in contempt of softnes, and delicacie, they lie on the naturally hard boords of that naked tree; and will your worship assure them rewards fit for persons of their freight.
PLVT. Dost thou doubt my reward beeing pleased?
CAPR. I know Sir, a man may sooner win your reward, for pleasing you, then deseruing you. But you great wise persons, haue a fetch of State; to employ with countenance, and encouragement, but reward with austerity and disgrace, saue your purses, and lose your honours.
PLVT. To assure thee of reward, I will now satisfie thee touching the miraculous cause, both of my sight and wit, and which consequently moues mee to humanity, and bounty; And all is, onely this; my late being in loue, with the louely Goddesse Honor.
CAPRIC. If your Worshipp loue Honor, indeed, Sir you must needes be bountifull. But where is the rare Goddesse you speake of to be seene?
PLVTVS. In that Rich Temple, where Fortune fixt those her goulden wings, thou seest; And that rowling stone she vs'd to tread vpon, for signe shee would neuer for-sake this Kingdome; There is ador'd, the worthy Goddesse Honor. The swetnesse of whose voice, when I first heard her perswasions, both to my self, and the *Virginian* Princes arriu'd here, to doe honor and homage, to these heauenly Nuptialls, so most powerfully enamour'd mee, that the fire of my loue flew vp to the sight of mine eyes: that haue lighted within mee a whole firmament of Bounty, which may securely assure the, thy reward is certaine: & therefore call thy accomplisht company to their Antemaske.
CAPRIC. See Sir, The time, set for their apperance, being expir'd; they appeere to their seruice of them-selues.

Enter the Baboones after whose dance, being Anticke, and delightful, they returned to their Tree, when Plutus *spake to* Capriccius.

86 THE CAMPION, CHAPMAN, AND BEAUMONT MASQUES

Example 2.1 Antimasque—Baboons: *The Babboons Dance*, BL 10444/5, no. 27; Brade (1617), no. 9, *Intrada der Jungen Princessinnen*.

Example 2.1 Continued

PLVTVS. Gramercy now *Capriccio*, take thy men of complement, and trauaile with them to other marriages. My Riches to thy Wit; they will get something some-where.

CAPR. Whats this?

PLVT. A straine of Wit beyond a Man of Wit. I haue imployd you, and the grace of that, is reward enough; hence; packe, with your complemental Fardle: The sight of an attendant for reward, is abominable in the eyes of a turne-seru'd Politician, and I feare, will strike me blinde againe. I can not abide these bellowes of thy head, they and thy men of wit haue melted my Mines with them, and consum'd me, yet take thy life and be gone. *Neptune* let thy predecessor, *Vlysses*, liue after all his slaine companions, but to make him die more miserably liuing; gaue him vp to ship wracks, enchantments; men of wit are but enchanted, there is no such thing as wit in this world. So, take a tree, inure thy souldiers to hardnes, tis honorable, though not clinkant.[49]

CAPR. Can this be possible?

PLVT. Alas! poore man of wit, how want of reward daunts thy vertue? But because I must send none away discontented, from these all-pleasing Nuptials; take this wedge of golde, and wedge thy selfe into the world with it, renouncing that loose wit of thine, t'will spoile thy complexion.

CAPR. Honor, and all *Argus* eyes, to Earths all-commaunding Riches. Pluto *etiam cedit* Iupiter [Even Pluto gives way to Jupiter].

Exit Capr.

After this lowe Induction, by these
succeeding degrees, the chiefe Maskers
were aduanc't to their discouerie

PLVTVS.[50] These humble obiects can no high eyes drawe,
Eunomia? (or the sacred power of Lawe)
Daughter of *Joue*, and Goddesse Honors Priest;
Appeare to *Plutus*, and his loue assist.
EVN.[51] What would the god of Riches?

---

[49] clinkant = glittering
[50] Marginal note: Plutus, cals to Eunomia.
[51] Marginal note: Eunomia in the Temple gates.

THE MEMORABLE MASQUE 89

PLVT. Ioine with Honor:
In purpos'd grace of these great Nuptials;
And since to Honor none should dare accesse,
But helpt by vertues hand (thy selfe, chaste *Loue*
Being *Vertues* Rule, and her directfull light)
Help me to th'honor of her speech and sight.

EVN. Thy will shal straight be honour'd; all that seek
Accesse to Honor, by cleer virtues beame,
Her grace preuents their pains, and comes to them.

    Loud Musick, and Honor appears,
descending with her Herrald Phemis, *and*
Eunomia (her Priest) *before her.*

Example 2.2 Antimasque—Loud Music: *The second [of the Temple Anticke]*, BL 10444/5, no. 123; Adson (1621), no. 8.

Example 2.2 Continued

The Musique ceasing *Plutus* spake.

PLVT. Crowne of all merit, Goddess, and my Loue;
Tis now high time, that th'end for which we come
Should be endeuor'd in our vtmost right,
Done to the sweetnes of this Nuptiall night.

HON. P*lutus*? The Princes of the Virgine land,
Whom I made crosse the Britan Ocean
To this most famed Ile, of all the world,
To do due homage to the sacred Nuptials
Of *Loue* and *Beauty*, celebrated here,

By this Howre of the holy Eeuen I know,
Are ready to performe the rites they owe
To setting *Phoebus*; which (for greater State
To their apparance) their first act aduances.
And with songs Vshers their succeeding dances,
Herrald! giue summons to the Virgine Knights,
No longer to delay their purpos'd Rites.

HER. Knights of the Virgine Land, whom bewties lights
Would glorifie with their inflaming sights;
Keep now obscur'd no more your faire intent,
To adde your Beames to this nights ornament,
The golden-winged *Howre* strikes now a Plaine,
And calls out all the pompe ye entertaine;
The Princely Bride-groome, and the Brides bright eyes,
Sparkle with grace to your discoueries.

> At these words, the Phoebades (or Priests of
> the Sunne) appear'd first with six Lutes, and six
> voices, and sung to the opening of the Mine and
> Maskers discouery, this ful Song.

The first Song.

Example 2.3 *Ope Earth thy womb of golde*, set to *What poore Astronomers are they*, from Dowland's *Third Booke of Songs* (1603).

Example 2.3 Continued

Ope Earth thy wombe of golde,
    Shew Heauen thy cope of starres.
All glad Aspects vnfolde,

Shine out, and cleere our Cares:
Kisse Heauen and Earth, and so combine
In all mixt ioy our Nuptiall Twine.

This Song ended, a Mount opened, and spred like a Skie, *in which appear'd a* Sunne *setting; beneath which, sate the twelue Maskers, in a Mine of golde; twelue Torch-bearers holding their torches before them, after which* Honor, *&c.*

    HON. Se now the setting Sun, casts vp his bank,
    And showes his bright head at his Seas repaire,
    For signe that all daies future shall be faire.

    PLVT. May he that rules the nightes & dayes confirme it.

    HON. Behold the Sunnes faire Preists the *Phaebades*,
    Their euening seruice in an Hymne addresse
    To *Phoebus* setting; which we now shall heare,
    And see the formes of their deuotions there.

THE MEMORABLE MASQUE 93

The Phoehades sing the first Stance of the
second song, vt sequitur. [as follows]

Example 2.4a *Descend (faire Sun) and sweetly rest,* set to *There is a lady sweet and kind,* from Ford's *Musicke of Sundrie Kindes* (1607).

One alone 1.

[1.] *Descend (faire Sun) and sweetly rest,*
  In Tethis *Cristal armes, thy toyle,*
Fall burning on her Marble brest,
  And make with Loue her billowes boyle.

Another alone. 2.

Blow blow, sweet windes, O blow away,
  Al vapours from the fined ayre:
That to this golden head no Ray,
  May languish with the least empaire.

CHO.

Dance Tethis, *and thy loues red beames,*
  Embrace with Ioy he now discends:
Burnes burnes with loue to drinke thy streames,
  and on him endles youth attends.

After this Stance, Honor &c.

HON. This superstitious Hymne, sung to the Sunne,
Let vs encounter with fit duties done
To our cleere Phoebus; whose true piety, —
Enioyes from heaven an earthly deity.

Other Musique, and voyces;
and this second Stance *was sung,*
directing their obseruance
to the King.

One alone 1.
[2.] *Rise, rise O Phoebus, euer rise,*
  descend not to th'inconstant streame,
But grace with endles light, our skyes,
  to thee that Sun is but a beame.

Another 2.
Dance Ladies in our Sunnes bright rayes,
  in which the Bride and
  Bridegroome shine:
Cleere sable night with your eyes dayes,
  and set firme lights on Hymens shrine.
CHO.
O may our Sun not set before,
  he sees his endles seed arise:
And deck his triple crowned shore,
  with springs of humane Deities.

This ended the Phoebades *sung*
the third Stance.

[3.] 1. *Set Set (great Sun) our rising loue*
  shall euer celebrate thy grace:
Whom entring the high court of Ioue,
  each God greetes rising from his place.

2. *When thow thy siluer bow dost bend,*
  all start aside and dread thy draughtes:
How can we thee enough commend,
  commanding all worlds with the shafts?
CHO.
Blest was thy mother bearing thee,
  and Phoebe th at delights in darts:
Thou artful Songes dost set; and sheewinds horns,
  loues hounds, & high pallmd harts.

After this Honor.
HON. *Againe our Musique and conclude this Song,*
To him, to whom all Phoebus beames belong:

The other voyces sung to other Musike the third stance.

[4.] 1 *Rise stil (cleere Sun) and neuer set,*
  but be to Earth her only light:
All other Kings in thy beames met,
  are cloudes and darke effects of night.

2. *As when the Rosie Morne doth rise,*
  Like Mists, all giue thy wisedome waie;
A learned King, is, as in skies,
  To poore dimme stars, the flaming day.
CHO.
Blest was thy Mother, bearing Thee,
  Thee only Relick of her Race,
Made by thy vertues beames a Tree,
  Whose armes shall all the Earth embrace.

Example 2.4b *Descend (faire Sun) and sweetly rest*, alternative setting to *As by the streames of Babilon*, from Campion's *First Booke of Ayres* (1613).

Example 2.4c *Descend (faire Sun) and sweetly rest,* alternative setting to *Sweet Cupid, ripen her desire,* from Corkine's *Ayres to Sing and Play to the Lvte and Basse Violl* (1610).

THE MEMORABLE MASQUE 97

Example 2.4d *Descend (faire Sun) and sweetly rest*, alternative setting to *Now O now I needs must part*, from Dowland's *First Booke of Songes or Ayres* (1597).

Example 2.4d Continued

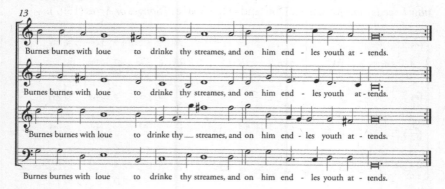

This done *Eunomia* spake to the Maskers set
yet aboue.

EVN. Virginian Princes, ye must now renounce
Your superstitious worship of these Sunnes,
Subiect to cloudy darknings and descents,
And of your fit deuotions, turne the euents
To this our Britan *Phoebus*, whose bright skie
(Enlightned with a Christian Piety)
Is neuer subiect to black Errors night,
And hath already offer'd heauens true light,
To your darke Region, which acknowledge now;
Descend, and to him all your homage vow.

[Loude Mus(ick)][52] With this the Torch-bearers descended, and
performed another Antemaske, dancing with
Torches lighted at both ends;

---

[52] The University of Illinois copy of the 1613 quarto inserts a manuscript annotation here: "Loude Mus[ick]," which may mean some kind of fanfare, or that the winds played at least the beginning of the antemasque. On the annotations, which Blakemore Evans implies may be by Chapman himself; see Evans, *The Plays of George Chapman*, 559–60.

Example 2.5 Antemasque—Torchbearers: *Essex Anticke Masque*, BL 10444/5, no. 92; Adson (1621), no. 4.

Example 2.5 Continued

which done, the Maskers descended, and fell into their dances, two of which being past, and others with the Ladies, . . .

Example 2.6 First Measure: *The first of the Temple*, BL 10444/5, no. 39; Brade (1617), no. 21, *Auffzug der Kauffleute*.

Example 2.6 Continued

Example 2.7 Second Measure: *The second of the Temple*, BL 10444/5, no. 40; Brade (1617), no. 26, *Der Irlender Tantz*.

Example 2.7 Continued

THE MEMORABLE MASQUE   103

[Revels 1]

Honor spake.

Musique! your voyces, now tune sweet and hie,
And singe the Nuptiall *Hymn* of Loue, and Beauty.[53]
Twinns, as of one age, so to one desire
May both their bloods giue, an vnparted fire.
And as those twinns that Fame giues all her prise,
Combind their lifes power in such *Symphathies*;[54]
That one being merry; mirth the other grac't:
If one felt sorrow, th' other griefe embrac't.
If one were healthfull; Health the other pleasd:
If one were sicke: the other was diseasd;
And all waies ioynd in such a constant troth
That one like cause had like effect in both,
So may these Nuptiall Twynnes,[55] their whole liues store,
Spend in such euen parts, neuer grieuing more,
Then may the more set off their ioyes diuine;
As after clouds, the Sunne, doth clerest shine.

This sayd, this Song of *Loue*, and
Bewty was sung; single.

Example 2.8 *Bright Panthaea borne to Pan*, set to *Now I see thy lookes were fained*, from Ford's *Musicke of Sundrie Kindes* (1607).

---

[53] Marginal note: The Bride and Bride groome were figured in Loue and Beauty.
[54] Marginal note: Twinns of which Hippocrates speakes.
[55] Marginal note: Called Twynns being both of an Age [i.e., both sixteen years old].

Example 2.8 Continued

1. Bright *Panthaea* borne to Pan,
   Of the Noblest Race of Man,
Her white hand to *Eros* giuing,
   With a kisse, ioin'd Heauen to Earth
And begot so faire a birth,
   As yet neuer grac't the liuing.
CHO: A Twinne that all worlds did adorne,
For so were *Loue* and *Bewty* borne.

2. Both so lou'd, they did contend
   Which the other should transcend,
Doing either, grace, and kindnes;
   Loue from *Bewty* did remoue,

Lightnes call'd her staine in loue,
   Bewtie took from *Loue* his blindness.
CHO: *Loue* sparks made flames in *Bewties* skie,
And *Bewtie* blew vp *Loue* as hie.

3. Virtue then commixt her fire;
   To which *Bountie* did aspire,
Innocence a Crowne conferring;
   Mine, and Thine, were then vnusde,
All things common: Nought abusde,
   Freely earth her frutage bearing.
CHO: Nought then was car'd for, that could fade,
And thus the golden world was made

This sung, the Maskers danc't againe with
the Ladies,

[Revels 2]

       after which *Honor*.
HON. Now may the blessings of the golden age,
Swimme in these Nuptials, euen to holy rage,
A Hymn to Sleep prefer, and all the ioyes
That in his Empire are of dearest choice,
Betwixt his golden slumbers euer flow,
In these; And Theirs, in Springs as endless growe.

   This sayd, the last Song was sung full.
     The last Song.

Example 2.9a *Now sleepe, binde fast, the flood of Ayre*, set to *Unto the temple of thy beauty*, from Ford's *Musicke of Sundrie Kindes* (1607).

Example 2.9a Continued

Now sleepe, binde fast, the flood of Ayre,
    strike all things dumb and deafe,
And, to disturbbe our Nuptiall paire,
    Let stir no Aspen leafe.
Send flocks of golden Dreames

That all true ioyes presage,
    Bring, in thy oyly streames,
The milke and hony Age.
    Now close the world-round
        sphere of blisse,
    And fill it with a heauenly kisse.

Example 2.9b *Now sleepe, binde fast, the flood of Ayre*, alternative setting to *Your faire lookes enflame my desire*, from Campion's *A Booke of Ayres* (1601).

After this *Plutus* to the Maskers.

PLVT. Come Virgine Knights, the homage ye haue done,
To *Loue* and *Bewty*, and our Britan Sun,
Kinde *Honor*, will requite with holy feasts
In her faire Temple; and her loued Guests,
Giues mee the grace t'inuite, when she and I
(*Honor* and *Riches*) will eternally
A league in fauour of this night combine,
In which *Loues* second hallowed Tapers shine;
Whose Ioies, may Heauen & Earth as highly please
As those two nights that got great *Hercules*.

The speech ended; they concluded with a dance, that brought them off; *Plutus*, with *Honor* and the rest conducting them vp to the Temple of *Honor*.

Example 2.10 Third Measure: *The third of the Temple*, BL 10444/5, no 41; Brade (1617), no. 22, *Auffzug vor Grienwitsch*.

THE MEMORABLE MASQUE   109

Example 2.10 Continued

FINIS.

A Hymne to Hymen for the most time-
fitted Nuptialls of our
thrice gracious Princesse
Elizabeth. &c.

Example 2.11 *Singe, Singe a Rapture to all Nuptial eares*, epithalamium set to *My deerest Mistrisse, let vs liue and loue*, from Corkine's *Second Booke of Ayres* (1612).

Singe, Singe a Rapture to all Nuptial eares,
Bright *Hymens* torches, drunke vp *Parcaes* tears:
Sweete *Hymen*; *Hymen*, Mightiest of Gods
Attoning of all-taming blood the odds;
Two into One, contracting; One to Two
Dilating, which no other God can doe.

Mak'st sure, with change, and lett'st the married try,
Of Man and woman, the Variety.
And as a flower, halfe scorcht with daies long heate   *Simil.*
Thirsts for refreshing, with Nights cooling sweate,
The wings of *Zephire*, fanning still her face,
No chere can ad to her heart-thirsty grace;
Yet weares she gainst those fires that make her fade,
Her thicke hayrs proofe, al hyd, in Midnights shade;
Her Helth, is all in dews; Hope, all in showres,
Whose want bewailde, she pines in all her powres:
So Loue-scorch't Virgines, nourish quenchles fires;
The Fathers cares; the Mothers kind desires;
Their Gould, and Garments, of the newest guise,
Can nothing comfort their scorcht Phantasies,
But, taken rauish't vp, in *Hymens* armes,
His Circkle holds, for all their anguish, charms:
Then, as a glad Graft, in the spring Sunne shines,   *Simil. ad*
That all the helps, of Earth, and Heauen combines   *eandem ex-*
In Her sweet grouth: Puts in the Morning on   *plicat.*
Her cherefull ayres; the Sunnes rich fires, at Noone;
At Euen the sweete deaws, and at Night with starrs,
In all their vertuous influences shares;
So, in the Bridegroomes sweet embrace; the Bride,
All varied Ioies tasts, in their naked pride:
To which the richest weedes: are weedes, to flowres;
Come *Hymen* then; com close these Nuptial howres
With all yeares comforts. Come; each virgin keepes
Her odorous kisses for thee; Goulden sleepes
Will, in their humors, neuer steepe an eie,
Till thou inuit'st them with thy Harmony.
Why staiest thou? see each Virgin doth prepare
Embraces for thee; Her white brests laies bare
To tempt thy soft hand; let's such glances flie
As make starres shoote, to imitate her eye.
Puts Arts attires on, that put Natures doune:
Singes, Dances, sets on euery foote a Crowne,
Sighes, in her songs, and dances; kisseth Ayre
Till Rites, and words past, thou in deedes repaire;
The whole court Io sings: Io the Ayre:
Io the flouds and fields: Io, most faire,

Most sweet, most happy *Hymen*; Come: away;
With all thy Comforts come; old Matrons pray,
With young Maides Languors; Birds bill, build, and breed
To teach thee thy kinde, euery flowre and weed
Looks vp to gratulate thy long'd for fruites;
Thrice giuen, are free, and timely-granted suites:
There is a seed by thee now to be sowne,
In whose fruit Earth, shall see her glories show'n,
At all parts perfect; and must therfore loose
No minutes time; from times vse all fruite flowes;
And as the tender Hyacinth, that growes *Simil.*
Where *Phoebus* most his golden beames bestowes,
Is propt with care; is water'd euery howre;
The sweet windes adding their encreasing powre,
The scattered drops of Nights refreshing dew,
Hasting the full grace, of his glorious hew,
Which once disclosing, must be gatherd straight,
Or hew, and Odor both, will lose their height;
So, of a Virgine, high, and richly kept,
The grace and sweetnes full growne must be reap't,
Or, forth her spirits fly, in empty Ayre;
The sooner fading; the more sweete and faire.
Gentle, O Gentle *Hymen*, be not then
Cruell, that kindest art to Maids, and Men;
These two, One Twynn are; and their mutuall blisse,
Not in thy beames, but in thy Bosome is.
Nor can their hands fast, their harts ioyes make sweet;
Their harts, in brests are; and their Brests must meete.
Let, there be Peace, yet Murmur: and that noise,
Beget of peace, the Nuptiall battailes ioyes.
Let Peace grow cruell, and take wrake of all,
The warrs delay brought thy full Festiuall.
Harke, harke, O now the sweete Twyn murmur sounds;
Hymen is come, and all his heate abounds;
Shut all Dores; None, but *Hymens* lights aduance.
No sound styr; let, dumb Ioy, enioy a trance.
Sing, sing a Rapture to all Nuptiall eares,
Bright *Hymens* Torches, drunke vp *Parcaes* teares.

FINIS.

The Masque of the Inner Temple and Gray's Inn

Francis Beaumont

Plate 3.1 Francis Beaumont, *The Masque of the Inner Temple and Gray's Inn*, Title Page (1613) Courtesy of the Huntington Library.

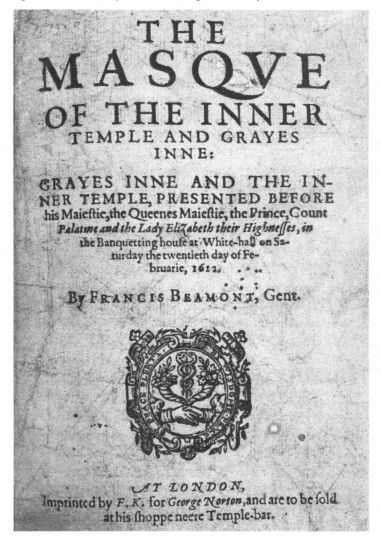

Introduction

The financial records for this event have not survived in the extant Inner Temple or Gray's Inn accounts,[1] so we are ignorant of payments to creative artists and performers. Francis Beaumont is listed as the author on the title page of the quarto,[2] and it seems very likely that the dances, at least, were composed by John Coprario, since the presumed first masque dance survives in BL 10444/5 with the title *Cuperaree or Graysin*.[3] Three main dances are extant, in addition to two antimasques that may have come from this masque. Ensemble versions also exist in Brade's 1617 *Newe Ausserlesene liebliche Branden*,[4] and the first masque dance additionally in the six-voice partbooks of Cambridge, Fitzwilliam Museum, Mu. MS 734 (formerly MSS 24.E.13–17), the so-called Fitzwilliam Wind Manuscript.[5] This would make sense because we know that "Hoboyes, Cornets, &c." took part in the masque performance,[6] and that winds normally played six-part, rather than five-part, ensemble music, as has been documented by Thurston Dart, among others.[7]

Even conceding that Coprario composed the dances, however, we have no evidence for who composed the songs. Given the division of labor in other masques, it does not seem likely that Coprario made the songs as well. One

---

[1] See John R. Elliott Jr, "Invisible Evidence: Finding Musicians in the Archives of the Inns of Court, 1446–1642," *Royal Musical Association Research Chronicle* 26 (1993), 45–57, at 47, https://doi.org/10.1080/14723808.1993.10540961.

[2] The original title page (STC: 1663), shown in Plate 3.1, actually says "Francis Beamont," and a version with a replacement title page (STC: 1664) was issued where the name was removed. On the title page issue, see Philip Edwards's Introduction to his edition of the masque in *A Book of Masques*, 127. The "Beamont" spelling actually suggests some widely used variant pronunciation, different from the French-based one of today. That would be congruent with the Beauchamp Tower at the Tower of London being pronounced traditionally as the "Beecham Tower." Beamont occurs in more than a dozen seventeenth-century printed sources and a similar number of literary manuscripts (along with a half-dozen of the variant, "Beamond"). Fellow-playwright, Thomas Heywood, gives his name as "Bewmont," which suggests a tradition alongside the English pronunciation of "beauty." See *The Hierarchie of the Blessed Angells* (London: Adam Islip, 1635; STC: 13327), 206. One clue to what may have been a standard pronunciation of "Beamont" comes from a 1685 broadside entitled *A Pack of Hell-Hounds* (Wing P154), whose third stanza begins: "The next's a Lieutenant, / Yet *Fletcher* nor *Beamont*…" which suggests a pronunciation tradition with "ea" as in "heaven" or "bread."

[3] Fols. 28v–29r.

[4] See Sabol, *Four Hundred Songs and Dances*, Nos. 269–75.

[5] No. 22.

[6] The quarto of the masque notes at one point (sig. C2v) that "the Musicke changed from Violins to Hoboyes, Cornets, &c."

[7] See Thurston Dart, "The Repertory of the Royal Wind Music, *Galpin Society Journal* 11 (1958), 70–7, https://doi.org/10.2307/842105. See also Holman, *Four and Twenty Fiddlers*, 189; Ross W. Duffin, "'Cornets & Sagbuts': Some Thoughts on Early Seventeenth-Century English Repertory for Brass," in *Perspectives in Brass Scholarship: Proceedings of the International Historic Brass Symposium, Amherst, 1995*, ed. Stewart Carter (New York, 1997), 47–70, at 55–57.

thing we know for certain is that the "songs" were all ensemble settings, since they uniformly involved a crowd of singing, lute-playing Priests.

As with *The Memorable Masque*, some background information appears in John Chamberlain's 18 February 1613 letter to Alice Carleton—actually predating the performance, which was delayed until 20 February from its scheduled date on the 16th. Chamberlain's account explains the delay:

> On teusday yt came to Grayes ynne and the inner Temples turne to come wth theyre mask, wherof Sr Francis Bacon was the cheife contriuer, and because the former came on horse backe and open shariots, they made choise to come by water from Winchester place in Southwark (wch suted well enough wth theyre deuise, wch was the mariage of the riuer of Thames to the Rhine), and theyre shew by water was very gallant by reason of infinite store of lights very curiously set and placed: and many boats and barges wth deuises of light and lampes, wth three peales of ordinance, one at theyre taking water, another in the Temple garden, and the last at theyre landing: wch passage by water cost them better than three hundred pound. they were receued at the priuie stayres: and great expectation thayre was they shold euery way exceed theyre competitors that went before them, both in deuise, daintines, of apparell, and aboue all in dauncing (wherin they are held excellent) and esteemed for the properer men, but by what yll planet yt fell out I know not, they came home as they went wthout doing anything, the reason whereof I cannot yet learne thoroughly, so but only that the hall was so full that yt was not possible to auoyde yt or make roome for them, besides that most of the Ladies were in the galleries to see them land, and could not get in, but the worst of all was that the king was so wearied and sleepie wth sitting vp almost two whole nights before, that he had no edge to yt ... but wthall gave them very goode wordes and appointed them to come again on Saterday, but the grace of thayre maske is quite gon, when theyre apparell hath ben alredy shewed and theyre deuises vented so that how yt will fall out God knowes, for they are much discouraged and out of countenance, and the world sayes yt comes to passe after the old prouerb: the properer men, the worse luck.[8]

A follow-up letter from Chamberlain to Sir Dudley Carleton on 25 February reports that the disappointed masquers "on Saterday last performed

---

[8] National Archives, SP 14/72, fols. 47r–47v. Chamberlain may have been especially sympathetic because he was a former student at Gray's Inn.

theyre parts exceedingly well and wt great applause and approbation both from the king and all the companie."[9] They were probably also buoyed by permission to present it in the Banqueting House, rather than the Hall used by *The Memorable Masque*, as originally planned.

The first musical event of the *Masque of Inner Temple and Gray's Inn* is an antimasque danced by the "Nymphs of the Fountains," or "Naiades," who "fall into a Measure, daunce a little, then make a stand." This suggests something graceful, not grotesque, and also something brief. BL 10444/5 contains *The Nymphes Dance* (no. 53), which seems to connect admirably to the situation. It also occurs in Brade's 1617 collection as *Mascharada der Edelfrauen* (no. 10). The problem is the "daunce a little" description, combined with the fact that the Nymphs dance three more times in the masque, and only after the last does the text say, "and so concluded the first Anti-masque." In other words, the first antimasque seems to have four distinct episodes. The second episode occurs when five "Hyades" descend in a cloud to dance with the Nymphs, and the third when four Cupids "ioyne with the Nymphes and the *Hyades* in another daunce." As an end to the first antimasque, four statues enter, with "the Musicke changed from Violins to Hoboyes, Cornets, &c. And the ayre of the Musicke was vtterly turned into a soft time, with drawing notes, excellently expressing their natures, and the Measure likewise was fitted vnto the same." What I propose is that the first part of *The Nymphes Dance* (no. 3.1a) be played and repeated twice more for the first three dance episodes,[10] and then, for the fourth instance of dancing, the second part of *The Nymphes Dance* (no. 3.1b) be played, with long ("drawing") notes matching the description, and a change from strings to winds in the instrumentation. Felicitously, this second part of the dance ends with the same musical phrase as the first part, so there is a kind of musical rhyme between them, drawing them together into a single antimasque.[11] The text of the masque later notes that King James had so enjoyed this dance that he asked for it to be repeated at the end, but one of the statues was by then undressed, so it could not be done.

The performers were able to repeat the second antimasque at the king's request, however. It featured a gaggle of rural folk, clowns, and shepherds, May

---

[9] National Archives, SP14/72, fol. 102v.
[10] This dance would, thus, be analogous to strophic song stanzas separated by dialogue, like *Powerfull Jove* (no. 4) and *Breathe you now* (no. 10) in *The Lords' Masque*, and *Descend (faire Sun)* (no. 4) in *The Memorable Masque*.
[11] The reprised closing section occurs only in Brade.

Lord and Lady, he-fool and she-fool, servingman, chambermaid, along with a pair of baboons (which seem to have been in vogue).[12] The music to this "May-daunce" was "extremely well fitted, hauing such a spirit of Countrey iollitie as can hardly be imagined; but the perpetuall laughter and applause was aboue the Musicke." In other words, the audience reaction to the dancing and May-game pantomime by "the Dancers, or rather Actors" was so raucous that the music could scarcely be heard. Because of the favor shown by the king, a dance known in some keyboard sources as *The Kings Morisco* would seem to fit admirably, since Morris dancing was and is a prime feature of country dances.[13] Significantly, that particular piece survives in BL 10444/5 as *The Maypole* (no. 70), and in a five-part arrangement in Brade's 1617 collection as *Der Satyrn Tantz* (no. 18).

After this, the "Maine Masque" begins, with fifteen Olympian knights and twelve priests, all of whose elaborate costumes are described in detail in the text. The priests descend first, "euery Priest playing vpon a Lute" and singing. Their song, *Shake off your heauy traunce*, consists of a single six-line stanza, unusually beginning with a trimeter rhyming couplet followed by a cross-rhymed ballad-meter quatrain (aabcbc 334343). There is no extant musical setting with that precise versification, but a small number of songs exist with an aabcbc rhyme scheme. The only one of those that works for this masque song is *Good men shew if you can tell* (no. 3.3a), from Thomas Campion's *Second Booke of Ayres* (1613).[14] Here is the masque song in parallel with the first stanza of Campion's song:

Inner Temple / Gray's Inn Masque	Campion: *Second Booke of Ayres* (1613)
Shake off your heauy traunce,	Good men shew if you can tell,
And leape into a daunce,	Where doth humane pity dwell?
Such as no mortals vse to treade,	Farre and neere her would I seeke,
Fit only for *Apollo*	So vex'd with sorrow is my brest.
To play to, for the Moone to lead,	She they say to all is meeke,
And all the Starres to follow.	And onely makes th'vn happy blest.

---

[12] An almost identical list of country folk danced a "Morris" in *Two Noble Kinsmen*, 3.5 (1634), sig. G3v: "the Lord of May and Lady bright, The Chambermaid and Servingman ... mine Host and his fat Spouse ... the beast eating Clowne, and next the foole, The *Bavian* [i.e., Baboon] with long tayle ..." *Two Noble Kinsmen* was first produced ca.1613–14, so Beaumont's country group seems to have made an impression.

[13] On the Morris tune in general, and the morisco in particular, see John M. Ward, "The Morris Tune," *Journal of the American Musicological Society* 39 (1986), 294–331, at 314, https://doi.org/10.2307/831532. An anonymous keyboard arrangement is in the Fitzwilliam Virginal Book (Cambridge, Fitzwilliam Museum Mu MS 168), no. 247, pp. 358–59.

[14] No. 9, sig. K1v.

Campion's original song is for Cantus, Altus, and Bassus with lute, so the Tenor part here is editorial. The octave leap in the second measure of the Cantus part seems especially apt for setting "leape into a daunce."

A second setting to *Shake off your heauy traunce* can be made to Campion's *Now let her change and spare not* (no. 3.3b), from his *Third Booke of Ayres* (1617).[15] This is the same song used above to set the final song in Campion's masque (see the discussion for no. 14 in *The Lords' Masque*, above). Unlike the masque song, *Now let her change* has a six-line stanza entirely in rhyming couplets, but its versification is 334443, which is close to the 334343 of *Shake off your heauy traunce*, so lyric and music match well.

Immediately after that song, the knights descend and "daunce their first Measure." It is generally accepted that the music to this dance is the one given in BL 10444/5 as *Cuperaree or Graysin*, connecting John Coprario to the Gray's Inn masque and apparently confirming him as the composer for the dances in Beaumont's masque. A five-part version appears in Brade's 1617 collection as *Des Rothschencken Tantz* (no. 28), so that is given as the first version here (no. 3.4a). Another ensemble version survives in a source known as the Fitzwilliam Wind Manuscript,[16] which has been identified as containing repertory from the Royal Wind Band in the early seventeenth century.[17] Although missing one part, which has been reconstructed here (no. 3.4b), its six-voice texture and lower key conform to what is known about wind ensemble versions of pieces also written for violin band, and we know from the first antimasque description that "Hoboyes, Cornets, &c." (certainly including sackbuts) took part in the masque performance.

The first measure of the masquers is followed directly by the second song, *for Joue doth pause*.[18] Again, this is just a single stanza, consisting of six lines in tercets: aabccb 442443. No extant song has this precise versification, but it resembles Shakespeare's *O mistress mine*, and a group of three lutesongs that are constructed in the same way, with six tetrameter lines in two tercets.[19] One of those that works well for setting this masque song is

---

[15] No. 2, sig. B1r.

[16] Cambridge, Fitzwilliam Museum, Mu. MS 734 (formerly MSS 24.E.13–17), no. 20.

[17] See Thurston Dart, The Repertory of the Royal Wind Music," *Galpin Society Journal* 11 (1958), 70–77, https://doi.org/10.2307/842105; Ross W. Duffin, "'Cornets & Sagbuts': Some thoughts on the early seventeenth-century English repertory for brass," in *Perspectives in Brass Scholarship*, ed. Stewart Carter (New York, 1997), 47–70.

[18] On "measures" as dances for masques, see Ward, "Newly Devis'd Measures," 111–42.

[19] See Duffin, "Thomas Morley, Robert Johnson, and Songs for the Shakespearean Stage," 356–86, at 382–85, https://doi.org/10.1093/oxfordhb/9780190945145.013.12.

O my poor eies that sun whose shine, from *The First Booke of Songes & Ayres* (1600), by Robert Jones.[20] Here is the masque lyric in parallel with the first stanza of Jones's song:

Inner Temple / Gray's Inn Masque	Jones: *First Booke of Songes & Ayres* (1600)
On blessed youthes, for *Joue* doth pause	O my poor eies that sun whose shine
Laying aside his grauer lawes	Late gaue you light doth now decline
For this deuice,	And set to you to others riseth,
And at the wedding such a paire,	She who would sooner die then change,
Each daunce is taken for a praier,	Not fearing death delights to range,
Each song a sacrifice.	And now O now my soule despiseth.

The longer third and sixth line of the model requires some text repetition in the masque song, though Jones's song already has much text repetition at "And now O now" in the last line. The lyric otherwise fits well (no. 3.5a), and the four voices of Jones's setting serve for the multiple singers.

Another of the three extant aabccb tetrameter lutesongs makes a good alternative setting: Dowland's *Wofull hart with griefe oppressed* from his *Second Booke of Songs or Ayres* (1600).[21] It suffers from the same issue with the shorter third and sixth lines in the masque song, but it still makes a fine setting (no. 3.5b), with all four parts given in Dowland's print. There is a sign of congruence in the three lower parts, omitted from the lute and top part in the original, but words and music may be reprised from there.

That song is followed by the knight's "second Measure," (no. 3.6) which seems likely to have been the dance in BL 10444/5 that follows *Cuperaree or Graysin*, namely, *[Graysin] The second* (no. 51). It appears also in Brade's 1617 collection as *Comoedianten Tantz* (no. 37). Once again, the faster notation in BL 10444/5 for the final triple section has been preferred here, even though this is not an antimasque dance.

The Second Measure is followed by the third song, *More pleasing were these sweet delights*, in which the knights are directed to choose ladies in the audience for the revels. Consisting of a single stanza of eight tetrameter lines in rhyming couplets, with the last two set off as a chorus, this is again sung by the Priests, as the last line of the lyric affirms. The first six lines, however, are marked "Single," as opposed to the chorus couplet, which is marked "All,"

---

[20] Sigs. E1v–E2r.
[21] STC: 7095: no. 16, sig. I2v–K1r.

making clear that the first part of the song is sung by solo voice with instrumental accompaniment. There is a handful of songs from the lutesong repertoire that could set this lyric, but the best match seems to be Campion's song, *Mistris since you so much desire*, from Rosseter's 1601 *A Booke of Ayres*,[22] the same song used above for *Svpported now by Clouds descend*, no. 5 from *The Lords' Masque*. The Campion ayre calls for a reprise of the last couplet, and that would work well for the chorus in the masque song (no. 3.7). Here are the two lyrics in parallel:

Inner Temple / Gray's Inn Masque	Campion/Rosseter: *A Booke of Ayres* (1601)
More pleasing were these sweet delights,	Mistris since you so much desire,
If Ladies mou'd as well as Knights;	to know the place of Cupids fire,
Runne eu'ry one of you and catch	in your faire shrine that flame doth rest,
A Nymph in honor of this match;	yet neuer harbourd in your brest,
And whisper boldly in her eare,	it bides not in your lips so sweete
Joue will but laugh, if you forsweare.	nowhere the rose and lillies meete,
All: And this daye's sinnes he doth resolue	But a little higher, but a little higher,
That we his Priests should all absolue.	There there, O there lies Cupids fire.

Because both Campion's original 1601 song, and his 1617 version (as *Beauty, since you so much desire*) are set for solo voice with lute and an untexted Bassus, the inner parts here are editorial, along with the texting of the Bassus in the chorus.

As expected, that third song is followed by the revels (branles, galliards, corantos, etc), where the "Knights take their Ladies to daunce." The revels end when "loude Musicke sounds," followed immediately by the fourth song, *Ye should stay longer if we durst*. The loud music could be simply a flourish of trumpets, interrupting the dancing and calling the masquers to take their roles again, but it could also be a loud ensemble previewing the music for the next song. Consisting of ten lines, that song begins with a tetrameter quatrain in rhyming couplets (aabb), followed by two tercets: ccdeed 443443. That versification is not perfectly matched by any surviving song, but two songs have an identical rhyme scheme, and one of them, Dowland's *Thinkst thou then by thy faining*, works very well (no. 3.8),[23] although it uses

---

[22] No. 16, sig. F1r.
[23] (1597), no. 10, sigs. E2v–F1r. The other song with the same versification is *I will not force my thoughts*, by Thomas Greaves, from *Songes of Sundrie Kindes* (1604; STC: 12210), sig. C1r. Its line lengths are mostly much too long to work with Beaumont's masque song, however.

trimeters throughout and, thus, requires subdivision of some notes to make the masque lyric fit. Most important, the unusual structure of the song is preserved. Here are the two lyrics in parallel:

Inner Temple / Gray's Inn Masque	Dowland: *First Booke of Songes* (1597)
Ye should stay longer if we durst,	Thinkst thou then by thy fayning,
Away, alas that he that first	Sleepe with a proude disdaining,
Gaue Time wilde wings to fly away,	Or with thy craftie closing,
Hath now no power to make him stay.	Thy cruell eyes reposing,
But though these games must needs be plaid,	To driue me from thy sight,
I would this Paire, when they are laid,	When sleepe yeelds more delight,
And not a creature nie them,	Such harmles beauty gracing.
Could catch his scythe, as he doth passe,	And while sleepe fayned is,
And cut his wings, and breake his glasse,	May not I steale a kisse,
And keepe him euer by them.	Thy quiet armes embracing.

After that fourth song, the knights "daunce their parting measure." Although not consecutive in BL 10444/5 like the first two measures from this masque, at least the manuscript does have a later dance entitled *Grayes Inne Masque* that seems to fit the situation (no. 3.9). The complication is that Gray's Inn and "The Temple" (meaning The Middle Temple of the Inns of Court), had frequent events with dancing aside from these Palatine wedding masques, so we cannot be sure that one Gray's Inn dance is intended for this masque, or another. In fact, the *Grayes Inne Masque* in BL 10444/5 (no. 133) is followed by a different dance with an identical title (no. 134). The no. 133 dance occurs also in Brade's 1617 collection, as *Heynen sein Tantz* (no. 38); given how many other dances from the wedding masques are collected there, this seems a likelier prospect.

Finally, "the Priests sing the fifth and last Song." The timing is slightly ambiguous because the Priests are said to sing while the knights are putting on their swords and belts, presumably after dancing. *Peace and silence be the guide* is obviously a full song, with all of the Priests singing. It consists of a single eight-line stanza, with a tetrameter rhyming couplet and two 443 tercets: aabbcddc 44443443. That versification is unique, but comes closest to *Scinthia Queen of seas and lands*, from *Ultimum Vale* (1605), by Robert Jones.[24] The lyric appeared originally in the Entertainment at Harefield, from

---

[24] No. 8, sigs. E2v–F1r. Jones dedicated that collection to Prince Henry.

Queen Elizabeth's last summer progress, in 1602, although it is not clear that this is the musical setting used for that event.[25] Its versification is 44443343, which misses only the tetrameter in the third last line, and its rhyme scheme is aabbcded, with the last three lines forming a refrain in Jones's song. The original song also repeats words and phrases, so the versification is somewhat flexible. Here is the masque song in parallel with the first stanza of Jones's song:

Inner Temple / Gray's Inn Masque	Jones: *Ultimum Vale* (1605)
Peace and silence be the guide	Scinthia Queene of seas and lands,
To the Man, and to the Bride,	That fortune euery where commands,
If there be a ioy yet new	Sent forth fortune to the sea,
In mariage, let it fall on you,	To trye her fortune euery way:
That all the world may wonder.	Ther did I Fortune meete,
If we should stay, we should doe worse,	Which makes mee now to sing,
And turne our blessing to a curse,	There is no fishing to the Sea,
By keeping you asunder.	Nor seruice to a King.

Since Jones's song is in four voices, it works well for the Priests (no. 3.10). Its final section may be reprised from the sign of congruence.

---

[25] On the music for that entertainment, see Ross W. Duffin, "Framing a Ditty for Elizabeth: Thoughts on Music for the 1602 Summer Progress," *Early Music History* 39 (2020), 115–48, https://doi.org/10.1017/S0261127920000066.

Table of Musical Contents for The *Inner Temple & Gray's Inn Masque*

Song / Dance	Model	Source
3.1a. Antimasque – Nymphs	*The Nymphes Dance* (pt. 1 x 3)	BL10444:53; Brade (1617), no. 10
3.1b. Antimasque – Nymphs & Statues	*The Nymphes Dance* (pt. 2)	BL10444:53; Brade (1617), no. 10
3.2. Antimasque – May-daunce	*The Maypole*	BL10444:70; Brade (1617), no. 18
3.3. *Shake off your heavy traunce*	*Good men shew if you can tell*	Campion: *Second Booke of Ayres* (1613)
	Now let her change and spare not	Campion: *Third Booke of Ayres* (1617)
3.4. First Measure	*Cuperaree or Graysin*	BL10444:50; Brade (1617), no. 21; Fitzwilliam MS 734, no. 20
3.5. *On blessed youthes for Joue doth pause*	*O my poor eies that sun whose shine*	Jones: *First Booke of Songes* (1600)
	Wofull hart with griefe oppressed	Dowland: *Second Booke of Songs* (1600)
3.6. Second Measure	*[Graysin] The second*	BL10444:51; Brade (1617), no. 37
3.7. *More pleasing were these sweet delights*	*Mistris since you so much desire*	Campion: *A Booke of Ayres* (1601)
Revels		
3.8. *Ye should stay longer if we durst*	*Thinkst thou then by thy fayning*	Dowland: *First Booke of Songes* (1597)
3.9. Third Measure	*Grayes Inne Masque*	BL10444:133; Brade (1617), no. 38
3.10. *Peace and silence be the guide*	*Scinthia Queene of seas and lands*	Jones: *Ultimum Vale* (1605)

THE MASQVE
OF THE INNER
TEMPLE AND GRAYES
INNE:
GRAYES INNE AND THE INNER
TEMPLE, PRESENTED BEFORE
his Maiestie, the Queenes Maiestie, the Prince, Count
Palatine and the Lady Elizabeth their Highnesses, in
the Banquetting house at White-hall on
Saturday the twentieth day of
Februarie, 1612 [1613].
By FRANCIS BEA[U]MONT, Gent.
AT LONDON,
Imprinted by *F[elix] K[ingston]* for George Norton, and are to be sold
at his shoppe neere Temple-bar.

THE MASKE OF
THE INNER TEMPLE AND
GRAYES INNE, GRAYES INNE
and the Inner Temple, presented before his
Maiestie, the Queenes, &c.

This Maske was appointed to haue beene presented the Shroue-Tuesday before, at which time the Maskers with their attendants and diuers others gallant young Gentlemen of both houses, as their conuoy, set forth from Winchester house which was the *Rende vous* towards the Court, about seuen of the clocke at night.

This voyage by water was performed in great Triumph. The gentlemen Maskers being placed by themselues in the Kings royall barge with the rich furniture of state, and adorned with a great number of lights placed in such order as might make best shew.

They were attended with a multitude of barges and gallies, with all variety of lowde Musicke, and seuerall peales, of Ordnance. And led by two Admiralls.

Of this shew his Maiesty was gratiously pleased to take view, with the Prince, the Count *Palatine*, and the Lady *Elizabeth*: their highnesses at the windowes of his priuy gallerie vpon the water, till their landing, which was at the priuy staires; where they were most honorablie receiued by the Lord Chamberlaine, and so conducted to the Vestry.

The Hall was by that time filled with company of very good fashion, but yet so as a very great number of principall Ladies, and other noble persons were not yet come in, wherby it was foreseen that the roome would be so scanted[26] as might haue been inconuenient. And there vpon his Maiesty was most gratiously pleased with the consent of the gentlemen Maskers, to put off the night vntil Saturday following with this special fauour and priuiledge, that there should bee no let, as to the outward ceremony of magnificence vntill that time.

At the day that it was presented, there was a choice roome reserued for the gentlemen, of both their houses, who comming in troope about seuen of the clocke, receiued that speciall honor and noble fauour, as to be brought to their places, by the Right Honourable the Earle of Northampton, Lord Priuie Seale.

TO THE WORTHIE
SIR FRANCIS BACON, HIS
MAIESTIES SOLLICITOR GENERALL,
and the graue and learned Bench
of the anciently allied houses of Grayes
Inne, and the Inner Temple, the Inner
Temple, and Grayes Inne.

Yee that spared no time nor trauell, in the setting forth, ordering, & furnishing of this Masque, being the first fruits of honor in this kinde, which these two societies haue offered to his Maiestie: Will not thinke much now to looke backe vpon the effects of your owne care and worke: for that whereof the successe was then doubtfull, is now happily performed and gratiously accepted. And that which you were then to thinke of in straites of time, you may now peruse at leysure: And you Sir Francis Bacon *especially, as you did then by your countenance, and louing affection aduance it, so let your good word grace it, and defend it, which is able to adde value to the greatest, and least matters.*

THE DEVISE OR
ARGVMENT OF THE
MASQVE.

[26] scanted = crowded

Jvpiter and *Juno* willing to doe honour to the Mariage of the two famous Riuers *Thamesis* and *Rhene*, imploy their Messengers seuerally, *Mercurie* and *Iris* for that purpose. They meete and contend: then *Mercurie* for his part brings forth an Anti-masque all of Spirits or diuine Natures; but yet not of one kinde or liuerie (because that had been so much in vse heretofore) but as it were in consort like to broken Musicke:[27] And preseruing the proprietie of the deuise; for that Riuers in nature are maintained either by Springs from beneath, or Shewers from aboue: He raiseth foure of the *Naiades*[28] out of the Fountaines, and bringeth downe fiue of the *Hyades*[29] out of the Cloudes to daunce; hereupon *Iris* scoffes at *Mercurie* for that hee had deuised a daunce but of one Sexe, which could haue no life: but *Mercurie* who was prouided for that exception, and in token that the Match should be blessed both with Loue and Riches calleth forth out of the Groues foure *Cupids*, and brings downe from *Jupiters* Altar foure *Statuaes* of gold and siluer to daunce with the Nymphes and Starres: in which daunce the Cupids being blinde, and the *Statuaes* hauing but halfe life put into them, and retaining still somewhat of their old nature, giueth fit occasion to new and strange varieties both in the Musick and paces. This was the first Anti-masque.

Then *Iris* for her part in scorne of this high-flying deuise, and in token that the Match shall likewise be blessed with the loue of the Common People, calles to *Flora* her confederate (for that the Moneths of flowers are likewise the Moneths of sweete shewers, and Raine bowes) to bring in a May-daunce or Rurall daunce, consisting likewise not of any suted persons, but of a confusion or commixture of all such persons as are naturall and proper for Countrey sports. This is the second Anti-masque.

Then *Mercurie* and *Iris* after this vying one vpon the other, seeme to leaue their contention; and *Mercurie* by the consent of *Iris* brings downe the *Olympian* Knights, intimating that *Jupiter* hauing after a long discontinuance reuiued the *Olympian* games, and summoned thereunto from all parts the liueliest, & actiuest persons that were, had enioyned them before they fell to their games to doe honour to these Nuptials. The *Olympian* games portend to the Match, Celebritie, Victorie, and Felicitie. This was the maine Masque.

The Fabricke was a Mountaine with two descents, and seuered with two Trauesses.[30]

---

[27] broken Musicke = music with ornamental divisions of notes
[28] Naiades = water-nymphs
[29] Hyades = group of stars near the Pleiades
[30] Trauesses = traverses, curtains

At the entrance of the King.

The first Trauers was drawne, and the lower descent of the Mountaine discouered, which was the Pendant of a hill to life, with diuers boscages and Grouets[31] vpon the steepe or hanging grounds thereof; and at the foote of the Hill, foure delicate Fountaines running with water and bordered with sedges and water flowers.

Iris first appeared, and presently after *Mercurie* striuing to ouertake her.

Iris apparelled in a robe of discoulored[32] Taffita figured in variable colours, like the Raine-bowe, a cloudie wreath on her head, and Tresses.

Mercurie in doublet and hose of white Taffita, a white hat, wings on his shoulders and feet, his Caduceus in his hand, speaking to *Iris* as followeth:

MERCVRIE. Stay, Stay.
Stay light foot *Iris*, for thou striuest in vaine,
My wings are nimbler then thy feete.

IRIS. Away,
Dissembling *Mercury*; my messages
Aske honest haste, not like those wanton ones
Your thundring father sends.

MERCVRIE. Stay foolish Maid,
Or I will take my rise vpon a hill,
When I perceiue thee seated in a cloud,
In all the painted glorie that thou hast,
And neuer cease to clap my willing wings,
Till I catch hold of thy discolour'd Bow,
And shiuer it beyond the angry power
Of your curst Mistresse, to make vp againe.

IRIS. *Hermes* forbeare, *Juno* will chide and strike;
Is great *Joue* iealous that I am imploy'd
On her loue errands? she did neuer yet
Claspe weake mortalitie in her white armes,
As he hath often done: I onely come
To celebrate the long wisht Nuptials,

---

[31] boscages and Grouets = thickets and small groves
[32] discoulored = variously colored

Heere in *Olympia*, which are now perform'd
Betwixt two goodly Riuers, which haue mixt
Their gentle rising waues, and are to grow
Into a thousand streames, great as themselues;
I need not name them, for the sound is lowde
In heauen and earth, and I am sent from her
The Queene of Mariage, that was present heere,
And smil'd to see them ioyne, and hath not chid
Since it was done: good *Hermes* let me go.

MERCVRIE. Nay you must stay, *Joues* message is the same,
Whose eies are lightning, and whose voice is thunder,
Whose breath is any winde, he will, who knowes
How to be first on earth as well as heauen.

IRIS. But what hath he to doe with Nuptiall rights?
Let him keepe state vpon his starry throne,
And fright poore mortals with his thunderbolts,
Leauing to vs the mutuall darts of eyes.

MERCVRIE. Alas, when euer offer'd he t'abridge
Your Ladies power, but onely now in these,
Whose match concernes his generall gouernment?
Hath not each god a part in these high ioyes?
And shall not he the King of gods presume
Without proud *Junoes* licence? let her know
That when enamor'd *Joue* first gaue her power
To linke soft hearts in Vndissolued bonds,
He then foresaw, and to himselfe reseru'd
The honor of this Mariage: thou shalt stand
Still as a Rocke, while I to blesse this feast
Will summon vp with my all charming rod,
The Nymphes of fountains, from whose watry locks
Hung with the dew of blessing and encrease,
The greedie Riuers take their nourishment.
You Nymphes, who bathing in your loued springs,
Beheld these Riuers in their infancie,
And ioy'd to see them, when their circled heads
Refresht' the aire, and spread the ground with flowers:
Rise from your Wells, and with your nimble feete

Performe that office to this happie paire;
Which in these plaines, you to *Alpheus* did;
When passing hence through many seas vnmixt,
He gain'd the fauour of his *Arethuse*.

> Immediatlie vpon which speech, foure *Naiades* arise gentlie out of their seuerall Fountaines, and present themselues vpon the Stage, attired in long habits of sea-greene Taffita, with bubbles of Christall intermixt with powdering of siluer resembling drops of water; blewish Tresses on their heads, garlands of Water-Lillies. They fall into a Measure, daunce a little, then make a stand.

Example 3.1a First Antimasque—Nymphs: *The Nymphes Dance*, first part, BL 10444/5, no. 53; Brade (1617), no. 10, *Mascharada del Edelfrauen*.

Example 3.1a Continued

IRIS. Is *Hermes* growne a louer, by what power
Vnknowne to vs, calls he the *Naiades*?

MERCVRIE. Presumptuous *Iris*, I could make thee daunce
Till thou forgott'st thy Ladies messages,
And rann'st backe crying to her, thou shalt know
My power is more, onely my breath, and this
Shall moue fix'd starres, and force the firmament
To yeeld the *Hyades*, who gouerne showers,
And dewie clouds, in whose dispersed drops
Thou form'st the shape of thy deceitfull Bow.
You maids, who yearely at appointed times,
Aduance with kindly teares, the gentle flouds,
Descend, and powre your blessing on these streames,
Which rolling downe from heauen aspiring hils,
And now vnited in the fruitfull vales;
Beare all before them rauisht with their ioy,
And swell in glorie till they know no bounds.

> Fiue *Hyades* descend softly in a cloud from the firmament, to the middle part of the hill, apparelled in skie coloured Taffita robes, spangled like the Heauens, golden Tresses, and each a faire Starre on their head; from thence descend to the Stage, at whose sight the *Naiades* seeming to reioyce, meete and ioyne in a dance. [repeat 3.1a]

IRIS. Great witte and power hath *Hermes* to contriue
A liuelesse dance, which of one sexe consists.

MERCVRIE. Alas poore *Iris, Venus* hath in store
A secret Ambush of her winged boyes,
Who lurking long within these pleasant groues;
First strucke these Louers with their equall darts,
Those *Cupids* shall come forth, and ioyne with these,
To honor that which they themselues begun.

>Enter foure *Cupids* from each side of the Boscage, attired in flame coloured Taffita close to their bodie, like naked Boyes, with Bowes, Arrowes, and wings of gold; Chaplets of flowers on their heads, hoodwinckt[33] with Tiffiny scarfs, who ioyne with the Nymphes and the *Hyades* in another daunce. [repeat 3.1a]

>That ended, *Iris* speakes.[34]

IRIS. Behold the Statuaes which wise *Vulcan* plac'd
Vnder the Altar of Olympian *Ioue*,
Shall daunce for ioy of these great Nuptialls:
And gaue to them an Artificiall life,
See how they moue, drawne by this heauenly ioy,
Like the wilde trees, which follow'd *Orpheus* Harpe.

>The *Statuaes* enter, supposed to be before descended from *Ioues* Altar, and to haue been prepared in the couert with the *Cupids*, attending their call.

These *Statuaes* were attired in cases of gold and siluer close to their bodie, faces, hands and feete, nothing seene but gold and siluer, as if they had been solid Images of mettall, Tresses of haire as they had been of mettall imbossed, girdles and small aprons of oaken leaues, as if they likewise had been carued or molded out of the mettall: at their comming, the Musicke changed from Violins to Hoboyes, Cornets, &c. And the ayre of the Musicke was vtterly turned into a soft time, with drawing notes, excellently expressing their natures, and the Measure likewise was fitted vnto the same, and the *Statuaes* placed in such seuerall postures, sometimes all together in the Center of the daunce, and sometimes in the foure vtmost Angles, as was very gracefull besides the noueltie: and so concluded the first Anti-masque.

---

[33] hoodwinckt = blindfolded

[34] Although it appears this way in both the quarto and the later Beaumont and Fletcher folio, Philip Edwards regards this as an error, ascribing the speech instead to Mercury. See *A Book of Masques*, 137, 148.

Example 3.1b First Antimasque concludes: Winds—*The Nymphes Dance*, second part.

MERCVRIE. And what will *Junoes Iris* do for her?

IRIS. Iust match this shew; or my Inuention failes,
Had it beene worthier, I would haue inuok'd
The blazing Comets, Clouds and falling Starres,
And all my kindred Meteors of the Ayre
To haue excell'd it, but I now must striue
To imitate Confusion, therefore thou
Delightfull *Flora*, if thou euer felt'st
Encrease of sweetnesse in those blooming plants,
On which the hornes of my faire bow decline;
Send hither all the Rurall company,
Which decke the May-games with their Countrey sports;
Juno will haue it so.

THE MASQUE OF THE INNER TEMPLE   133

The second Anti-masque rush in, daunce their Measure, and as rudely depart; consisting of a Pedant, May Lord, May Lady, Seruingman, Chambermaide, A Countrey Clowne, or Shepheard, Countrey Wench, An Host, Hostesse, A Hee Baboone, Shee Baboone, A Hee Foole, Shee Foole vshering them in.

All these persons apparelled to the life, the Men issuing out of one side of the Boscage, and the Woemen from the other: the Musicke was extremely well fitted, hauing such a spirit of Countrey iolitie, as can hardly be imagined; but the perpetuall laughter and applause was aboue the Musicke.

The dance likewise was of the same strain; and the Dancers, or rather Actors expressed euery one their part so naturally, and aptly, as when a Mans eye was caught with the one, and then past on to the other, hee could not satisfie himselfe which did best. It pleased his Maiestie to call for it againe at the end, as he did likewise for the first Anti-masque; but one of the *Statuaes* by that time was vndressed.

Example 3.2 Second Antimasque—May-Dance: *The Maypole*, BL 10444/5, no. 70; Brade (1617), no. 18, *Der Satyrn Tantz*.

Example 3.2 Continued

Example 3.2 Continued

MERCVRIE. *Iris* we striue,
Like windes at libertie, who should do worst
Ere we returne. If *Juno* be the Queene
Of Mariage, let her giue happie way
To what is done, in honor of the State
She gouernes.

IRIS. *Hermes*, so it may be done
Meerely in honor of the State, and these
That now haue prou'd it, not to satisfie
The lust of *Jupiter*, in hauing thankes
More then his *Juno*, if thy snakie rod
Haue power to search the heauens, or sound the sea,
Or call together all the ends of earth,
To bring in any thing that may do grace
To vs, and these: do it, we shall be pleas'd.

MERCVRY. Then know that from the mouth of *Ioue* himselfe,
Whose words haue wings, and need not to be borne;
I tooke a message, and I bare it through
A thousand yeelding clouds, and neuer stai'd
Till his high will was done: the Olympian games
Which long haue slept, at these wish'd Nuptials,
He pleas'd to haue renew'd, and all his Knights

Are gathered hither, who within their tents
Rest on this hill, vpon whose rising head.
Behold *Joues* Altar, and his blessed Priests
Mouing about it: come you holy men,
And with your voices draw these youthes along,
That till *Joues* musicke call them to their games,
Their actiue sports may giue a blest content
To those, for whom they are againe begun.

The Maine Masque

The second Trauers is drawne, and the higher ascent of the Mountaine is discouered; wherein vpon a leuell after a great rise of the Hill, were placed two Pauilions: open in the front of them, the Pauilions were to sight as of cloth of gold, and they were trimmed on the inside with rich Armour and Militarie furniture hanged vp as vpon the walles; and behind the Tents there were represented in prospectiue, the tops of diuers other Tents, as if it had been a Campe. In these Pauilions were placed fifteene *Olympian* Knights, vpon seates a little imbowed neere the forme of a Croisant,[35] and the Knights appeared first, as consecrated persons all in vailes, like to Coapes, of siluer Tiffinie, gathered, and falling a large compasse about them, and ouer their heads high Miters with long pendants behind falling from them; the Miters were so high, that they receiued their hats and feathers, that nothing was seene but vaile: in the midst betweene both the Tents vpon the very top of the hill, being a higher leuell then that of the Tents, was placed *Jupiters* Altar gilt, with three great Tapers vpon golden Candlesticks burning vpon it: and the foure *Statuaes*, two of gold, and two of siluer, as supporters, and *Jupiters* Priests in white robes about it.

Vpon the sight of the King, the vailes of the Knights did fall easilie from them, and they appeared in their owne habit.

The Knights attire

Arming doublets of Carnation satten embrodered with Blazing Starres of siluer plate, with powderings of smaller Starres betwixt, gorgets of siluer maile, long hose of the same, with the doublets laide with siluer lace spangled,

---

[35] Croisant = crescent

and enricht with embroderie betweene the lace: Carnation like stockins imbrodered all ouer, garters and roses sutable: Pumpes of Carnation satten imbrodered as the doublets, hats of the same stuffe and embroderie cut like a helmet before, the hinder part cut into Scallops, answering the skirts of their doublets: the bands of the hats were wreathes of siluer in forme of garlands of wilde Oliues, white feathers with one fall of Carnation; Belts of the same stuffe and embrodered with the doublet: Siluer swords, little Italian bands[36] and cuffes embrodered with siluer, faire long Tresses of haire.

The Priests habits.

Long roabes of white Taffita, long whiteheads of haire. The high-Priest a cap of white silke shagge close to his head, with two labels at the eares, the midst rising in forme of a Pyramis, in the top thereof a branch of siluer, euery Priest playing vpon a Lute: twelue in number.

The Priests descend and sing this song following, after whom the Knights likewise descend: first laying aside their vailes, belts, and swords.

The first Song.

Example 3.3a *Shake off your heauy traunce*, set to *Good men shew if you can tell*, from Campion's *Second Booke of Ayres* (1613).

---

[36] little Italian bands = Italian lace collars

Example 3.3a Continued

    Shake off your heauy traunce,   Fit only for *Apollo*
      And leape into a daunce,   To play to, for the Moone to lead,
    Such as no mortals vse to treade,   And all the Starres to follow.

Example 3.3b *Shake off your heauy traunce*, alternative setting to *Now let her change and spare not*, from Campion's *Third Booke of Ayres* (1617).

Example 3.3b Continued

The Knights by this time are all descended and fallen into their place, and then daunce their first Measure.

Example 3.4a First Measure: *Cuperaree or Graysin*, BL 10444/5, no. 50; Brade (1617), no. 21, *Des Rothschencken Tantz*.

Example 3.4a Continued

Example 3.4b First Measure: *Almande* [*Cuperaree*], Fitzwilliam Wind Manuscript, no. 20.

Example 3.4b Continued

The second Song.

Example 3.5a *On blessed youthes, for Joue doth pause*, set to *O my poor eies that sun whose shine*, from the *The First Booke of Songes & Ayres* (1600), by Robert Jones.

Example 3.5a Continued

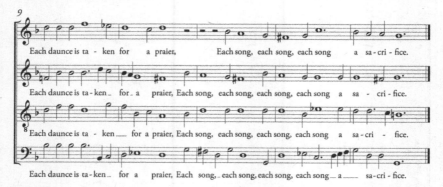

On blessed youthes, for *Joue* doth pause
Laying aside his grauer lawes
  For this deuice,

And at the wedding such a paire,
Each daunce is taken for a praier,
  Each song a sacrifice.

Example 3.5b *On blessed youthes, for Joue doth pause*, alternative setting to *Wofull hart with griefe oppressed*, from the *The Second Booke of Songs or Ayres* (1600), by John Dowland.

THE MASQUE OF THE INNER TEMPLE   143

Example 3.5b Continued

The Knights daunce their second Measure.

Example 3.6 Second Measure: *[Graysin} The second*, BL 10444/5, no. 51; Brade (1617), no. 37, *Comoedianten Tantz*.

Example 3.6 Continued

The third Song.

Example 3.7 *More pleasing were these sweet delights,* set to *Mistris since you so much desire,* from Campion's *A Booke of Ayres* (1601/1617).

Example 3.7 Continued

Single.
More pleasing were these sweet delights,
If Ladies mou'd as well as Knights;
Runne eu'ry one of you and catch
A Nymph in honor of this match;

And whisper boldly in her eare,
Joue will but laugh, if you forsweare.
All.
And this daye's sinnes he doth resolue
That we his Priests should all absolue.

The Knights take their Ladies to daunce with them Galliards, Durets,[37] Corantoes, &c. and leade them to their places.

[Revels]

Then loude Musicke sound's, supposed to call them to their *Olympian* games.

The fourth Song.

Example 3.8 *Ye should stay longer if we durst*, set to *Thinkst thou then by thy fayning*, from Dowland's *First Booke of Songes or Ayres* (1597).

[37] Michael Praetorius included a dance, *La Durette*, among the "Courantes" (corantos) in *Terpsichore* (1612), no. 103. It was mentioned also in the revels for Campion's *The Maske of Flowers* for Twelfth Night (1614; STC: 17625), sig. C3v: "Measures, Corantoes, Durettoes, Moriscoes, Galliards."

THE MASQUE OF THE INNER TEMPLE   147

Example 3.8 Continued

Ye should stay longer if we durst,
Gaue Time wilde wings to fly away,
Hath now no power to make him stay.
But though these games must needs be plaid,
I would this Paire, when they are laid,

Away, alas that he that first
   And not a creature nie them,
Could catch his scythe, as he doth passe,
And cut his wings, and breake his glasse,
   And keepe him euer by them.

The Knights daunce their parting Measure and ascend, put on their Swords and Belts,

Example 3.9 Third Measure: *Grayes Inne Masque*, BL 10444/5, no. 133; Brade (1617), no. 38, *Heynen sein Tantz*.

Example 3.9 Continued

during which time, the Priests sing the fifth and last Song.

Example 3.10 *Peace and silence be the guide*, set to *Scinthia Queene of seas and lands*, from Jones's *Ultimum Vale* (1605).

Example 3.10 Continued

Peace and silence be the guide
To the Man, and to the Bride,
If there be a ioy yet new
In mariage, let it fall on you,

    That all the world may wonder.
If we should stay, we should doe worse,
And turne our blessing to a curse,
    By keeping you asunder.

Conclusion

Aside from Andrew Sabol's 1993 attempt to provide a complete performance score of *The Lords' Masque*, the songs from the three Palatine wedding masques of 1613 have not been available as reconstructions, so it has not been possible to consider performances of the masques, spectacular entertainments though they were. Since the first song in *The Lords' Masque* survives as a *contrafactum* of a 1613 song by Thomas Campion, poet-composer and deviser of the masque, this study has begun from the premise that the other songs from the Palatine wedding masques—all of them, significantly, required for just a single performance—may also have been *contrafacta*, their models unrecognized in period song collections for over four centuries. Using versification markers and sometimes verbal connections, it has been possible to find models from Campion himself, as well as composer/performers John Dowland and Thomas Ford, who were involved in Chapman's *Memorable Masque*, William Corkine, who was paid for making music at Middle Temple just days before the wedding, and Robert Jones, who was a partner with Philip Rosseter of the Children of the Queen's Revels acting company from 1610 to 1613.[1] Besides authoring *The Lords' Masque*, furthermore, Campion was himself a former student at Gray's Inn,[2] so he may have taken an interest in that masque as well.

Setting these masque lyrics to period song models is not an arbitrary exercise. Of the hundreds of songs in the lutesong repertoire, there is sometimes only a single extant song whose music could reasonably fit a certain masque lyric. This does not guarantee that the music to that particular song was used in the masque performance in 1613, though it is possible, and for anyone

---

[1] See Linda Phyllis Austern, *Music in English Children's Drama* (Philadelphia, 1992), 10. Lutenist-composer Rosseter was, in fact, the payee for four plays acted at court by the company in late 1612 and early 1613, including three under the patronage of Princess Elizabeth and the Elector Frederick. See Lucy Munro, *Children of the Queen's Revels: A Jacobean Theatre Repertory* (Cambridge, 2005), 190–91. Rosseter was also among the musicians for *The Memorable Masque*, which lends support to Anne Daye's speculation that the baboons in that masque were from his company. See Daye, "'Graced with Measures,'" 309.

[2] See "Gray's Inn Admissions Lists," British Library, Harley MS 1912, fol. 91, for 27 April 1586. See also *The Register of Admissions to Gray's Inn, 1521–1889*, ed. Joseph Foster (London, 1889), 69.

who wishes to perform these masques with songs today, it does provide a musical solution that is appropriate to both the lyric and the period.

As for the dances, there is evidence that the main dances survive for each of these three masques, and arguments can be made for the antimasque dances as well, though the choice is often more conjectural than for the measures. Nevertheless, the five-part versions provided here, whether extant in Brade or Adson, or reconstructed from BL 10444/5, seem to furnish something close to the dance music for the original productions, and offer a starting point for anyone attempting to mount a performance.

Enormous resources are required to perform Jacobean masques like those for the Palatine wedding: reconstructed sets, costumes, dances, and music, as well as actors, dancers, and musicians. But now, at least, modern performers can avoid the situation in the otherwise laudable performance of Chapman's *Memorable Masque* in 2011, where the song lyrics were spoken, rather than sung.[3]

Index to Song Sources for Part I

L = *Lords' Masque*; M = *Memorable Masque*; G = *Inner Temple/Gray's Inn Masque*

Thomas Campion:

A Booke of Ayres (1601) with Philip Rosseter		
XVI	*Mistris since you so much desire*	L6, G7
XVII	*Your faire lookes enflame my desire*	M9
First Booke of Ayres (1613)		
V	*View mee Lord, a worke of thine*	L7
XIV	*As by the streames of Babilon*	M4
Second Booke of Ayres (1613)		
III	*Harden now thy tired heart*	L10
V	*Where she her sacred bowre adornes*	L4
IX	*Good men shew if you can tell*	G3
XVII	*Come away, arm'd with loues delights*	L3

---

[3] See Peter Kirwan's blog review: https://blogs.warwick.ac.uk/pkirwan/entry/the_memorable_masque/.

Description of a Maske (1614)
 V Wooe her and win her   L8
Third Booke of Ayres (1617)
 II Now let her change and spare not   L15
Fourth Booke of Ayres (1617)
 I Leaue prolonging, thy distresse   L13
 XXII Beauty since you so much desire   L6, G7

John Dowland:

First Booke of Songes or Ayres (1597)
 VI Now O now I needs must part   M4
 X Thinkst thou then by thy fayning   G8
Second Booke of Songs or Ayres (1600)
 XVI Wofull hart with griefe oppressed   G5
Third and Last Booke of Songs or Aires (1603)
 XX What poore Astronomers are they   M5

Thomas Ford:

Musicke of Sundrie Kindes (1607)
 III Unto the temple of thy beauty   M9
 IV Now I see thy lookes were fained   M8
 IX There is a lady sweet and kind   M4

Robert Jones:

First Booke of Songes & Ayres (1600)
 III She whose matchles beauty stayneth   L12
 XIII O my poor eies that sun whose shine   G5
Ultimum Vale (1605)
 VIII Scinthia Queene of seas and lands   G10
A Musicall Dreame, or the Fourth Booke of Ayres (1609)
 IV Will saide to his mammy   L14

William Corkine
Ayres to Sing and Play to the Lvte and Basse Violl (1610)
 VII Sweet Cupid, ripen her desire   M4

Second Booke of Ayres (1612)
   XI   My deerest Mistrisse   M11

First Line Index
to Masque Songs and Models in Part I

L = Lords' Masque; M = Memorable Masque; G = Inner Temple/Gray's Inn Masque

Aduance your Chorall motions now	L2
As by the streames of Babilon	M2
Beauty since you so much desire	L3, G3
Breath[e] you now while Io Hymen	L6
Bright Panthaea borne to Pan	M3
Cease, cease you revels, rest a space	L7
Come away, arm'd with loues delights	L1
Come away, bring thy golden theft	L1
Come triumphing, come with state	L8
Dance and visit now the shadowes	L9
Descend (faire Sun) and sweetly rest	M2
Good men shew if you can tell	G1
Harden now thy tired heart	L6
Leaue prolonging, thy distresse	L8
Mistris since you so much desire	L3, G3
More pleasing were these sweet delights	G3
My deerest Mistrisse, let vs liue and loue	M11
No longer wrong the night	L10
Now I see thy lookes were fained	M3
Now let her change and spare not	L10, G1
Now O now I needs must part	M2
Now sleepe binde fast the floode	M4
O my poor eies that sun whose shine	G2
On blessed youthes for Ioue doth pause	G2
Ope Earth thy womb of golde	M1
Peace and silence be the guide	G5
Powerfull Ioue, that of bright starres	L4
Scinthia Queene of seas and lands	G5

Shake off your heauy traunce   G1
She whose matchles beauty stayneth   L7
Singe, singe a Rapture to all Nuptiall eares   M11
Svpported now by Clouds descend   L3
Sweet Cupid, ripen her desire   M2
There is a lady sweet and kind   M2
Thinkst thou then by thy fayning   G4
Unto the temple of thy beauty   M4
View mee Lord, a worke of thine   L4
What poore Astronomers are they   M1
Where she her sacred bowre adornes   L2
Will saide to his mammy   L9
Wofull hart with griefe oppressed   G2
Wooe her and win her   L5
Ye should stay longer if we durst   G4
Your faire lookes enflame my desire   M4

Plate 1 Inigo Jones, *Torchbearer: An Indian*, from Chapman's *The Memorable Masque* (1613). Reproduced by permission of Chatsworth Settlement Trustees / Bridgeman Images.

Plate 2 Map of the World. Abraham Ortelius, *Theatrum Orbis Terrarum* (London, 1608), sig. 1v. Courtesy of the Huntington Library.

Plate 3 Map of Europe. Abraham Ortelius, *Theatrum Orbis Terrarum* (London, 1608), sig. 2v. Courtesy of the Huntington Library.

Plate 4 Europa. *Was uns die Jahrzeiten und Monate weise* (17th century), Huntington Library MS HM 1016. Courtesy of the Huntington Library.

Plate 5 Map of Asia. Abraham Ortelius, *Theatrum Orbis Terrarum* (London, 1608), sig. 3v. Courtesy of the Huntington Library.

Plate 6 Map of Africa. Abraham Ortelius, *Theatrum Orbis Terrarum* (London, 1608), sig. 4v. Courtesy of the Huntington Library.

Plate 7 Asia. *Was uns die Jahrzeiten und Monate weise* (17th century), Huntington Library MS HM 1016. Courtesy of the Huntington Library.

Plate 8 Africa. *Was uns die Jahrzeiten und Monate weise* (17th century), Huntington Library MS HM 1016. Courtesy of the Huntington Library.

Plate 9 Side-by-side: Europa. *Was uns die Jahrzeiten und Monate weise* (17th century), Huntington Library MS HM 1016. Courtesy of the Huntington Library; Queen Elizabeth Stuart, after Michiel Janszoon van Mierevelt. Private Collection, Scotland. Used with permission. Photo: Antonia Reeve.

Plate 10 America. *Was uns die Jahrzeiten und Monate weise* (17th century), Huntington Library MS HM 1016. Courtesy of the Huntington Library.

PART II
THE MASQUE OF TRUTH

The Masque of Truth

Introduction

Beginning with his 1978 Oxford dissertation,[1] and then in a 1986 article in the inaugural issue of the journal *Seventeenth Century*,[2] David Norbrook introduced an entertainment that he dubbed *The Masque of Truth*,[3] and deftly placed it in its historical context. Like the masques in Part I, this event celebrates the marriage of Princess Elizabeth Stuart, the only daughter of King James I of Britain, and Frederick V, Elector-in-waiting of the Palatinate, which was a bastion of Calvinism on the Rhine in southwestern Germany.[4]

At the time of the wedding, Elizabeth's importance as the young-adult daughter of King James was magnified because Prince Charles was still only twelve and somewhat sickly as the heir apparent. Indeed, just two months before the wedding, a Venetian diplomat in Florence observed that Prince

---

[1] David Norbrook, "Panegyric of the Monarch and Its Social Context under Elizabeth I and James I" (D.Phil. diss., Oxford University, 1978), https://ora.ox.ac.uk/objects/uuid:514b9c61-be87-4832-a397-cdda040dcd06.

[2] David Norbrook, "'The Masque of Truth': Court Entertainments and International Protestant Politics in the Early Stuart Period," *Seventeenth Century* 1 (1986), 81–110, https://www.tandfonline.com/doi/abs/10.1080/0268117X.1986.10555252?journalCode=rsev20. See also David Norbrook, "The Reformation of the Masque," in David Lindley, ed., *The Court Masque* (Manchester, 1984), 94–110; Kevin Curran, "James I and Fictional Authority at the Palatine Wedding Celebrations," *Renaissance Studies* 20 (2006), 51–67, at 57–58, https://doi.org/10.1111/j.1477-4658.2006.00113.x. A version of this also appeared in Curran, *Marriage, Performance, and Politics at the Jacobean Court* (Farnham, 2009); Anne Daye, "'Graced with Measures': Dance as an International Language in the Masques of 1613," in *The Palatine Wedding of 1613: Protestant Alliance and Court Festival*, ed. Sara Smart and Mara R. Wade (Wiesbaden, 2013), 289–318; and Martin Wiggins and Catherine Richardson, *British Drama, 1533–1642: A Catalogue, Volume VI: 1609–1616* (Oxford, 2015), 252–56. This last source dubs the masque "Projected Court Masque of Muses and Geography."

[3] Though well established now, Norbrook's title is slightly problematic since the entertainment is not a masque in the usual sense of the word. For an allegorical presentation with songs and dances, however, the word "masque" is the closest English term. The nearest French equivalent is the *ballet de cour*, and even at the time, the terms were sometimes used interchangeably; but there are differences between the masque and the *ballet de cour*, most notably that the French entertainment was primarily a succession of dances with an occasional song. On the differences between them, see Peter Walls, *Music in the English Courtly Masque, 1604–1640* (Oxford, 1996), 224–30.

[4] Frederick's father had died in 1610, but his son was underage and officially had a guardian until his majority in 1614, although he actually assumed his personal rule in 1613. The masque below refers to him as Elector, but most reports from England at the time call him "Count Palatine," or "the Palsgrave."

Charles was "weak and may not live long."[5] In the end, Charles did accede to the throne in 1625, but it was Elizabeth, rather than her brother, who became the conduit for the royal succession, even after the Stuart dynasty, since her grandson by her daughter Sophia (Electress of Hanover), became Britain's King George I, through whom the Royal Family is descended to this day. Thus, Elizabeth Stuart was—and is—important in the succession of the British crown, and her wedding was a moment, not only of heightened national anticipation, but of religious expectation as well. As George Webbe explained in a sermon in Wiltshire on the day of the wedding, justifying celebration so far from court:

> Wherefore let no man taxe it as a matter either ridiculous, or presumptuous, for vs that liue here in the Countrie, to participate in any sort with this daies triumph of the Court, seeing that not Court alone, but Countrie also, and (if I not much mistake my selfe) whole Christendome is interested in this dayes businesse: yea, I doubt not, but in forraine countries, as wel as here in ours, the confederate Nations, and all true-hearted Christians, whose hearts and minds are linked with the band of the same Religion together with vs, so many as heare of it, doe greatly ioy and reioyce in it.[6]

The ceremony took place at Whitehall Palace on Valentine's Day, 1613, and the source for *The Masque of Truth* is a 1613 quarto by D. Jocquet,[7] who published it in Heidelberg a few months later, following the royal couple's arrival there to take up residence.[8]

As noted in Part I, three famous masques are already connected to the nuptials: Thomas Campion's *Lords' Masque*, performed at the Whitehall

---

[5] Domenico Domenici to the Doge and Senate, 8 December (new style) 1612. *CSP Venetian*, vol. 12, no. 712.

[6] George Webbe, *The Bride Royall* (1613; STC: 25157), 2–3. For a recent overview of the national and international reactions to the wedding, see Clare Jackson, *Devil-Land: England under Siege, 1588–1688* (London, 2021), 144–48.

[7] D. Jocquet is otherwise unknown, but may be the author of the manuscript, "Le discours de l'entrée (7 nov. 1613) de Messeigneurs le duc d'Espernon et marquis de La Vallette en la ville de Metz, avec pourtraits des arc triomphaux," Paris, Bibliothèque Nationale, MS fonds fr. 24103. The author's name (fol. 1v) has been written over, and the library gives it as D. Jacquet, but it looks more like D. Jocquet.

[8] *Les Triomphes, Entrées, Cartels, Tournois, Ceremonies, et aultre Magnificences, faites en Angleterre, & au Palatinat, pour le Mariage & Receptions, de Monseigneur le Prince Frideric V. Comte Palatin du Rhin, Electeur du Sainct Empire, Duc de Baviere, &c. et de Madame Elisabeth, fille unique et Princesse de la Grande Bretagne, Electrice Palatine du Rhin &c. Son Espouse* (Heidelberg, 1613), sigs. H1r–H4v. In addition, the Bibliothèque Municipale de Lyon holds two copies (one imperfect) of a variant edition, printed there in 1613 by Jaques Mallet (sigs. G1r–G4r). The readings in the two editions are very close but not identical, with some variants, especially in the sung lyrics, noted below.

Banqueting House the evening of the wedding (a Sunday); George Chapman's *Memorable Masque of the Middle Temple and Lincoln's Inn*, presented at Whitehall on the following evening (Monday); and Francis Beaumont's *Masque of the Inner Temple and Gray's Inn*, scheduled for the Tuesday evening, but postponed at the king's request to the following Saturday. Those three masques were all printed in quarto in 1613,[9] and have long been known in modern times,[10] though music definitively associated with them is scarce.[11]

The Masque of Truth purports to have been performed on the Tuesday following the wedding, that is, 16 February 1613, presumably as a substitute for Beaumont's postponed event, but there is no evidence that it was actually performed at all. As David Norbrook commented, "Jocquet is giving a completely false account of the events of the Tuesday, and he seems to be doing so quite consciously."[12] Yet, its sequence of events, its lyrics for singing, and the placement of the dances, are all included in Jocquet's description. In this, it somewhat resembles the description of the other Palatine wedding masques, and other masques from the period, though—crucially—without the dialogue that is normally included.

The Masque of Truth, thus, appears to be a production that was conceived to be presented during the wedding celebrations but that was never seen by audiences, no matter how much the author(s) and sponsors might have wished it. This fact, plus Jocquet's failure to include any dialogue, may be why it has received very little attention since Norbrook's early studies.[13] Still, the description is sufficiently detailed that it seems to represent something

---

[9] *A Relation of the late Royal Entertainment... Whereunto is annexed the Description, Speeches, and Songs of the Lords Maske* (1613; STC: 4545); *The Memorable Maske of the two Honorable Houses or Inns of Court; the Middle Temple, and Lyncolns Inne* (1613; STC: 4981); *The Masque of the Inner Temple and Grayes Inne* (1613; STC: 1663 and 1664). Additionally, *The Memorable Maske* was issued a second time, probably in 1614 (STC: 4982), though without substantial variants, although the title was given as *The Memorable Masque*.

[10] Besides the original quartos, the texts were printed in John Nichols, *Progresses, Processions, and Magnificent Festivities of King James the First*, vol. 2 (London, 1828), 554–86 and 591–600.

[11] See the discussion of songs and dances in Walls, *Music in the English Courtly Masque*, 43–158. From the three wedding masques combined, several dances survive, along with two songs from Campion's *Lords' Masque* (really only one, plus a fairly obvious *contrafactum*). For those pieces, see Andrew Sabol, *Four Hundred Songs and Dances from the Stuart Masque* (Hanover, N.H., 1982), Nos. 18–19, pp. 72–75. For a new reconstruction of the songs in those masques, and their presumed dances, see Part I of this volume.

[12] Norbrook, "The Masque of Truth," 82.

[13] One interesting theory is that it formed the last of a planned group of four masques for the Palatine wedding, with "The Masque of Fire" (Campion), "The Masque of Earth" (Chapman), and "The Masque of Water" (Beaumont), completed by *The Masque of Truth* as "The Masque of Air." See Jerzy Limon, *The Masque of Stuart Culture* (Newark, 1990), 166–69.

that had been brought to an advanced state of preparation, though it reads misleadingly as a description of an entertainment that had actually taken place. Assuming it was fully prepared, the question I am seeking to answer here is whether it is possible to identify music that was used, or could plausibly be used, for setting its lyrics and accompanying its dancing.

Origins

The Palatine wedding was regarded by Protestants as tying Britain to Europe through the reformed religion shared with the Palatinate, and the "Truth" of the title refers to the truth of the gospel as preached in those countries, as well as the figure of Truth (Verité), onstage throughout. The intent was to persuade the holdouts in Europe, along with those "benighted" souls in Asia and Africa, to convert to the reformed religion. Without documentary evidence, one common theory of authorship is that it was instigated originally by Elizabeth's older brother, Prince Henry, a militant Protestant,[14] and that a primary author may have been Georg Rudolf Weckherlin, a German poet who had spent time in Paris and had close friends among Huguenots there.[15] Oddly, there has been a reluctance to regard Princess Elizabeth as a possible patron. As Norbrook says, "Elizabeth was only sixteen when the wedding took place, and both as a political figure and as an artistic patron she was overshadowed by her brother Prince Henry."[16] Nevertheless, it seems likely that this is the event referred to in the report of the Venetian ambassador, Antonio Foscarini, for 30 October 1612: [The Princess] "is preparing a sumptuous ballet of sixteen maidens, of whom she will be one."[17] *The Masque of Truth* does, indeed, have sixteen princesses, though ultimately, Elizabeth was not described as taking part. Nonetheless, she was the dedicatee of Jocquet's quarto, and he further described her as "le premier mobile" of the event;[18] her recent biographer, Nadine Akkerman, sees Elizabeth as

---

[14] On Prince Henry as the personification of militant Protestantism, see Jason White, *Militant Protestantism and British Identity, 1603–1642* (London, 2012), 28–32, https://doi.org/10.4324/9781315656052.

[15] See Norbrook, "The Masque of Truth," 97. Weckherlin later became a high-ranking civil servant in England.

[16] Norbrook, "The Masque of Truth," 89. For a contrary view, see Akkerman, *Elizabeth Stuart, Queen of Hearts*, 425–26, n. 39.

[17] Antonio Foscarini to the Doge and Senate, 9 November (new style) 1612. *CSP Venetian*, vol. 12, no. 680.

[18] Sigs. A2r–A3v.

having had "more than a hand in its invention,"[19] something that would be in the tradition of her mother, Queen Anna.[20] Foscarini reported in January 1613, in fact, that four masques were in preparation for the wedding, the last being "of lovely maidens," so *The Masque of Truth* may still have been on the agenda and in rehearsal within weeks of the ceremony.[21]

The Venetian dispatch of 30 October, incidentally, reports widespread use of the French language at the English Court at the time. Speaking of the Count Palatine, Foscarini notes:

> He is frequently with the Princess, with whom he is now very familiar. He speaks French to her and to every one else, and knows the language excellently well, as does the King and the rest of the royal family sufficiently. Since his arrival hardly any other language has been used at Court, as it is the language of all his suite.[22]

Moreover, it happens that all of the extant correspondence between Elizabeth and Frederick, during their courting period in 1612, was in French on both sides.[23] This emphasis on the French language is fascinating because one thing that sets *The Masque of Truth* apart from the others for the royal wedding is that it is written in French. Claude-François Menestrier, the only commentator in the seventeenth-century to say anything about its authorship, attributed it to proselytizing "Ministres Protestans" who were "trying to turn entertainments into subjects of instruction."[24]

---

[19] Akkerman, *Elizabeth Stuart, Queen of Hearts*, 77–84. Akkerman asserts that the masque was originally intended for performance on the day before the wedding, which, because of the cancellation, became a rest day.

[20] As Jemma Field points out, Ben Jonson "unequivocally credited Anna with the conceit of *The Masque of Blackness*," and for its companion piece, *The Masque of Beauty*, "onlookers explicitly ascribed the occasion to Anna and the Venetian ambassador identified her as the 'authoress of the whole.'" See Jemma Field, *Anna of Denmark: The Material and Visual Culture of the Stuart Courts, 1589–1619* (Manchester, 2020), 5, https://doi.org/10.7765/9781526142504. See also *CSP Venetian*, vol. 11, no. 154: 24 January 1608.

[21] Antonio Foscarini to the Doge and Senate, 11 January (new style) 1613, *CSP Venetian*, vol. 12, no. 734. See also Clare McManus, *Women on the Renaissance Stage: Anna of Denmark and Female Masquing in the Stuart Court, 1590–1619* (Manchester, 2002), 141.

[22] *CSP Venetian*, vol. 12, no. 680.

[23] See Nadine Akkerman, ed., *The Correspondence of Elizabeth Stuart, Queen of Bohemia, Volume 1, 1603–1631* (Oxford, 2015), 103–13, https://doi:10.1093/actrade/9780199551071.book.1. In fact, while growing up in the Harington household, Elizabeth had a French Huguenot writing master, Jean de Beau-Chesne. See Akkerman, *Elizabeth Stuart, Queen of Hearts*, 38.

[24] C.-F. Menestrier, *Des Ballets Anciens et Modernes selon les Règles du Théatre* (Paris, 1682), 114 (see Appendix 1.2). See also Norbrook, "The Masque of Truth," 84. Menestrier includes a description of the event, and reproduces three of the lyrics, so he must have been working from Jocquet's print (the Heidelberg edition), though his authority for the information on the Protestant ministers is unknown. Menestrier's account, in turn, was quoted at length in Jacques Bonnet's *Histoire*

It is often assumed, nevertheless, that *The Masque of Truth* was translated from an English original. David Norbrook, indeed, speculates that it was,[25] and Wiggins and Richardson state it more emphatically.[26] The original language is not entirely clear, however, just as the authorship is unclear. If the event truly had its genesis months earlier, in the circle of either Prince Henry or Princess Elizabeth,[27] or both, and had been completed in preparation for performance at Whitehall, Jocquet's work might have been translated from an English original, but as it survives, it appears to me to be constructed in French,[28] which would make sense if the immediate sponsors were French Protestant ministers.[29] Of course, they may have taken the idea of a Protestant masque, officially abandoned at some point after Prince Henry's death, and developed it more fully in their own language. Indeed, if it was first conceived around 30 October 1612, English organizers had virtually no time to work on it before Henry's sudden death on 6 November, just one week later.

Lyrics

Wiggins and Richardson further characterize *The Masque of Truth* as a translation by referring to the surviving lyrics as "incipits,"[30] implying that the complete English lyrics were longer, and those that survive in French are just the opening stanzas. *Quittez vos anciennes querelles*, on the other hand, consists of four six-line stanzas, so presumably that is not just an incipit. Furthermore, all of the single-stanza lyrics are self-contained, accomplishing their mission of summoning the various queens, or counseling adherence to the reformed religion, so there is no evidence that anything is lacking. In the aftermath of the assassination of King Henry IV in 1610, and the recent

---

Générale de la Danse, Sacrée et Profane (Paris, 1723), 101–6, though it wrongly places the event after the Restoration.

[25] See Norbrook, "The Masque of Truth," 84, 86.
[26] Wiggins and Richardson, *British Drama*, 6:255.
[27] On the connections to the circle of Prince Henry in particular, see Norbrook, "The Masque of Truth," 89.
[28] See the discussion of the lyrics below, as well as the note about Archimedes after the masque's first lyric.
[29] A French origin would help to explain why it differs from extant English court masques in format, though it also differs from French *ballets de cour* from the period, giving the impression of a unique hybrid, or a newly invented form.
[30] Wiggins and Richardson, *British Drama*, 6:255.

death of Prince Henry,[31] French Protestants had good reason for supporting a Protestant alliance between England and Europe[22] and for celebrating it in the language known to be preferred by the wedding couple.[33]

A French origin is also supported by the lyrics' versifications, which have no comparable examples in English poetry, except among the 1632 translations of French metrical psalms by John Standish.[34] The French metrical psalms of Clément Marot and Théodore de Bèze were the basis for much of the English metrical psalter of *The Whole Booke of Psalmes* (1562), but the English versions mostly do not precisely match the versifications of their French models. The French psalter itself was known in England long before Standish's translated versions, however: Philip and Mary Sidney almost certainly grew up listening to French metrical psalms since their family home in Threadneedle Street adjoined St. Anthony's, London's French Protestant church,[35] and three of Philip's psalms appear in John Standish's 1632 collection as singable translations of the French psalter.[36] Moreover, a painting at Hardwick Hall, dated 1591, shows a young woman (perhaps Lady Grace Cavendish, née Talbot) beside whom is an open volume showing French Psalm 16 with mensural music—apparently the monophonic metrical psalm in spite of the oblong format more typically used for polyphonic partbooks.[37] Last, the French psalm tunes were also known in Germany, and particularly in the Palatinate. In Heidelberg in 1572, Paul Schede (writing as Melissus) published a German translation of fifty French psalms to their tunes: *Di Psalmen Davids nach Französischer melodei in hoch-Teutsche*

---

[31] As the Venetian Ambassador in Paris, Zorzi Giustinian, wrote to the Doge and Senate on 27 November (new style) 1612: "The Huguenots are grieved, as they built their hopes on the Prince, and had already chosen him as their chief support and head." See *CSP Venetian*, vol. 12, no. 696.

[32] For an exploration of French support for the marriage, see Norbrook, "The Masque of Truth," 84–85.

[33] Reinforcing the view that the masque was no longer planned by the time of the wedding is the detailed report of the French ambassador, Samuel Spifame. If any whiff of a French masque being cancelled was in the air, his nose for precedence and diplomatic slights would undoubtedly have caused him to mention it. See Marie-Claude Canova-Green, "'Particularitez des Resjoyssances Publiques et Cérémonyes du Mariage de la Princesse': An Ambassadorial Account of the Palatine Wedding," in *The Palatine Wedding of 1613*, 353–69.

[34] *All the French Psalm Tunes with English Words* (1632; STC: 2734).

[35] See Katherine Duncan-Jones, *Sir Philip Sidney, Courtier Poet* (New Haven, 1991), 25–6.

[36] Jim Doelman, "A Seventeenth-Century Publication of Three of Sir Philip Sidney's Psalms," *Notes and Queries* 38 (1991), 162–63, https://doi.org/10.1093/nq/38.2.162. See also Hannibal Hamlin, "'The Highest Matter in the Noblest Forme': The Influence of the Sidney Psalms," *Sidney Journal* 23 (2005), 146.

[37] For a reproduction and discussion of this painting, see Linda Phyllis Austern, "'For Musicke Is the Handmaid of the Lord': Women, Psalms, and Domestic Music-Making in Early Modern England," in *Psalms in the Early Modern World*, ed. Linda Phyllis Austern et al. (Farnham, 2013), 89–92, https://doi.org/10.4324/9781315602783.

reymen. Schede became librarian to the Elector Palatine in 1586. Also, the humanist and jurist Ambrosius Lobwasser published translations of the French psalms with Claude Goudimel's polyphonic versions of their tunes in Leipzig in 1573, and in Heidelberg the following year. They were then reprinted and used throughout Protestant Germany for 200 years, alongside the psalms and hymns of Martin Luther.[38]

A reasonable inference from this bilateral familiarity is that the lyrics in *The Masque of Truth* were written using French metrical psalms as models, with the expectation that they would be sung in French to those tunes. To say that this is unexpected for Jacobean masque song lyrics is an understatement, but psalm tunes impart a measure of solemnity to the musical settings, appropriate to the dignity of the task the *Masque of Truth* lyrics were attempting to fulfill in the service of the reformed religion. Furthermore, they work naturally in collective performance, as here, with three to nine (or more) singers for each lyric. Some existing French secular songs from the period would match the versifications, such as selections in Gabriel Bataille's *Airs de differents autheurs* (Paris, 1613),[39] but the character of those songs does not suit the gravity of the lyrics here, nor so readily allow collective participation.[40] It is possible, of course, that more song-like settings were intended for these lyrics but have been lost. The gravity of the lyrics, their religious purpose, and the fact that they are sung by multiple singers, however, all reinforce the idea that psalm tunes might have been the expected melodies here, even though they are completely different from song settings in other Jacobean masques. In many ways, *The Masque of Truth* is not like other Jacobean masques, however, and there is no question that psalm tunes were sometimes used in English plays of the time, especially for chorus lyrics.[41]

---

[38] *Der Psalter dess Königlichen Propheten Dauids* (1573). See Dieter Gutknecht, "Vergleichende Betrachtung des Goudimel-Psalters mit dem Lobwasser-Psalter," *Jahrbuch für Liturgik und Hymnologie* 15 (1970), 132–45, https://www.jstor.org/stable/24193786.

[39] See, for example, *C'est à tort qu'on dit que l'absence* for no. 5.1; *Belle je vous ayme d'amour* for no. 5.5; *Puisqu'en nostre tendre jeunesse* for nos. 5.8 and 5.13; and *Belle qui de peur d'une enflure* for no. 11, below.

[40] Solving the collective singing issue, if not the character problem, are selections from Pierre Guédron's *Airs de cour, a quatre & cinq parties* (Paris, 1608), where *Ov luis-tu soleil de mon ame?* could set no. 5.1, below, and *J'ayme les bois tant seulement* could set no. 5.5, below. Bataille and Guédron, along with Antoine Boësset, also composed extant music for songs in the 1617 royal *ballet de cour* entitled *La Délivrance de Renaud*, though none of the versifications there match lyrics in *The Masque of Truth*. On this work, see *La Délivrance de Renaud: Ballet danced by Louis XIII*, ed. Greer Garden (Turnhout, 2010). One 1614 *ballet de cour* has two song lyrics whose versification matches nos. 5.8 and 5.13 below, though no musical settings survive: *Le Ballet des dix verds* (Paris, 1614), *Il nous faut quitter ce parterre* (sigs. A3r–A3v), and *Mes Dames, ceste ieune bande* (sigs. B3v–B4r).

[41] On French metrical psalms adapted for English use in Elizabethan tragedies, see Duffin, "Hidden Music," 20–34. That study mostly concerns mid-sixteenth-century plays, but see Elizabeth

The lyrics in *The Masque of Truth* all use six-line stanzas of tetrameters, some quatrain-couplet, others tercet-tercet, but distinguished from English tetrameter lyrics by the frequent use of nine-syllable lines. Even English metrical psalms based on French models almost never use nine-syllable lines[42] whereas they are quite common in the French repertoire, although persistently (and inaccurately) described as octosyllabic.[43] It thus seems unlikely that Jocquet's lyrics are translated from English originals since they would fit awkwardly to whatever tunes were used, whereas the lyrics resemble selections from the French psalter, sometimes matching precisely, sometimes fitting with only minimal adjustment. For example, the first lyric sung by the Muses, *Le Monde Te vient faire hommage*, has 988–988 syllables in tercets, a versification matched by Théodore de Bèze's *Entre vous conseillers qui estes*, Psalm 58 from *Les Pseaumes mis en Rime Françoise*, of 1562, the French equivalent of *The Whole Booke of Psalmes*.

Metrical psalms were often sung monophonically and in unison, with all of the singers sounding together on the tune in whatever octave was most comfortable for them. But even as early as the mid-1560s, with Claude Goudimel's *Les pseavmes mis en rime françoise*, attempts were made to create harmonized versions of the French psalter.[44] Since we know that multiple singers with unknown ranges were to take part in *The Masque of Truth*, and also that instruments accompanied that first lyric and probably others, it makes sense to use harmonized settings of the psalm tunes. One source for these close to the time of the masque is Claude le Jeune's *Les Cent Cinquante*

Cary's *The Tragedie of Mariam* (1613; STC: 4613), where the act-ending choruses seem very likely to have used music from the metrical psalter.

[42] One exception is John Craig's *Give to the Lord all praise and honour*, Psalm 118 from the *Forme of Prayers* (Edinburgh. 1564; STC: 16577), based on the tune for Clément Marot's *Rendez à Dieu louange et gloire*, from the 1551 *Octantetrois Pseaumes de Dauid*. Both feature an eight-line stanza, however.

[43] French versification does not recognize the final unaccented syllable of a line as having any poetic value, but musical settings always give such syllables a note, so it definitely exists as far as the music is concerned. See, for example, the dozens of categories in the versification table in Pierre Pidoux, *Le Psautier Huguenot* (Basel, 1962), 253–60, where only Psalm 138 (Calvin's *Louange et grace je te rendray*) is recognized as having nine-syllable lines (and not for feminine endings in that case).

[44] Goudimel published a partial edition of harmonized psalms in 1562 and his first complete edition in 1564, though both are imperfectly preserved. His most famous complete four-voice psalter was printed in 1565; other composers with four-voice harmonizations of the French psalter include Philibert Jambe de fer (1564), and Hugues Sureau (1565).

Pseaumes de David, first published posthumously in 1601, and reprinted several times, including the same year as *The Masque of Truth*.[45]

Authorship

Georg Rudolf Weckherlin has already been mentioned as a possible author of *The Masque of Truth*. He was in court circles in 1612 and had ties to the newlyweds even after their removal to Heidelberg.[46] He certainly had the ability to write in French, though that has not been the assumption for his involvement.[47] For example, two drafts for a masque (*ballet*) in French survive from him from sometime in the period 1626–33, the most complete of which is "un ballet digne d'estre representé par la Reyne de la Grande Bretagne." Unfortunately, even this larger draft is nothing more than a summary or outline.[48] There are other writers who come to mind as possible authors in French, though no single person can be positively identified in that role.

Another writer who fits the profile is Josuah (Joshua) Sylvester. He was in the circles of both Princess Elizabeth and Prince Henry, and was active translating French writings and poetry in the years before the wedding.[49] Poems in his "small workes" name many of the rivers featured in *The Masque of Truth*, including the Nile, Tiber, Jordan, Ganges, Tigris, and Euphrates.[50] After Henry's death, moreover, he published an epitaph saying that the death of France's King Henry IV left England's Prince Henry as "an Atlas," carrying "the World of Hope," but that he was ultimately crushed by the weight of "England's sinnes."[51] In *The Masque of Truth*, therefore, the central figure of

---

[45] Because of the clearer text setting in all voices, these would have been preferable, I believe, to the more motet-like settings in Paschal L'Estocart, *Cent Cinquante Pseaumes de David*, printed in both Paris and Geneva in 1583. Also, unlike Le Jeune's psalm collection, L'Estocart's does not appear to have been reprinted.

[46] See Rudolf Weckherlin, *Triumphall Shews, Set forth lately at Stutgart, written First in German, and now in English* (Stuttgart, 1616; STC: 25186).

[47] See Norbrook, "The Masque of Truth," 97.

[48] See Leonard Forster, "Two Drafts by Weckherlin of a Masque for the Queen of England," *German Life and Letters* 18 (1965), 258–63, https://doi.org/10.1111/j.1468-0483.1965.tb00078.x. See also Jennifer Nevile, *Footprints of the Dance: An Early Seventeenth-Century Dance Master's Notebook* (Leiden, 2018), 83.

[49] He also contributed thirteen singing translations of French psalms to Standish's *All the French Psalm Tunes with English Words* (1632; STC: 2734). See Doelman, "A Seventeenth-Century Publication," 162. Sylvester's psalm translations are listed by William Drummond in Edinburgh, National Library of Scotland, MS 2060, fol. 150r: psalms 2, 3, 4, 5, 6, 7, 8, 9, 81, 117, 127, 128, and 129.

[50] See Josuah Sylvester, *All the small Workes of that famous Poet Iosuah Siluester* (1620; STC: 23575.5), passim. Sylvester died in 1618.

[51] See Sylvester, *The Parliament of Vertues Royal* (1614; STC: 23581), 297.

Atlas could be seen as Prince Henry, unable to sustain the task, and passing the weight of the world to Truth (perhaps representing Princess Elizabeth), "à cause de leurs pechez, qui est vng insupportable fardeau."[52] The use of this analogy, presumably within weeks of the wedding, could be seen as support for Sylvester's authorship.

A third potential author for *The Masque of Truth* is Abraham Aurelius. He was born in London, becoming pastor of the French Protestant church there, after his Italian-born father before him. A published poet, Aurelius contributed a Latin epithalamium on the 1613 wedding, *In Nuptias*, that mentions some of the same rivers as *The Masque of Truth*: the Thames, the Rhine, the Tagus and the Ganges. Indeed, Christof Ginzel remarks on Aurelius's "tuneful verse with its pastoral commonplaces and the recurrent image of a union of rivers swelling to become a second deluge."[53] That certainly accords with the many rivers in the masque and their coming together in unity at the end.

Another possibility for involvement—particularly among those who qualify as "Ministres Protestans"—is Pierre du Moulin. A Cambridge-trained Frenchman, he was in and out of England and, in fact, carried on a correspondence with King James about the unification of Protestants in Europe and beyond. Du Moulin is not known for poetry, but in 1612–13, he was directly in touch with the king and, on 1 March 1613, two weeks after the wedding, sent him a twenty-one point plan for the unification of the Protestant church.[54] In a 1615 sermon before King James—in French, but printed in translation in 1620—du Moulin said, "It is good that God be glorified in euery language, and that you should know the joy and fellow feeling that forraine Churches haue of the blessings that God hath accumulated vpon you, and of the vnion which is betweene vs all in the very same Doctrine and Faith."[55] That hoped-for outcome is central to *The Masque of Truth*.

One last person deserves mention here as a potential sponsor: Henri de la Tour d'Auvergne, Duc de Bouillon, the preeminent Protestant noble in

---

[52] See *The Masque of Truth*, after no. 5.12, below. In fact, the device of Atlas supporting the globe had been used for the Spanish betrothal ceremony in Paris in April 1612, an event that an anonymous correspondent related to Prince Henry (British Library, MS Harley 7015, fol. 268r). On the Paris ceremony, see André Stegman, "La Fête Parisienne à la Place Royale en Avril 1612," in *Les Fêtes de la Renaissance*, vol. 3, ed. J. Jacquot and E. Kongson (Paris, 1975), 373–92, at 385.

[53] Christof Ginzel, *Poetry, Politics, and Promises of Empire* (Göttingen, 2009), 183.

[54] See W. B. Patterson, "Pierre du Moulin's Quest for Protestant Unity, 1613–18," *Studies in Church History* 32 (1996), 235–50, https://doi.org/10.1017/S0424208400015436.

[55] *A Sermon preached before the King's Maiesty at Greenwich the 15. of Iune 1615* (Oxford, 1620; STC: 7338), 35.

France and former Maréchal under Henry IV. His principality of Sedan in northeast France remained the foremost Protestant stronghold there, well into the reign of Louis XIII. Frederick, Count Palatine, was the Duc de Bouillon's nephew (his wife's sister's son), and had been raised in his court, which is why he spoke French so fluently. It was the duke who first proposed the marriage of Frederick and Elizabeth in 1608,[56] with negotiations beginning in earnest in 1611,[57] and he arrived in England to finalize the match in April 1612. King James wrote to him on multiple occasions (in French) concerning religious affairs in France, addressing him each time as "Mon cousin," and they frequently discussed the union of Protestants.[58] It seems possible that the Duc de Bouillon may have helped sponsor an entertainment to celebrate the Palatine wedding—both its French connections and the newly strengthened ties among Protestants that it represented.

Dances

The Masque of Truth also lacks music for the many dances specified throughout the event. For a conjectural reconstruction here, what I propose is the use of selections from *Terpsichore* (1612), published in Wolfenbüttel by Michael Praetorius. At first glance, dance music published in Germany might seem incongruous for a French entertainment purportedly presented in England. But Praetorius proclaims on the title page that the repertoire is French rather than German: *Terpsichore, Musarum Aoniarum, Darinnen Allerley Französische Dânze und Lieder . . . von den Französischen Danzmeistern in Franckreich.* The repertoire is decidedly French, therefore, rather than German, with "French dances" from "French dancing masters in France." Dating from 1612, furthermore, just a year before *The Masque of Truth*, the contents appear to be French dances that were circulating internationally when the masque was conceived.[59] It is also striking that the Praetorius collection is entitled *Terpsichore* (the Muse of Dance), since she is among the first Muses named in the text, the Muses being important actors and singers throughout.

---

[56] Akkerman, *Elizabeth Stuart, Queen of Hearts*, 49.
[57] The duke's February 1611 memorandum listing Frederick's assets and advantages as a suitor survives as Kew, National Archive, SP 81/11, fol. 35. See also the *Report on the Manuscripts of the Marquess of Downshire*, vol. 3, 25.
[58] British Library, MS Stowe 174, fol. 232r.
[59] On French dances and the relationship between the French *ballet de cour* and the English masque, see Walls, *Music in the English Courtly Masque*, 224–55. On the Praetorius collection in general, see Peter Holman, "*Terpsichore* at 400: Michael Praetorius as a Collector of Dance Music," *Viola da Gamba Society Journal* 6 (2012), 34–51.

It is felicitous too that many of the dances Praetorius calls *Ballets* (from the French *ballet de cour*—the French counterpart to the masque) are in four voices, since that matches the number of parts in the Le Jeune psalm harmonizations. The specified instrumental accompaniment of the first song in *The Masque of Truth*, thus, makes the integration of vocal and instrumental music seamless for modern performers. It also happens that a book of festival images from Stuttgart,[60] sixty miles from Heidelberg, shows a four-part costumed violin band as part of a masque procession in 1609 (see Plate II.1), so although the English court violin band normally performed in five parts,[61] the tradition of the French *ballet de cour* and the Stuttgart masque image combine to make a basic four-part violin band seem ideal or, at least, defensible.

Last, some titles in the Praetorius collection seem to evoke characters or situations in *The Masque of Truth*. His *Bransle de la Torche*, for example,

Plate II.1 Violin band of four masquers costumed *à l'antique*. *Repraesentatio der Fürstlichen Auffzug vnd Ritterspil* (Stuttgart, [1611]), p. 125. Courtesy of the Huntington Library.

---

[60] Balthasar Küchler, *Repraesentatio der Fürstlichen Auffzug vnd Ritterspil* (Stuttgart, [1611]). On the festival depicted, see *Europa Triumphans: Court and Civic Festivals in Early Modern Europe*, ed. J. R. Mulryne, Helen Watanabe-O'Kelly, and Margaret Shewring, vol. 2 (Aldershot, 2004), 58–73. Stuttgart was, coincidentally, the birthplace and long-time home of Georg Rudolf Weckherlin.

[61] Peter Walls, *Music in the English Courtly Masque*, 30–33, and Peter Holman, *Four and Twenty Fiddlers: The Violin at the English Court, 1540–1690* (Oxford, 1993), 184–89.

172   THE MASQUE OF TRUTH

seems a felicitous choice for the "avant-ballet" of the torchbearers in the train of Queen Europa,[62] and his *Ballet des Amazones* for the "antibalet" of Queen Africa's dancing pages, which specifically included one dressed "à la façon ... des Amazonnes."[63] The *Terpsichore* pieces were not composed for this masque, obviously, but they were available when the masque was conceived and written, and might have struck the author(s) or the dance directors as the kind of dance music that would be appropriate at those moments in the entertainment.[64] In the absence of specific information, that seems enough of a connection to propose them as possibilities, at least, for those dances in the masque.

Resources

As David Norbrook points out,[65] Jocquet's attempt to portray *The Masque of Truth* as an event for the royal wedding included a close translation of the following passage, printed in England very shortly after the events of Tuesday:

> The night proceeding, much expectation was made of a stage play to be acted in the great Hall by the Kings Players, where many hundreds of people stood attending the same: but it hapned contrarie, for greater pleasures were preparing, which in this manner were performed, as vpon the night before a most famous maske came to court, by the Gentlemen and students of the lawe, from the Roles Office, by land, so some three hundred Gentlemen more, of the same estate and calling, by water, to equall them in statelines, came likewise vp the Thames by water, with a maske to White Hall....[66]

In trying to fabricate an authentic context for *The Masque of Truth*, Jocquet seems to have found it expedient to re-use some of this language.[67] His version

---

[62] See the discussion of this dance below, in the Notes on the Music.
[63] Abraham Ortelius, *Theatrum Orbis Terrarum* (1608; STC: 18855), places the Kingdom of the Amazons, not in South America, where we might expect, but in modern-day Kenya.
[64] Indeed, almost all of the dance directors for masques at the English court around this time were French, including Jerome Heron (Herne), Jacques Cordier (alias Bochan), and Nicolas Confais (Confesse). See Daye, "'Graced with Measures,'" 292; Walls, *Music in the English Courtly Masque*, 41–42.
[65] See Norbrook, "The Masque of Truth," 82.
[66] *The Mariage of Prince Fredericke, and the Kings daughter, the Lady ELIZABETH* (1613; STC: 11359), sig. B4r. An earlier edition with the same title (STC: 11358) described events only up to Monday night and did not include this description, which may be compared with the beginning of *The Masque of Truth* below.
[67] Similar language appears in a report of this masque from *Mercure François*, apparently based on Jocquet's account. See Appendix 1.1.

certainly makes it seem as if the "three hundred gentlemen" from the Inns of Court were there to present the French masque, rather than the *Masque of the Inner Temple and Gray's Inn*, actually scheduled for Tuesday. In reality, three hundred persons were not necessary for the performance of *The Masque of Truth*, although it still calls for more onstage personnel than any other masque for the 1613 royal wedding. It also demands that a majority of the onstage characters are women. Women did sometimes perform as masquers (noble participants) in English masques following the lead of Queen Anna,[68] and Foscarini's report of "a sumptuous ballet of sixteen maidens" supports that intention here, although Jocquet's inference about the Inns of Court, implies that the actors were all expected to be cross-dressing men.[69] We do not know for sure. At any rate, here is a list of characters named during the course of the event,[70] beginning with Truth herself, although she is described as a statue:

Dramatis Personae

Truth, or Aletheia – a statue[71]
9 Muses, dressed as nuns or vestals, with instruments
Atlas
Queen Europa, with
    5 princesses: France, Spain, Germany, Italy, Greece
    2 Admiral Ocean with his wife, Mediterranean Sea

---

[68] The title page of Ben Jonson's Masques of Blackness and Beauty (1608) states: "THE CHARACTERS of Two royall Masques. The one of BLACKNESSE, The other of BEAVTIE. *personated* By the most magnificent of Queenes ANNE Queene of great Britaine, &c. *With her honorable Ladyes*, 1605. and 1608. *at White hall.*" Also, Jonson's *Workes* (1616; STC:14752), 945–64, includes THE MASQVE OF QVEENES, *Celebrated* From the house of FAME: *By the* QVEENE *of great* BRITAINE, *with her Ladies.* AT WHITE-HALL, *Febr.* 2. 1609 [1610]. Jonson's autograph manuscripts of the first two survive as British Library, Royal MS 17 B XXXI, and of the latter as Royal MS 18 A XLV.

[69] See McManus, *Women on the Renaissance Stage*, 148. See also Clare McManus, "When Is a Woman Not a Woman? Or, Jacobean Fantasies of Female Performance (1606–1611)," *Modern Philology* 105 (2008), 437–74, https://doi.org/10.1086/591257. In the French *ballet de cour*, which might have been a relevant model in this case, women were commonly seen onstage all through this period. See Melinda J. Gough, *Dancing Queen: Marie de Médicis' Ballets at the Court of Henri IV* (Toronto, 2019), https://doi.org/10.1080/0268117X.2021.1991677; and Margaret McGowan, *"L'Art du Ballet de Cour en France, 1581–1643* (Paris, 1963). For a detailed examination of a single event with an eyewitness description, see Melinda J. Gough, "Marie de Medici's 1605 *ballet de la reine*: New Evidence and Analysis," *Early Theatre* 15 (2012), 109–44, https://www.jstor.org/stable/43499606.

[70] Not all, but most of the countries, regions, and rivers are named in *Theatrum Orbis Terrarum*, by Abraham Ortelius, with several editions during this period.

[71] In Campion's *The Lords' Masque*, eight statues are brought to life by Jove, and it is likely that the statue in this case was also portrayed by a real person, especially since she is described as persuading the Muses to sing (just before no. 5.11, below). Intriguingly, there was a prominent noblewoman in England, Aletheia Howard (née Talbot—niece of Grace Talbot cited above), though ironically, she married Thomas Howard, Earl of Arundel, from one of the premier Catholic families in England. That

>   5 vassal rivers: Loire, Boedo, Rhine, Tiber, Achelous[72]
>   15 torch-bearing pages to the princesses, to dance
>   5 princes, to dance with the princesses
> Queen Asia,[73] with
>   7 princesses: Syria, Palestine, Mesopotamia, Chaldea, Assyria, Arabia, Half-Persia
>   3 Admiral Bay of Bengal with 2 wives: Red Sea, Caspian Sea
>   7 vassal rivers: Tigris, Indus, Ganges, Euphrates, Jordan, Jadoc, Tata
>   21 torch-bearing pages to the princesses, to dance
>   7 princes, to dance with the princesses
> Queen Africa, with
>   4 princesses: Barbary, Numidia, Libya, Ethiopia
>   3 wife of Prester John and Admiral Oceans Atlantic and Ethiopian[74]
>   4 vassal rivers: Nile, Zambesi, Niger, Agaise [Zaire?][75]
>   11 pages, to dance
>   4 princes, to dance with the princesses
> Angel with a flaming sword
> many stars, angels, cherubim
> violins, lutes,
> "haute" (loud) music[76]

Even without the complicated stage machinery required to open and close the giant globe, such a lot of people would have made the show difficult and expensive to present. In all, 118 individuals are named, each with a distinctive costume, in addition to the "plusieurs Estoilles, Anges & Cherubins"

did not preclude their involvement in the royal wedding, however, and the two of them accompanied the bride and bridegroom to Heidelberg in April 1613. The name Aletheia was reportedly given to her by her godmother, Queen Elizabeth, "out of true consideration and judgement that the house of the Talbots was ever loyall to the Crown." See Thomas Fuller, *The Holy State* (Cambridge, 1642; Wing: F2443), 299. On the couple's involvement in court masques, see Peter Parolin, "The Venetian Theater of Aletheia Talbot, Countess of Arundel," in *Women Players in England, 1500–1660: Beyond the All-Male Stage*, ed. Pamela Allen Brown and Peter Parolin (Aldershot, 2005), 219–40, at 223–35.

[72] A river in Thessaly, the largest in Greece, flowing down from the Pindus mountains.
[73] The masque uses "Asia" mostly to refer to what might today be called "Western Asia" or the "Near East," though the Ganges River and the Bay of Bengal are in South Asia.
[74] Prester John was the mythical ruler of Abyssinia. Why his wife appears but not him is unclear, though it may be just that he was Christian and she was not. The only period reference to his wife, in fact, is the memorable "*Skinckimurra Brachia del Pegoe*, Wife of *Prester-John*," in Thomas Durfey's comedy *Sir Barnaby Whigg* (1681; Wing: D2778), sig. F1r.
[75] For this river, Wiggins and Richardson (*British Drama*, 6:253) propose the Nile tributary "Tagasi" (known today as the Black Nile, or Atbarah River) or its tributary, the "Tekezé." L'Agaise is actually a town in the Belgian province of Hainaut, though what its connection might be to a river in Africa is unknown. I have suggested the Zaire, the early modern name for the Congo River, because it is the second longest river in Africa, after the Nile, and before the Niger and Zambesi.
[76] See the notes to no. 5.14, the final piece in the masque, below.

surrounding Truth towards the end, and the ensembles of violins, lutes, and loud music that are mentioned as participating. It would have made a spectacular show, but the staggering number of necessary personnel and costumes would probably have rendered the entertainment, as it survives, unsuitable for performance at court during the week of the wedding.[77] As the Venetian ambassador reported afterward, "The expenses have been so great that, in spite of their being very rich, they will feel it for some time."[78] Complicated and expensive, *The Masque of Truth*'s prospects would have been further diminished because its praise of King James was "overshadowed by apocalyptic excitement."[79] Someone might have failed to explain to an enthusiastic but non-native author that Jacobean court masques should never let Truth get in the way of a good glory, as it were, and especially not in French. As David Norbrook points out. "James and Charles were both suspicious of religious enthusiasm and were anxious to establish reverence for the monarchy as a counterweight to the potentially disruptive forces of Puritan or Jesuit radicalism."[80] With Prince Henry gone, a proselytizing Protestant masque had no champion at court with sufficient influence to bring it to the stage.

Performance

Even if the requirements of personnel and materiel for *The Masque of Truth* were available, it cannot be performed complete today because the dialogue does not survive. On the other hand, it could be performed as a pantomime, perhaps accompanied by a reading of the description in French or English translation, along with performance of the dances and singing of the lyrics.[81] At its most basic (and inexpensive) level, the pantomime could be omitted, leaving the spoken description and the musical events as a programmatic concert for dancers, singers, and instrumentalists.[82]

---

[77] Although noble masquers had previously paid for their own costumes, and the Inns of Court were covering much of the cost of Chapman's and Beaumont's masques for the 1613 wedding (about £2,000 each), the court was still bearing the entire cost of the *Lords' Masque* (in addition to the other considerable expenses for the wedding) and, as Anne Daye argues, "The English coffers were not bottomless." See Daye, "'Graced with Measures,'" 297.

[78] Antonio Foscarini to the Doge and Senate, 1 March (new style) 1613, *CSP Venetian*, vol. 12, no. 775.

[79] See Norbrook, "The Reformation of the Masque," 100.

[80] See Norbrook, "The Masque of Truth," 86.

[81] A pantomime could still require an enormous expenditure for costumes.

[82] Even omitting the pantomime, a concert performance would presumably require costumes for the dancers. One further possibility in this day and age, of course, is an animated version.

In spite of the fact that it was never performed at the time and could not be fully realized in performance today, it is possible to reconstruct a musical version of *The Masque of Truth*, and valuable, I believe, to do so in order to understand what it may have been intended to sound like, notwithstanding the text's reinforcement of outdated cultural and imperialist stereotypes. That is something that modern producers might choose to address with their audiences. But its triumphant and optimistic Protestant outlook, its position as a French production among English masques celebrating the same event, indeed, its ironic situation as a Calvinist "entertainment" with singing and dancing, make it unique among period stage productions and worthy of reconstruction for that reason alone.

Calvinists considered singing to be frivolous, as a rule, though Calvin came to appreciate the metrical psalms, whose tunes he endorsed in his preface to the psalter:

> And in truth we know by experience that singing has vigor to move and inflame the hearts of men to invoke and more vehement and ardent zeal. Care must always be taken that song be neither light nor frivolous: but that it have weight and majesty.... But when anyone wishes to judge correctly of the [music of the psalms] here presented, we hope that it will be found holy and pure, seeing that it is simply directed to the edification of which we have spoken.[83]

Those psalm tunes might therefore have helped the singing, as given here, seem more acceptable to Calvinists, and apt for the edification and conversion of the peoples of the world.[84]

Dancing, however, was (and remains) anathema in Calvinism: "For there is alway such vnchaste behauiour in dauncing: that of it selfe ... it is nothing else but an enticement to whoredome."[85] Calvin says further: "It

---

[83] "Et à la verité, nous cognoissons par experience, que le chant a grande force & vigueur d'esmouuoir & enflamber le cœuer des hommes, pour inuoquer & louer Dieu d'vn zele plus vehement & ardent. Il y a tousiours à regarder, que le chant ne soit leger ni volage: mais qu'il ait poids & maiesté.... Or quand on voudra droitement iuger de la forme qui est ici exposee, nous esperons qu'on la trouuera saincte & pure, veu qu'elle est simplement reiglee à l'edification dont nous auons parlé." Written in 1543, this is from Calvin's preface to the psalter, here quoted from Goudimel, *Les pseavmes mis en rime françoise* (Geneva, 1565), sigs. A4v–5r, with the translation from Charles Garside Jr., "Calvin's Preface to the Psalter: A Re-Appraisal," *Musical Quarterly* 37 (1951), 566–77, at 568, https://www.jstor.org/stable/739611. On Calvin and music, see also H. P. Clive, "The Calvinist Attitude to Music, and Its Literary Aspects and Sources," *Bibliothèque d'Humanisme et Renaissance* 19 (1957), 80–102, https://www.jstor.org/stable/20673881.

[84] On Calvin and psalm singing, see also Beth Quitslund, *The Reformation in Rhyme: Sternhold, Hopkins and the English Metrical Psalter, 1547–1603* (Aldershot, 2008), 10.

[85] *Sermons of Master Iohn Caluin, vpon the booke of Iob.* Translated out of French by Arthur Golding (1574; STC: 4445), Sermon on Job 21, p. 409.

is well known that dances can only be preambles to debauchery, that they serve to open the door in particular to Satan, and to shout that he comes, and that he enters boldly."[86] Thus, although *de rigueur* for a masque in England,[87] the dancing must have been galling for the sponsors of *The Masque of Truth*, all the more so because it involved musical instruments, which Calvin also disdained.[88] Whatever the opinion on this matter of the bridegroom, "the most militantly Calvinist of the German princes,"[89] this was clearly not the attitude of the English bride: Princess Elizabeth reportedly "combined Protestant zeal with a love of masques and dancing,"[90] so this entertainment would have suited her perfectly. Unfortunately, she never got to enjoy it.

Nevertheless, a few months after the Palatine wedding, Jocquet wanted his readers to believe that this grand event had been presented as described. Whether the intended musical settings and dance insertions were already lost at that point is unknown, but in order to hear echoes of the spectacle from that time, and even to make it performable today, after a fashion, this reconstruction suggests plausible music based on the available evidence. Those choices arise from my contention that *The Masque of Truth* was intended to be presented in French, and that is a fundamental conjecture, though I believe the evidence to support it is substantial, and validates a reconstruction from that point of view.

What follows is a Table of Musical Contents, then a transcription of *The Masque of Truth* as preserved in Jocquet's 1613 print, with my parallel English translation, and the music inserted as stipulated. Notes on the individual musical items follow the text, along with an appendix consisting of two third-party reports.

---

[86] "Or on sait bien que les danses ne peuuent estre sinon des preambules à paillardise, qu'elles sont pout ouvrir la porte notamment à Satan, et pour crier qu'il vienne, et qu'il entre hardiment." Jean Calvin, *Sermon de M. Jean Caluin sur le V. livre de Moyse nommé Deuteronome* (Geneva, 1567), Sermon XXXVIII, p. 216. See also H. P. Clive, "The Calvinists and the Question of Dancing in the 16th Century," *Bibliothèque d'Humanisme et Renaissance* 23 (1961), 296–323, https://www.jstor.org/stable/20674294.

[87] On the dances for the Palatine wedding masques, see Anne Daye, "'Graced with Measures.'"

[88] See Clive, "The Calvinist Attitude to Music," 90–92.

[89] This characterization is from Peter Holbrook, "Jacobean Masques and the Jacobean Peace," in *The Politics of the Stuart Court Masque*, ed. David Bevington and Peter Holbrook (Cambridge, 1998), 67–87, at 69. Frederick was the leader of the German Evangelical Union, founded by his father in 1608, and with which King James signed a treaty in 1612. See Patterson, "Pierre du Moulin's Quest for Protestant Unity, 1613–18," 250.

[90] Norbrook, "The Masque of Truth," 89. See also Deanne Williams, *Shakespeare and the Performance of Girlhood* (New York, 2014), chapter 5, "A Dancing Princess," 127–48, https://link.springer.com/content/pdf/10.1057/9781137024763_6.pdf.

Table of Musical Contents

Lyrics & Dances	Music Source	Final & Signature
5.1. *Le Monde Te vient*: all nine Muses sing & play	Psalm 58	G –
5.2. *Sortez Europe*: Urania, Clio, & Terpsichore sing	Psalm 112	D –
5.3. European torch-bearing pages dance/sing? "avant-ballet"	*Bransle de la Torche* (MP 15)*	D –
5.4. European Princes & Princesses dance "grand ballet"	*Ballet* (MP 268)	G –, G♭
5.5a. *Sortez Reyne*: Calliope, Melpomene, & Erato sing	Psalm 28	G♭
5.5b.	*Cantique d'Anne*	G –
5.6. Asian torch-bearing pages dance "advant-ballet"	*Ballet des feus* (MP 279)	C –
5.7. Asian Princes & Princesses dance "grand ballet"	*Ballet* (MP 269)	G –, G♭
5.8. *Sortez Affrique*: last 3 muses sing	Psalm 80	G♭
5.9. African torch-bearing pages dance "Antibalet"	*Ballet des Amazones* (MP 270)	G♭
5.10. African Princes & Princesses dance "grand Balet"	*Ballet* (MP 259)	D –
5.11. *Quittez vos*: Muses sing 3 x 3, then all together	Psalm 112	D –
5.12. Queens et al. adore Aletheia "comme en dançant"	*Ballet des Anglois* (MP 271)	G♭
5.13. *Que ceux à qui*: Stars et al. sing with instruments	Psalm 28	G♭
5.14. All led into paradise "au son de haute Musique"	*Ballet des Princesses* (MP 277)	C –

* MP = Michael Praetorius, *Terpsichore* (1612). There appear to be three parallel groupings of close-following musical items in the midst of the masque, consisting of avant-ballet, grand ballet, and air: Nos. 5.3–5, 5.6–8, and 5.9–11.

The Masque of Truth

Le mardy d'apres on avoit dressé des eschaffaux, pour faire jouer les Comediens du Roy, de sorte que plusieurs milliers de peuples s'estoyent ia assemblés. Mais il arriva le contraire. Car le Roy les remit à vne aultre fois, & donna ceste nuit entrée à environ trois cents gentilshommes, estudians au Droit & d'autre honnorable Profession, qui arriverent par la Thamise, vestus tous differemment, comme sont toutes les Nations du Monde, & furent introduits en la Sale, ou on avoit joué le ballet precedant; y ayant fact preparer pour leur scene, vne grande statue ressemblant à vne Vierge, à demy couchée; tenant en sa main gauche, vng Globe terrestre aussy grand quasi qu'une Montagne; & sur la droite elle appuyoit sa teste, environnée de rayons, & regardoit dedans vne grande Bible, posée sur vng pulpitre aupres d'elle. De l'autre costé estoient les Armes d'Angleterre, & celles de l'Electeur Palatin, ou il a vng Monde.

L'Argument de leur Ballet estoit: Que la [H1v] Religion avoit joint le Monde avec l'Angleterre. Car encor que les Poëtes disent, *divisus ab orbe Britannus*:[92] toutesfois le mariage, faict au Ciel, & consommé en Terre, de la fille vnique

On the Tuesday following [the wedding], scaffolds had been erected for the King's Players, so several thousand people already gathered there. But the opposite happened. For the King rescheduled them for another time, & gave entry this night to about three hundred gentlemen, students of Law & other honorable Professions, who arrived by the Thames, dressed completely differently, as are all Nations of the World, & were introduced in the Hall, where the preceding dance had been performed; and there was prepared for their scene, a large statue resembling a Virgin, half reclining; holding in her left hand a terrestrial Globe almost as big as a Mountain; & on the right hand she leaned her head, surrounded by rays, & was intently reading a large Bible, placed on a lectern next to her. On the other side were the Arms of England, and those of the Elector Palatine, where there is an Orb.[91]

The Argument of their *Ballet* was: That Religion had united the World with England. Because still the Poets say, *Britain is divided from the world*: nevertheless, the marriage, made in Heaven & consummated on Earth, of the only

---

[91] See the coats of arms of Frederick and Elizabeth in the frontispiece, at the upper left.
[92] Originally from Vergil's Eclogue 1.66 as "divisos ab orbe Britannos" (see also the Menestrier account in Appendix 1 2), this singular phrase is borrowed directly from Chapman's *Memorable*

de ce Sage ROY de la grand Bretagne, avec le Serenissime Prince FRIDERIC V. Electeur Palatin (qui porte en ses Armes, & en son office Electoral, le Monde d'or: qui est maintenant joint aux Armes d'Angleterre) a donné occasion de contredire le Poëte, & de croire, qu'un jour, s'il plaist à Dieu, le Monde (quittant ses erreurs) se viendra rendre à la cognoissance de la Verité,[93] qui est purement preschée en Angleterre & au Palatinat. Ce qui les a meu de faire venir Atlas, pour se descharger du Globe Terrestre entre les mains d'Alithie, c'est à dire la Verité, qui a choisy sa demeure en ceste Isle. Duquel Globe sortent les trois parties du Monde, asçavoir l'Europe, l'Asie, & l'Afrique, estans sommées par les Trompettes de la Verité, qui sont les Muses diuines, & par son Lieutenant Atlas, de venir apprendre d'Alithie, & de son Protecteur, le ROY de ceste Isle heureuse,[94] le droit chemin de Salut, par lequel chacun doit aller consacrer son Ame à la gloire du Grand DIEV.

daughter of this Wise King of Great Britain, with the Most Serene Prince Frideric V, Elector Palatine (who bears in his Arms, & in his Electoral office, the golden Orb: which is now joined to the Arms of England) has given the opportunity to contradict the Poet, and to believe that one day, if it pleases God, the World (renouncing its errors) will come to acknowledge Truth, which is righteously preached in England & the Palatinate. This moved them to bring Atlas to relinquish the Terrestrial Globe into the hands of Aletheia, that is to say Truth, who has chosen to make her home in this Isle. From this Globe proceed the three parts of the world, namely Europe, Asia, & Africa, being summoned by the Trumpets of Truth, who are the divine Muses, & by her Lieutenant Atlas, to come and learn from Aletheia, & her Protector, the King of this happy Isle, the true path of Salvation, which each must follow to consecrate his Soul to the glory of the Great God.

Masque, performed on 15 February 1613: "That this Ile is (for the excellency of it) diuided from the world (*diuisus ab orbe Britannus*) and that though the whole World besides moues; yet this Ile stands fixt on her owne feete, and defies the Worlds mutability, which this rare accident of the arriuall of Riches, in one of his furthest-off-scituate dominions, most demonstratiuely proues." See Chapman, *The Memorable Masque*, sig. B3r. The singular Latin phrase had a further precedent in Thomas Watson, *Amintae Gavdia* (1592; STC: 25117), Epistola Quinta, sig. D1v.

[93] Mallet has "la verité Chrestienne."
[94] The phrase about the Protector and King is not in Mallet.

THE MASQUE OF TRUTH   181

Premierement parurent les Neuf Muses, habillées en Religieuses ou Vestales, jouans de leurs instrumens: & chanterent toutes ensemble melodieusement ces vers devant le Roy: [H2r]	First appeared the Nine Muses, dressed as Nuns or Vestals, playing their instruments: & all sang together melodiously these lines before the King:

Example 5.1 *Le Monde Te vient faire hommage*, set to Psalm 58 from *Les Cent Cinquante Pseaumes de David*, by Claude le Jeune (Paris, 1601).

Le Monde Te vient faire hommage,
Grand Roy, de sa fertilité:
Puis qu'icy loge la Beauté,
   Et l'Amour, l'Honneur de nostre aage.
Il vient cercher la Verité
Chez Toy, ou son temple est planté.

The World comes to pay you,
Great King, the homage of its fertility:
For Beauty lodges here,
   And Love, the Honor of our age.
The World comes to seek Truth
In your realm, where her temple stands.

Puis vient ATLAS, qui se plaignant de lassitude, dit; qu'ayant apprins d'Archimede, que si on luy donnoit vn point ferme, qu'il souleuroit ceste Machine,[95] qui luy avoit tant donné de peine: et qu'estant las de la porter, aussy bien que Hercules, qui l'avoit soulagé quelque temps; il estoit venu en ceste Isle, laquelle avoit ceste qualité requise, sinon elle mesme, au moins le doigt d'une Vierge incontaminée, qu'on appelloit ALITHIE, qui faisoit sa demeure en Angleterre.[96]

Sur lequel il l'avoit posé, & pour recognoissance en venoit remercier son Protecteur le ROY de ceste Isle; luy promettant, que toutes les Nations de la Terre viendroient faire hommage à la VERITE, par laquelle le Monde subsiste; ainsy que les Pucelles avoient n'agueres chanté; lesquelles luy servoyent de guide en ce Royaume, desirans aussy de suivre leur Maistresse ALITHIE; ayant donné conge au fol Amour, pour se choisir ce docte ROY leur Moecenas.

Then comes Atlas, who complaining of weariness, says; that having learned from Archimedes, that if someone gave him a fixed point, he could lift this celestial Burden which had given him so much trouble; and that being weary of carrying it, although Hercules had relieved him for a spell; he had come to this Isle, which had this requisite quality, if not itself, at least in the finger of a spotless Virgin, called Aletheia, who has made her home in England.

On this finger he had placed the globe, & for gratitude came to thank her Protector, the King of this Isle; promising him, that all the Nations of the Earth would come to pay homage to Truth, by which the World subsists; just as the Maidens had recently sung; these served him as guide in this Kingdom, also wishing to follow their Mistress Aletheia; having dismissed foolish Cupid, in order to choose this learned King as their Maecenas.

---

[95] This derives from the saying, attributed to Archimedes by Pappus of Alexandria, that if he had a fixed point (a fulcrum) and a big enough lever, he could move the earth. This was cited in both divine and scientific writings of the time, of which an English example is Robert Norton's *A Mathematicall Apendix* (1604; STC: 18675): "*Archimedes* affirmed that he could moue the whole Globe of the Earth out of her place, if he had any firme place in the Ayre, that could support his said Engine." A contemporary French example is found in *Les Diversitez de Messire Jean Pierre Camus*, vol. 9, book 31 (Paris, 1613–14), chapter 41, p. 436: "Archimede . . . ne demandoit qu'vn poinct ferme hors de la terre, pour enleuer hors de son centre toute la machine de la terre & de l'eau." The specific use of "poinct ferme" and "machine" may support a French origin for the passage in the masque, and thus, a French origin for the masque itself, as argued above.

[96] This last phrase, about making her home in England, is not in Mallet.

THE MASQUE OF TRUTH   183

AYANT dit ces paroles, il s'en retourna pres du Globe, ayant pris avec luy les trois Muses, Vranie, Clio, & Terpsichore, qui chanterent ces paroles:	Having thus spoken, he came back near the Globe, taking with him the three Muses, Urania, Clio, & Terpsichore, who sang these words:

Example 5.2 *Sortez EVROPE la premiere*, set to Psalm 112 from *Les Cent Cinquante Pseaumes de David*, by Claude le Jeune (Paris, 1601).

Sortez Evrope la premiere,	Come forth Europa first,
Puis que vostre ame a ia receu	Since your soul has already received
Quelques rayons de la lumiere	A few rays of light
Que le Sainct Esprit a conceu.	That the Holy Spirit has conceived.
Ammenez icy vos Princesses	Bring here your Princesses
Pour en recevoir les adresses.	To receive the [Holy Spirit's] attentions.

[H2v] AYANT finy, vne partie du Globe, ou estoit despeinte la Carte de l'EVROPE s'ouvrit. D'ou l'on vit sortir vne Reyne, habillée comme les peintres ont depeint l'EVROPE, ayant avec elle cinq Princesses, ses Filles: qui se nommoyent, France; Espagne, Allemagne, Italie, & Grece; avec vng Admiral & sa femme (nommez l'Occean & la Mer Mediterranée) avec leurs vassaux; le Loire, le Boete,[97] le Rhin, le Tibre, & Achelous; portant chacun, dans vne Corne d'Abondance, des fruits, qui croissent sur leurs rivages; desquels ilz vont faire offrande à l'Espouse & l'Espoux: ayant premierement faict reverence à ceste Vierge, qui soustient le Monde. Ces Princesses avoyent chacune trois pages: comme la Françoise, vng Basque, vng bas Breton, & vng Lorrain: l'Espagnol, vng Portugois, vng Arragonois, & vn Catelan; l'Allemagne, vn Hongrois, vng Boheme, & vng Danois: l'Italie, vng Napolitain, vng Venitien, & vng Bargamasch: la Grece, vng Turc, vng Albanois, & vng Bulgarois: chacun habillé à la façon de son pays, & portans en leur main chacun vn flambeau. L'offrande estant faite avec vng air, que l'on chanta,[98] les Porte-flambeaux dancerent l'avant-ballet.

Having finished, the part of the Globe where the Map of Europe was painted, opened. From whence we saw a Queen come forth, attired as painters have depicted Europa, having with her five Princesses, her Daughters: who were called, France; Spain, Germany, Italy, & Greece; with an Admiral & his wife (named the Ocean & the Mediterranean Sea) with their vassals; the Loire, the Boedo, the Rhine, the Tiber, & Achelous; each carrying a Cornucopia of fruits that grow on their shores; of which they go to make an offering to the Bride & Groom: having first made reverence to this Virgin who is holding the Globe. These Princesses each had three pages: like the French: a Basque, a Lower Breton, & a Lorraine; the Spaniard: a Portuguese, an Aragonese, & a Catalan; Germany: a Hungarian, a Bohemian, & a Dane; Italy, a Neapolitan, a Venetian, & a Bergamasque; Greece: a Turk, an Albanian, & a Bulgarian: each dressed in their traditional national garb, & each carrying a torch. The offering being made with an ayre, which was sung, the Torchbearers danced the avant-ballet.

---

[97] Menestrier changes "Boete" to "Guadalquivir." See *Des Ballets Anciens et Modernes*, 116, and Appendix 1.2.

[98] It is not clear what is happening here. The text says that an "air" was sung but no lyric is given. It seems possible that something was sung to the tune of the avant-ballet, since some songs in the other 1613 wedding masques were also dances. For two possibilities (5.3a and 5.3b), I have set selected verses from Clément Marot's *Rendez à Dieu louange & gloire* (Psalm 118), and Théodore de Bèze's *Vous tous qui la terre habitez* (Psalm 100) to the top line (see the notes to no. 5.3a and 5.3b, below).

THE MASQUE OF TRUTH   185

Example 5.3a *Bransle de la Torche* XV [15] from *Terpsichore,... Allerley Französische Dänze,* by Michael Praetorius (Wolfenbüttel, 1612), conjecturally setting Psalm 118 by Clément Marot (1545).

[1. Rendez à Dieu louange & gloire:
Car il est benin & clement:
Qui plus est, sa bonté notoire
Dure perpetuellement.

2. Qu'Israel ores se recorde
De chanter solemnellement,
Que sa grande misericorde
Dure perpetuellement.

26. Benit soit qui au Nom tresdigne
Du Seigneur est venu ici:
O vous de la maison Diuine,
Nous vous benissons tous aussi.

27. Dieu est puissant, doux et propice,
Et nous donra lumiere à gré:
Liez le bœuf du sacrifice
Aux cornes de l'autel sacré.]

1. To God giue thanks, all praises render,
Because so gracious good is he,
For his compassion, mercy tender,
Endureth sure eternally.

2. Let Israel make declaration,
And singing publish solemnly.
That his so great commiseration,
Most sure endures perpetually.

26. Who in Gods Name doth come is blessed,
We bid him welcome heartily:
Out of Gods house to you addressed,
From him we bles you willingly.

27. God is the Lord, his mercy minding,
He hath giuen vs light plenteously:
Bring offrings, them with cords fast binding,
To th'Altars hornes abundantly.

Example 5.3b *Bransle de la Torche* XV [15] from *Terpsichore,... Allerley Französische Dänze*, by Michael Praetorius (Wolfenbüttel, 1612), conjecturally setting Psalm 100 by Théodore de Bèze (1562).

Example 5.3b Continued

[1. Vous tous qui la terre habitez,
Chantez tout hait à Dieu, chantez,
Seruez à Dieu ioyeusement,
Venez deuant luy gayement.

2. Sachez qu'il est le Souuerain,
Qui sans nous, nous fit de sa main,
Nous, di-ie, son vray peuple acquis,
Et le toupeau de son pasquis.

All people dwelling on the earth,
Sing to the Lord with ioy and mirth:
The Lord adore with thankfull voyce,
Approach his presence, sing, reioyce.

2. Know ye the Lord is God, euen he
It is that made vs hath, not we,
We are his people, he doth keep
Vs safe, as his own pasture sheep.

3. *Entrez és portes d'iceluy,*
Louez-le, & celebrez chez luy,
Par tout son honneur auancez,
Et son tressainct Nom benissez.

3. *Then enter in his gates with praise,*
And in his courts giue thanks alwayes:
Vnto the Lord let vs confes,
His sacred Name with praises bles.

4. *Car il est Dieu plein de bonté,*
Et dure sa benignité
A iamais, voire du Tres-haut
La verité iamais ne faut.]

4. *For God is good, his clemency,*
His mercy and benignity,
His truth and his fidelity,
Endure to all eternity.

Pvis Atlas appella les Princes. Qui sortirent richement vestus à la façon de leurs Royaumes, & dancerent le grand ballet avec leurs Princesses.

Then Atlas called the Princes. These came forth richly dressed in the manner of their Kingdoms, and danced the grand ballet with their Princesses.

Example 5.4 *Ballet* CCLXVIII [268] from *Terpsichore,... Allerley Französische Dänze,* by Michael Praetorius (Wolfenbüttel, 1612).

Example 5.4 Continued

190　THE MASQUE OF TRUTH

Et s'estans retirez à part, Atlas prist trois aultres Muses, Calliope, Melpomene, & Erato, & les fist chanter au pres du Globe ces vers: [H3r]	And stepping aside, Atlas took three other Muses, Calliope, Melpomene, & Erato & made them sing these verses near the Globe:

Example 5.5a *Sortez Reyne, de qui les yeux*, set to Psalm 28 from *Les Cent Cinquante Pseaumes de David*, by Claude le Jeune (Paris, 1601).

THE MASQUE OF TRUTH   191

Example 5.5b *Sortez Reyne, de qui les yeux*, alternative setting to *Cantique d'Anne* from *Les Saincts Cantiques* (Geneva, 1595), in a reconstructed harmonization.

Sortez, Reyne, de qui les yeux
Ont veu plus cler que les Estoilles;
Mais maintenant plus tenebreux,
Que ne sont Les nuits eternelles.
Venez cercher vostre Clarté
Dans le puy de la Verite.

Come forth, Queen, whose eyes
Have seen more clearly than the Stars;
But now more shadowy
Than are the eternal nights.
Come seek your clarity
In the well of Truth.

Incontinent l'on vit sortir la Reyne Asie,[99] sans faire la reverence à Alithie, non plus que les Princesses ses filles, qui la suivoyent, nommées Syrie, Palestine, Mesopotamie, Caldée & Assyrie: vestues toutes comme l'on a accoustumé en leurs regions. Seulement les deux derniers differoyent. Car l'une estoit habillée richement d'ung costé, & de l'autre pauvrement, et se nommoit Arabie: l'autre estoit à demy Mede,[100] à demy Perse. Leur Admiral marchoit apres: quel on appelloit le Golfe de Bengale, avec ses deux femmes, la Mer Rouge & la Mer Caspie, suyvies de leurs vassaux; le Tigre, l'Inde, le Gange, l'Euphrate, le Iourdain, le Iadoc, & le Tanais; qui apporterent aussy des offrandes des fruits de leurs contrées. Les pages de ces Princesses suivirent; chacune en ayant trois, habillez à la Moscovite, à la Tartare, à l'Hotomane, à l'Indienne, a la Iuifue, à la Samaritaine, à l'Hircinie, à la Natolie, à l'Idumee, à l'Egitiaque, à la Scythie, à la Parthe, à l'Hircanie, à la Bythinie, à la Phrigienne, Dorique, Ionique & Corinthe, à la Licaonie, Pamphile & Cilicie. Car chacun avoit son habit particulier, & portoit vne torche, avec laquelle ils dancerent leur advant-ballet, (apres que les fleuves eurent fait l'offrande)

Straightway we saw Queen Asia come forth, without reverence to Aletheia, nor the Princesses her daughters, who followed her, called Syria, Palestine, Mesopotamia, Chaldea & Assyria: all dressed as accustomed in their regions. Only the last two differed. For one was richly dressed on one side, and poorly on the other side, and was called Arabia: the other was half-Mede, half-Persian. Their Admiral walked behind them: he was called the Bay of Bengal, with his two wives, the Red Sea & the Caspian Sea, followed by their vassals; the Tigris, Indus, Ganges, Euphrates, Jordan, Jadoc, & Tana; who also brought offerings of the fruits of their countries. The pages of these Princesses followed; each one having three, dressed as Muscovite, Tartar, Ottoman, Indian, Jewish, Samaritan, Hircinian, Anatolian, Idumean, Egyptian, Scythian, Parthian, Hyrcanian, Bythinian, Phrygian, Dorian, Ionian & Corinthian, Lycaonian, Pamphylian & Cicilian. For each one had their own particular dress, and carried a torch, with which they danced their avant-ballet, (after the rivers had made their offering);

---

[99] See Color Plates 5 and 7.
[100] The Medes and Persians were both groups of Indo-European Iranian speakers to the southwest of the Caspian Sea, in what is now Iran.

Example 5.6 *Ballet des feus* CCLXXIX [279] from *Terpsichore,...Allerley Französische Dänze*, by Michael Praetorius (Wolfenbüttel, 1612).

lequel fuit suivy du grand ballet [H3v] des Princes avec les Princesses, selon la Musique & la façon de dancer de leurs pays. Ce qui donna du plaisir extreme aux spectateurs.

this was followed by the grand ballet of the Princes with the Princesses, according to the Music and the dancing style of their countries. Which gave the spectators extreme pleasure.

Example 5.7 *Ballet du Roy* CCLXIX [269] from *Terpsichore,...Allerley Französische Dänze*, by Michael Praetorius (Wolfenbüttel, 1612).

Example 5.7 Continued

Et s'estans retirez, Atlas prit les trois dernieres Muses, & s'en alla querir l'autre Royne, la faisant appeller avec cest air:

And having withdrawn, Atlas took the last three Muses, & went to fetch the other Queen, summoning her with this ayre:

Example 5.8 *Sortez AFFRIQVE monstrueuse*, set to Psalm 80 from *Les Cent Cinquante Pseaumes de David*, by Claude le Jeune (Paris, 1601).

*Sortez, AFFRIQVE monstrueuse
En erreurs plus qu'er animaux,
Et cerchez en ceste Isle heureuse
Le repos à tous vos travaux.
C'est icy que la VERITE[101]
Veut que son temple soit planté.*

Soudain l'on vit sortir l'AFFRIQVE, habillée d'aultre sorte que les precedentes Reynes,[102] & suivie de 4. Princesses ses filles, asçavoir Barbarie, Numidie, Libye, Ethiopie, qui toutes oublierent à faire la reverence à ALITHIE: reservé la derniere, femme du Prestre Ian: avec leur Admiral, l'Occean Atlantique & Etiopique freres encor à marier; menans leur vassaux, qui sont le Nil, le Zambere, le Niger, & l'Agaise, qui sont aussy chargez de leur Abondance, à l'imitation de ceux qui les devancent: suivis des pages, qui marchent avec des flambeaux, & habillez à la Bresilienne, à la Madagascar, à la Guinée, à la Tunes, à la Fez, à la façon d'Algier, des Amazonnes, à la Sicilienne, à la Sardinienne, à la Moravie, & à la Mozambique. Lesquels dancerent aussy leur Antibalet.

*Come forth, Africa, prodigious
In errors more than in animals,
And seek in this happy Isle
The repose for all your labors.
It is here that Truth
Wants her temple to be established.*

Suddenly, Africa was seen to come forth, dressed differently from the previous Queens, & followed by 4 Princesses, her daughters, namely Barbary, Numidia, Libya, Ethiopia, all of whom forgot to pay reverence to Aletheia: last of all, the wife of Prester John: with their Admiral, the Atlantic & Ethiopian Ocean, brothers not yet married; leading their vassals, who are the Nile, the Zambesi, the Niger, & the Zaire[?], who are also responsible for their Abundance, in imitation of those who precede them: the pages followed, walking with torches, & dressed in Brazilian, Madagascan, Guinean, Tunisian, Fezian, Algierian, Amazonian, Sicilian, Sardinian, Moravian, & Mozambican style. These also danced their Antibalet.

---

[101] For "VERITÉ," Mallet has "Chrestienté."
[102] See Color Plates 6 and 8.

Example 5.9 *Ballet des Amazones* CCLXX [270] from *Terpsichore, ... Allerley Französische Dänze*, by Michael Praetorius (Wolfenbüttel, 1612).

Qui furent suyvis de leurs Maistres apres l'advertissement d'ATLAS.

These were followed by their Masters after Atlas's foretelling.

THE MASQUE OF TRUTH 199

Example 5.10 Ba!let CCLIX [259] from *Terpsichore,...Allerley Französische Dänze*, by Michael Praetorius (Wolfenbüttel, 1612).

Example 5.10 Continued

Et ayant dancé le grand Balet, les Mvses [H4r] chanterent cest air, trois a trois, à la persuasion d'Alithie se tournans vers les trois Reynes:

And having danced the grand Ballet, the Muses sang this ayre, in groups of three, at the persuasion of Aletheia, while turning to the three Queens:

Example 5.11 *Quittez vos anciennes querelles*, set to Psalm 112 from *Les Cent Cinquante Pseaumes de David*, by Claude le Jeune (Paris, 1601).

Example 5.11 Continued

Disant:	Saying:
Quittez vos anciennes querelles,	Set aside your ancient quarrels,
Vous Princes & Princesses belles	You beautiful Princes & Princesses
Pour mieux plaire à la Verité.	To better please Truth.
Accordez vous tous trois ensemble,	All three of you agree together,
Reynes, soubz qui le Monde tremble,	Queens, under whom the world trembles,
Et laissez l'opiniastreté.	And cease obstinacy.
II.	II.
Imitez ce Roy debonnaire[103]	Imitate this kindly King
Qui a tiré en Angleterre	Who drew forth in England
Le pure service divin.	Pure divine service.
Bruslez dans le feu de son zele	Burn, in the fire of his zeal,
Ceste religion nouvelle	This new religion
De Mahomet & de Iupin.	Of Mahomet & Jupiter.
III.	III.
Vous Empires & Republiques,	You Empires & Republics,
Amenez tous vos heretiques	Bring all your heretics
Aux pieds de ceste Verite.	To the feet of this Truth.
Affin qu'ayant sa cognoissance	So that recognizing her
Ilz soynt touché de Repentance	They be touched with Repentance
Et recherchent la Pureté.	And seek for Purity.
CHOR.	CHOR.
Vous Affrique, Europe, & Asie,	You Africa, Europe, & Asia,
Delaissez vostre Idolatrie,[104]	Let go of your idolatry
[H4v] Pour recognoistre l'Eternel.	In order to recognize the Lord.
Il nous concede ceste grace[105]	He grants us this grace
Qu'il a choysy en ceste place	That he chose in this place
Son sacré temple & son Autel.	His sacred temple & his Altar.
Ce qu'estant achevé, toutes ces Roynes, Princesses, Mers, Fleuves, & Nations estranges, se tournans devers ALITHIE, l'adorerent comme en dançant.	This having been completed, all these Queens, Princesses, Seas, Rivers, & foreign Nations, turning towards Aletheia, worshiped her as if dancing.

---

[103] For these three lines, Mallet has "Suyuez de ce Roy la sagesse / Qui attire par sa prouesse / Les Chrestiens d'vn zele diuin."

[104] For this line, Mallet has "Delaissez donc toute heresie."

[105] For these last three lines, Mallet has "C'est luy qui nous faict ceste grace / C'est luy qui les tenebres chasse / Et son renom est immortel."

THE MASQUE OF TRUTH 203

Example 5.12 *Ballet des Anglois* CCLXXI [271] from *Terpsichore,... Allerley Französische Dänze*, by Michael Praetorius (Wolfenbüttel, 1612).

Example 5.12 Continued

Soudain ATLAS les remercie, d'avoir quitté le monde, qui le chargoit si fort à cause de leurs pechez, qui est vng insupportable fardeau. Et lors soudain le MONDE s'ouvrant en deux, & disparoissant, l'on vit comme vn PARADIS: au devant du quel estoit vng Ange avec vne Espée

Suddenly, Atlas thanks them for having forsaken the world, which burdened him so much because of their sins, which is an unbearable burden. And then suddenly the Globe, splitting in two & disappearing, revealed a kind of Paradise: in front of which was an Angel

THE MASQUE OF TRUTH   205

flambante[106] & vne teste de mort à ses pieds: mais la Verité assise au milieu de plusieurs Estoilles, Anges & Cherubins. Qui avec l'armonie de Violes,[107] de Luths, & de Voix, inviterent ces Roynes & leur suite d'entrer en leur PARADIS, avec ces paroles:

with a flaming Sword, & a skull at his feet: but Truth sat in the midst of many Stars, Angels & Cherubim. These, with the harmony of Violins, Lutes, & Voices, invited these Queens & their retinue to enter their Paradise, with these words:

Example 5.13 *Que ceux, à qui la Repentance*, set to Psalm 28 from *Les Cent Cinquante Pseaumes de David*, by Claude le Jeune (Paris, 1601).

[106] Mallet has "flamboyante" for "flambante." The imagery comes from Genesis 3:24, glossed in Robert Wolcomb's *A Glasse for the Godly* (1612; STC 25941). 171, as follows: "the first *Adam* (for sin) was shut out of earthly *Paradise*, & the *Cherubims*, or Angels kept the gate thereof with a flaming sword." John Salkeld cites St. Ambrose's gloss on Psalm 118, interpreting "the fore-sayd flaming sword to be the fire of Purgatory, by which the soules that depart out of the world not altogether purified, are cleansed before their entrance into Heauen." See *A Treatise of Paradise* (1617; STC 21622), 232. Such purification seems to be the purpose of the flaming sword here.

[107] I have translated "Violes" as "Violins" because they are much more likely in this context and because the terms were somewhat flexible at the time. See Holman, *Four and Twenty Fiddlers*, 18–19, 168–69.

Example 5.13 Continued

Que ceux, à qui la Repentance
Et la Foy ont touché le coeur,
Et luy ont donné cognoissance,
Que Iesvs Christ est leur Sauveur:
Qu'ilz ne redoutent point la mort,
Pour entrer en cest heureux port.

That those, whose hearts Repentance
And Faith have touched,
And given them knowledge,
That Jesus Christ is their Savior:
Let them not fear death at all,
In entering into this happy refuge.

Ce qu'ayant entendu ces Nations, apres avoir derechef adoré la Verité; Atlas & les Neuf Muses les conduirent en ce Paradis au son de la haute Musique: d'ou desplaça ceste Espée de feu & ceste mort. Puis le Paradis se fermant, chacun se retira.

These Nations having heard this, having worshipped Truth again; Atlas & the Nine Muses led them into this Paradise to the sound of loud Music: from where were displaced this Sword of fire & this skull. Then, the Paradise closing, everyone withdrew.

Example 5.14 *Ballet des Princesses* CCLXXVII [277] from *Terpsichore,... Allerley Französische Dänze*, by Michael Praetorius (Wolfenbüttel, 1612).

Example 5.14 Continued

Notes on the Music

5.1. Le Monde Te vient. This first lyric is sung by all nine Muses. They enter playing their instruments, and apparently continue playing while they sing.[108] From this, we can infer that they all play string instruments (violins, lutes, harp, and so on), which can be carried, and do not affect singing, like wind instruments would. Viols are less likely here, even though the word "violes" could be used for viols as well as violins, because they do not readily allow walking while playing, being held between the legs.[109]

The lyric consists of a single six-line stanza: two tercets with an abc-abc rhyme scheme, and a versification of 988-988. A close match is found in Théodore de Bèze's Psalm 58, *Entre vous conseillers qui estes*, which has two tercets (abb-acc) with an identical 988-988 versification. It first appeared in *Les Pseaumes mis en Rime Françoise*, of 1562. Since instruments apparently accompany the singing, it seems very likely that a polyphonic version of the tune is being used, rather than the monophonic one originally composed. This harmonization, like all but one of the others here, is from Claude le Jeune's *Les Cent Cinquante Pseaumes de David*, first published posthumously in 1601, and reprinted several times, including the same year as *The Masque of Truth*. According to the usual practice, Le Jeune places the psalm tune in the tenor voice.

5.2. Sortez EVROPE. A trio of Muses, Urania, Clio, & Terpsichore, sing this second lyric,[110] which consists of six lines in an ababcc rhyme scheme and a 989899 versification.[111] Only two psalm tunes come close to this: Psalm 30 (also used for Psalm 76) which is 888899, and Psalm 112, which is 999999 (unique in the psalter). Because the first and third lines of Psalm 30 are not easily subdivided, as would be necessary, the best choice seems to be Psalm 112,

---

[108] See a similar scene in Plate II.2.

[109] Certain small viols could be played "up," however, since some surviving trebles originally had back folds in the lower bouts, making it easier for the instrument to be played at the shoulder like a violin. See Ephraim Segerman, "The Lower-bout Back Fold on English Treble Viols," *Fellowship of Makers and Restorers of Historical Instruments Quarterly* 24 (1981): Communication 352, 16–17, 52. For the larger viols, it would be possible to rig up a sling to carry the instrument while walking, as shown in an early seventeenth-century depiction of a violin band (Plate II.1). This is not standard playing technique for what is, after all, a "viola da gamba." On the musical instruments in such festival books and a connection to English repertoire, see Spohr, "English Masque Dances as Tournament Music?," in *The Palatine Wedding of 1613*, 546–65.

[110] See a similar scene in Plate II.3.

[111] Intriguingly, this is the same versification found in the "Song" for lutes and voices, *Ladies, why doe you spend your leasure*, by Weckherlin, from his *Triumphall Shews*, 12–13. It matches the versification of the German original, *Warumb, ihr frawen und jungfrawen*, from *Triumf Newlich bey der feyerlichen kindtauf zu Stutgart gehalten* (Stuttgart, 1616), 9.

Plate II.2 Seven women masquers with lutes, for the festival of Georg Fridrich, Margrave of Baden. *Repraesentatio der Fürstlichen Auffzug vnd Ritterspil* (Stuttgart, [1611]), p. 71. Courtesy of the Huntington Library.

Plate II.3 A trio of singing women masquers. *Repraesentatio der Fürstlichen Auffzug vnd Ritterspil* (Stuttgart, [1611]), p. 121. Courtesy of the Huntington Library.

O bien heureuse la personne, by Théodore de Bèze for *Les Pseaumes mis en Rime Françoise*, of 1562. This is so, even though Psalm 112 is organized in tercets: the phrase structure is not prominent in the music, and the lyric fits well. Once again, the tune is in the tenor voice, and the setting is from Le Jeune's *Les Cent Cinquante Pseaumes de David*.

The manuscript painting of Queen Europa bears a striking resemblance to the portrait of Elizabeth Stuart after Michiel Janszoon van Mierevelt, with the so-called Tudor Crown of England added afterward (see Color Plate 9).[112] The crown itself is distinctive, and the facial features—brow, lips, eyes, nose, hair poufed to the sides, and overall expression—are very similar, and suggest that the Europa artist may have used Elizabeth as a model—all the more apt for this edition of an event in her honor.

5.3a and 5.3b. Bransle de la Torche. The first dance in *The Masque of Truth* is called an "avant-ballet," which is a term that Jocquet (or some other author) made up, and which even Menestrier in 1682 felt compelled to remark upon.[113] It is similar to the English term "antimasque" ("Anticke Masque"), which typically involved grotesque gestures and was danced by professionals, and which was used for torchbearers in earlier masques. In this case, it seems more akin to Samuel Daniel's term "Ante-maske," from his 1610 *Tethys Festival* masque, where it was simply an introductory dance preceding (ante-) a main masque dance.[114] This sort of usage is found also in the first two Palatine wedding masques in 1613, where "torchbearers' dances were a serious prelude to the main entry, rather than a comic or grotesque counterpoint."[115] In the Palatine tradition, it should be noted, torchbearers solemnly processed to the accompaniment of trumpets and drums, but the torchbearers in *The Masque of Truth*, like those in *The Lords' Masque* and *The Memorable Masque*, are clearly dancing.[116]

---

[112] For the historical background and political implications behind this composite portrait, see Akkerman, *Elizabeth Stuart, Queen of Hearts*, 186–87.

[113] Menestrier, *Des Ballets Anciens et Modernes*, 116.

[114] Samuel Daniel, *Tethys Festival* (1610; STC: 13161), sig. E3r. See processing torchbearers in Plate II.4.

[115] See Anne Daye, "Torchbearers in the English Masque," *Early Music* 26 (1998), 246–62, at 259–61, https://www.jstor.org/stable/3128624. Daye also cites two choreographies for torchbearers in Cesare Negri's widely known *Le Gratie d'Amore* (1602).

[116] See Daye, "'Graced with Measures,'" 303. Trumpets at that time could play only fanfare-like flourishes (intrada, sennet, tucket = toccata), not melodies like those needed for dances. See, for example, Cesare Bendinelli's 1614 treatise, *Tutta l'arte della trombetta*, Verona, Biblioteca dell'Accademia Filarmonica, Mus. 128, and Vienna, Österreichische Nationalbibliothek, Cod. 10819. For a recent discussion of these techniques, see Peter Downey, "Understanding the Italian Trumpeters' Method: The Trumpet Ensemble Contribution to Schütz's Psalm Settings," Forschungsportal Schola Cantorum Basiliensis, 2021, http://www.forschung.schola-cantorum-basiliensis.ch/de/forschung/improvisation-trompeten-ensemble/downey-italian-trumpeters-method.html.

A brief *Branle de la Torche* was printed as a social dance in Thoinot Arbeau's *Orchésographie* (1589).[117] As a social dance, it might seem less appropriate for a court entertainment, but Arbeau states that some social dances were converted from dances in "mascarades," so the same might have happened here.[118] A choreography for the *Branle de la Torche* under the alternative title of *La Danse du Chandellier*, furthermore, appears in the roughly contemporary manuscript dance treatise, *Instruction pour dancer*,[119] apparently copied by French dancing master Anthoine Emeraud, and carried to the court of the Duke of Brunswick-Lüneburg, to whom Michael Praetorius ultimately dedicated his *Terpsichore* collection of 1612.[120]

It is difficult to know how well *Terpsichore* was known in England by early 1613, since the date is so soon after its publication in Wolfenbüttel. Intriguingly, this piece was copied into Margaret Board's lute manuscript (ca.1620),[121] apparently during the time that she was studying with John Dowland. A few pages later appears a masque dance from *The Lords' Masque* from the Palatine wedding, as well as one entitled *The La: Elyza: her masque*.[122] Dowland was at court during the 1613 wedding week, and was paid for playing lute in Chapman's *Memorable Masque* on the Monday night.

Thus, in spite of its history as a social dance, the *Bransle de la Torche* from *Terpsichore* may have seemed fitting for Queen Europa's fifteen Torchbearers in this court entertainment. Praetorius expanded the dance from Arbeau's tune, accompanying it with a combination of the *Passamezzo Antico* and *Romanesca* ground bass patterns (just like the English tune *Greensleeves*). He also set it in five voices—the only five-voice dance from the Praetorius collection used in this edition.

Finally, since the description seems to suggest that the torchbearers sang an "air," or that an air was sung while they danced ("L'offrande estant faite avec vng air, que l'on chanta, les Porte-flambeaux dancerent l'avant-ballet"), I have added

---

[117] (Langres, 1589), fols. 86r–87r. Precedents include a four-part *Bransle de la torche* in Jean d'Estrées, *Tiers Livre de Danseries* (Paris, 1559), fol. 7v, and *Branle de la torche* for four-course guitar solo in Pierre Phalèse, *Selectissima Elelgantissimaque... Carmina* (Antwerp, 1570), fol. 78r.

[118] See Arbeau, *Orchésographie*, fol. 82r. Furthermore, Italian dance theorist, Cesare Negri, included two choreographed torch dances in his 1602 treatise, *Le gratie d'amore*, thus demonstrating possibilities for a choreographed procession with torches. On these dances and their choreographies, see Pamela Jones, "Spectacle in Milan: Cesare Negri's Torch Dances," *Early Music* 14 (1986), 182–96, https://doi.org/10.1093/earlyj/14.2.182.

[119] Darmstadt University Library, MS Hs-304, fols. 4r–5r. This manuscript was published in facsimile, with commentary by Angene Feves et al. (Freiburg, 2000).

[120] It was Emeraud who brought Praetorius the French dance tunes that he then harmonized for his *Terpsichore* collection See Praetorius, *Terpsichore*, Cantus partbook, sig. (:)(:)1r.

[121] London, Royal Academy of Music, MS 603, fol. 23r. The title appears as *Brale delatroche*.

[122] This is a version of the first masque dance from *Oberon, the Faery Prince: A Masqve of Prince Henries* (1611), however, so it was not composed originally for Princess Elizabeth.

text to the top line of the dance music. Two different French metrical psalms seem highly appropriate alternatives for the context, and I have conjecturally set verses from them: 5.3a presents selections from Clément Marot's *Rendez à Dieu louange & gloire* (Psalm 118), and 5.3b features Théodore de Bèze's *Vous tous qui la terre habitez* (Psalm 100).[123] Psalm 118, with its pertinent call for offerings with singing, also matches the apparent versification requirements of the music well, with paroxytonic endings in the odd-numbered lines.[124] Théodore de Bèze's 1562 version of Psalm 100 is an excellent alternative, however, with its address to "All people dwelling on the earth," its call to sing, and enter the gates of heaven, as well as its concluding praise of "La verité." With four tetrameter quatrains, it can also be sung complete, but it lacks the paroxytonic line endings that make Psalm 118 such a good fit. In the end, either setting can work, but the use of a psalm text with the dance music is still conjectural.

5.4. Ballet. This dance is performed by the ten Princes and Princesses of Europe, shortly after the Torchbearers' dance, and is described as a "grand ballet."[125] Because of that "grandeur," *Ballet* 268 from *Terpsichore*, with two musical sections in contrasting keys, seems like a good choice. In fact, the preceding Torchbearers' bransle in D leads to this grand ballet in G (first without, then with a b signature), and then on to the Muses' chorus in G, which follows.

5.5a and 5.5b. Sortez Reyne. This third lyric is sung by the Muse trio of Calliope, Melpomene, and Erato, and serves to call forth Queen Asia from the globe. Like the previous lyric, its rhyme scheme is ababcc, but the versification this time is 898988. Again, the psalter does not contain a perfect match in versification, but Théodore de Bèze's Psalm 28, *O Dieu, qui est ma forteresse*, comes closest, with 999988. It was composed by Louis Bourgeois, and introduced in the landmark *Pseaumes Octantetrois de David*, of 1551. As noted above, most polyphonic psalms place the psalm tune in the tenor, but Le Jeune's setting places this one in the top voice, as did Claude Goudimel's

---

[123] Psalm 118 is the same psalm, moreover, that St. Ambrose cited for his discussion of the Angel with the "flaming sword." See the text before no. 5.13, above.

[124] The translations are from John Standish's 1632 *All the French Psalm Tunes with English Words*, sigs. K10v–K12r and I4v–I5r, and seem to be by Standish himself since they are not among the psalm translations ascribed to others by William Drummond in National Library of Scotland, MS 2060, fol. 150r. See also Doelman, "A Seventeenth-Century Publication of Three of Sir Philip Sidney's Psalms," 162–63.

[125] This term, at least, is taken directly from the French *ballet de cour*, where a *Grand Ballet* normally ended one or more *Entrées* (dance scenes). There are dozens of such examples in André Danican Philidor's late seventeenth-century manuscript collection of *Anciens Ballets*, Paris, Conservatoire, MS Rés. F. 496. On this repertoire, see David J. Buch, *Dance Music from the Ballets de Cour, 1575–1651: Historical Commentary, Source Study, and Transcriptions from the Philidor Manuscripts* (Stuyvesant, 1993).

early setting in his *Les Pseaumes, ... mis en musique à quatre parties* of 1565. Having leading tone motion in three of the six phrases of the tune, including the last, invites that sort of polyphonic treatment.

One other psalm-related piece comes close to the versification of this lyric, with ababcc 898999: Théodore de Bèze's *Le Seigneur est tout mon plaisir*, Cantique 5 (*Cantique d'Anne*), published with a musical setting in *Les Saincts Cantiques* (1595).[126] I could find no period harmonization for that anonymous tune, however, so I reconstructed the four-voice version given above, with the melody in the tenor voice as usual and the other parts shown at reduced size in the score. It serves as an alternative setting for this lyric.

5.6. Ballet des feus. This is a dance for Queen Asia's fifteen torchbearers, with the text describing it as an "advant-ballet," a variation on the "avant-ballet" of no. 5.3 (q.v.). In this case, "Ballet of the fires" seems another good choice for torchbearers.

Plate II.4 A procession of torchbearers for a masque. *Repraesentatio der Fürstlichen Auffzug vnd Ritterspil* (Stuttgart, [1611]), p. 127. Courtesy of the Huntington Library.

[126] P. 31. The 1597 edition (sig. B5v.) reverses the second and third pitches of the tenor melody.

5.7. Ballet du Roy. This dance is performed by the ten Princes and Princesses of Asia, shortly after the Torchbearers' dance, and is, once again, described as a "grand ballet." Because of that "grandeur," *Ballet* 269 from *Terpsichore*, with three musical sections in contrasting keys and meters, seems like a good choice. And as before, the succession of modal finals, from the antimasque through the grand ballet to the chorus that follows—C – G – G—works well.

5.8. Sortez AFFRIQVE. This lyric is sung by the last three Muses, Euterpe, Thalia, and Polyhymnia, although they are not named. It serves to call forth Queen Africa from within the globe. Beginning like no. 5.2 above, with a 9898 quatrain, it varies from no. 5.2 by closing with an 88 couplet. Two psalms come close to that versification with 998888 syllables: Psalm 80 and Psalm 105, both by Théodore de Bèze for *Les Pseaumes mis en Rime Françoise*, of 1562. Psalm 80, *O Pasteur d'Israel, escoute*, has been preferred here because of mode—G—as opposed to F for Psalm 105. The harmonization, once again, is from Claude le Jeune's *Les Cent Cinquante Pseaumes de David*, of 1601.

5.9. Ballet des Amazones. The (presumably) twelve torchbearing pages of Queen Africa dance this "antibalet,"[127] another made-up variation on the "avant-ballet" of no. 5.3 (q.v.). The music here has been chosen because one of the dancers is dressed "à la façon ... des Amazonnes."[128]

5.10. Ballet. This African dance parallels the "grand ballets" of European and Asian Princes and Princesses, though the term is not used, and the (presumably) eight grandees are described only as the "Masters" of the torchbearing pages. The D mode of this dance follows the G mode of the antibalet, and anticipates the D mode of the ensuing lyric. This is the only three-voice dance setting from Praetorius used here, and the fact that the chords at its cadence arrivals frequently lack thirds, suggests that it must have been accompanied by a chordal instrument, like a lute (or harp or keyboard, though those are not mentioned elsewhere). To fill in those missing harmonies, an editorial fourth part has been added in the tenor range, shown at a reduced size in the score.

5.11. Quittez vos anciennes. The four stanzas of this lyric are sung successively by the three trios of Muses heard previously, then by all nine of them together for the "Chorus" (as they had sung no. 5.1, above). This is the nub of

---

[127] Only eleven pages are named, but this assumes continuation of each princess having three pages.
[128] See notes to Praetorius dances, nos. 5.3 and 5.6, above. In his *Anciens Ballets* (Paris, Conservatoire MS Rés. F. 496, p. 70), Philidor gives 1607 as the date of the *Ballet des Amazonnes* at the French court. In addition, an English dance bears a similar name: *The Amazonians Masque*, found in British Library, Add. MSS 10444/5 (ca.1620), no. 71, among two-voice dances from the Inns of Court. Andrew Sabol speculates that it was intended for the abandoned *Masque of Amazons* (1618), sponsored by Lady Hay. See Sabol, *Four Hundred Songs and Dances*, no. 124, pp. 223, 578.

The Masque of Truth's argument, trying to persuade the three queens to have their populations embrace the "Truth" of the reformed religion. The rhyme scheme is tercets of aab-ccb and the versification is 998-998. The best choice seems to be the same tune used for no. 5.2, above: Psalm 112, *O bien heureuse la personne*, by Théodore de Bèze for *Les Pseaumes mis en Rime Françoise*, of 1562. In this case, the rhyme scheme matches perfectly, and the 999-999 versification needs only a little adjustment. The harmonization, once again, is from Claude le Jeune's *Les Cent Cinquante Pseaumes de David*, of 1601.

5.12. Ballet des Anglois. It is not clear that there is actual dancing at this point, but the peoples of the world are finally brought to worship Truth (Aletheia) "as if dancing." It makes sense, therefore, that dance music would be heard during a kind of pantomime, if they were not actually dancing, which may have been intended. I have used Praetorius's *Ballet des Anglois* here, both because it seems suitable for a court entertainment in England, and because it is fairly long, and could accommodate whatever pageantry takes place onstage involving a hundred or more members of the cast.

5.13. Que ceux à qui. This last lyric in *The Masque of Truth* is sung by untold numbers of "Stars, Angels, & Cherubim," accompanied by "Violins, Lutes, & Voices," inviting the three queens with their now-converted peoples to enter Paradise. We might guess that the "Stars, Angels, & Cherubim" numbered three of each, matching the number of Muses, but that is not clear. Additional voices apparently took part, in any case, along with bowed and plucked string instruments. The versification of ababcc and 989888 matches that for no. 5.8, above, which used Psalm 80 (998888), but in this case, the best choice seems to be the melody used for no. 5.5a, above: Théodore de Bèze's Psalm 28, *O Dieu, qui est ma forteresse*, from *Pseaumes Octantetrois de David*, of 1551. Its rhyming couplets fit the ababcc structure well, and the psalm's 999988 syllables mean that the setting needs only minimal adjustment to fit the tune. The harmonization, once again, is from Claude le Jeune's *Les Cent Cinquante Pseaumes de David*, of 1601, with the tune in the top voice.

5.14. Ballet des Princesses. This final musical selection, like no. 5.12 above, is not for dancing, but for the ceremonial entrance of the converted peoples into paradise, led by Atlas and the nine Muses. This action was accompanied by "haute Musique," which would have been understood as an ensemble of loud instruments,[129] probably cornetts and sackbuts, possibly with shawms

---

[129] Wiggins and Richardson translate "haute Musique" as "high music." See *British Drama*, 6:255. The seminal study of this issue is Edmund A. Bowles, "*Haut* and *Bas*: The Grouping of Musical Instruments in the Middle Ages," *Musica Disciplina* 8 (1954), 115–40, https://www.jstor.org/stable/20531877.

Plate II.5 A loud band of masquers, representing curtal, cornetti, shawm, and sackbut, from a festival procession for Margrave Christian of Brandenburg. *Repraesentatio der Fürstlichen Auffzug vnd Ritterspil* (Stuttgart, [1611]), p. 39. Courtesy of the Huntington Library.

(hautboys or hoboyes) as well (see Plate II.5).[130] It may be that the softer instruments, Lutes, Violins, etc. played along since they were present, but this is not specified.[131] I have chosen Praetorius's *Ballet des Princesses*, which suits the situation well, with its mode of C, coming from the G of the final chorus, and its brilliant, high tessitura, which seems an appropriately triumphant ending for *The Masque of Truth*.

---

[130] The quarto of Beaumont's *Masque of the Inner Temple and Gray's Inn*, for example, notes at one point (sig. C2v) that "the Musicke changed from Violins to Hoboyes, Cornets, &c."

[131] Payment records for Jacobean court masques make clear that ensembles of violins, lutes, and loud wind instruments were regular performers. See Walls, *Music in the English Courtly Masque*, 148–54.

APPENDIX 1
Reports on The Masque of Truth

from *Le Mercure François*, vol. 3, for 1613 (Paris, 1616), 77.

Le 16. les Comediens du Roy s'estoient preparez pour representer vne comedie, mais ils furent remis à vne autrefois; pource que sa M. voulut veoir les Ieux moraux de trois cent personnes de lettres qui les vindrent representer au Chasteau, estans tous vestus de diuerses sortes d'habits, & de toutes sortes de nations, auec des Statuës, des globes, des animaux, & de toutes sortes de Musiques. Leur subject estois de demonster, *Quod Religio orbem terrarum Angliae coniunxisset*: Contre l'ancien Prouerbe, *Diuisus ab orbe Britannus*: Et que l'Alitie, Vierge de Verité, residoit en l'Isle de Bretagne de laquelle le Roy estoit Defenseur. En ces ieux vn Atlas fit sortir d'vn globe les trois parties du monde, conduites chacune par trois Muses: auec les Habitans des Royaumes de chacune de ces parties, & leurs Fleuves, qui furent presenter aux Espousez des fruicts de leurs terres. Bref ce n'estoient que louanges & prieres de Felicité que lon leur desiroit.

On the 16th (of February), the Actors of the King were preparing to present a play, but they were put off to another time; because his Majesty wanted to see the allegorical play of three hundred literary persons who came to perform at the Palace, being dressed in varied sorts of attire from all sorts of nations, with statues, globes, animals, and all sorts of Music. Their goal was to demonstrate, *That the Religion of England has united the world*: countering the ancient proverb, *The Briton is divided from the world*: And that Aletheia, the Virgin of Truth, was residing in the Isle of Britain, of which the King was Defender. In this play, Atlas summoned the three parts of the world from a globe, each one led by three Muses: with the Inhabitants of the Realms of each of those parts, & their Rivers, who presented the Bride & Groom with the fruits of their lands. In short, it was nothing but praises and prayers for Happiness, which they desired for them.

from Claude-François Menestrier, *Des Ballets Anciens et Modernes selon les Règles du Théatre* (Paris, 1682), 114–18.

Deux jours aprés, trois cent Gentilshommes étudians au Droit, representerent toutes les nations du monde, & vinrent par la Tamise, jusqu'au Palais de Roy où ils danserent un Ballet Allegorique, dont le sujet opposé à cet ancien Vers. *Et toto divisos orbe Britannos*, étoit que la Religion avoit joint le monde avec l'Angleterre Les Ministres Protestans firent le dessein de ce Ballet, pour favoriser leur Religion, & dirent que le monde quittant ses erreurs se rendroit à la connoissance de la Verite qu'ils prétendoient n'être purement prêchée qu'en Angleterre, &

Two days later, three hundred Gentlemen, students of Law, represented all the nations of the world, and came via the Thames, to the Palace of the King, where they presented an Allegorical Masque, of which the subject opposed to this ancient proverb: *And Britons are divided from the entire Globe*, was that Religion had joined the world to England. Protestant Ministers devised this masque, to promote their Religion, and say that the world, abandoning its errors would acknowledge Truth, which they maintained was righteously preached only in England, and

dans le Palais qui s'unissoient par le moyen de cette Alliance. Pour cela ils feignirent qu'Atlas ne pouvant plus soûtenir le grand fardeau du monde dont il étoit chargé depuis longtemps, venoit le remettre entre les mains d'*Alithie*, qui est la Verité. La scene representoit le grand Globe du monde marqué de toutes les Provinces comme elles sont marquées sur les Globes,[1] & la Verité couchée auprés de ce Globe. Les Muses vêtuës en Vestales firent l'ouverture, & chanterent ces Vers au Roy,

Le Monde te vient faire Hommage
Grand Roy, de sa fertilité
Puisqu'icy loge la beauté,
Et l'Amour l'honneur de nôtre aage.
Il vient chercher la verité
Chez vous où son temple est planté.

Aprés quoi Atlas se plaignant de sa lassitude, dit qu'ayant appris d'Archimede, que si on lui donnoit un point ferme, il enleveroit toute la masse du monde qui lui avoit donné tant de peine à porter, il étoit venue dans la Bretagne qui étoit ce point fixe pour se décharger d'un si pesant fardeau sur Alithie, qui demeuroit dans cette Isle, ou le Roy l'avoit receuë si favorablement. Ayant fini son recit il s'approcha du Globe accompagné de trois des Muses Uranie, Clio, & Terpsicore qui chanterent ces Vers.

Sortez, Europe la premiere,
Puisque vôtre ame a ja receu
Quelque Rayons de la lumiere,
Que le saint Espris a conceu
Amenez icy vos Princesses,
Pou en recevoir les addresses.

in the [Palatinate] which were unified by means of this Alliance. To achieve this, they pretended that Atlas, no longer able to hold the great burden of the globe which has long been his responsibility, came to place it into the hands of *Aletheia*, or Truth. The scene represented the great Globe of the world with all the countries marked as they are on Globes, and Truth reclining near the Globe. The Muses, dressed as Vestals, began the proceedings, and sang these lines to the King,

The World comes to pay you,
Great King, the homage of its fertility:
For Beauty lodges here,
And Love, the Honor of our age.
The World comes to seek Truth
In your realm, where her temple stands.

After which Atlas, who complaining of weariness, says that having learned from Archimedes, that if someone gave him a fixed point, he could lift the whole weight of the world which had given him so much trouble to carry, he had come to Britain, which was this fixed point to unload such a heavy burden onto Aletheia, who has made her home in this Island, where the King had received her so favorably. Having finished his speech, he approached the Globe, accompanied by three Muses, Urania, Clio, & Terpsichore, who sang these lines.

Come forth Europa first,
Since your soul has already received
A few rays of light
That the Holy Spirit has conceived.
Bring here your Princesses
To receive the [Holy Spirit's] attentions.

---

[1] See Color Plate 2.

Aussitôt la partie du Globe ou l'Europe étoit décrite, s'ouvrit, l'Europe en sortit vêtuë en Reine avec cinq de ses Filles,[2] la France, l'Espagne, l'Allemagne, l'Italie, & la Grece, L'Ocean & la Mer Mediteranée l'accompagnerent avec cinq Rivieres, la Loire, le Guadalquivir, le Rhin, le Tibre & Acheloüs. Chaque Princesse avoit trois Pages. La France, un Basque, un bas Breton, & un Lorrain. L'Espagne un Portugais, un Arragonnois, & un Catalan. L'Allemagne un Hongrois, un Bohemien, & un Danois. L'Italie un Neapolitain, un Venitien, & un Bergamasque. La Grece un Turc, un Albanois, & un Bulgare, chacun habillé à la maniere de son pays & portant un flambeau en main, avec lequel ils danserent un avant Ballet, selon l'usage de ces temps là ou l'on ne manquoit jamais, d'introduire des Pages ou des Esclaves qui dansoient avec des flambeaux. Aprés cet avant-Ballet, des Princes sortirent du Globe, & danserent avec les Princesses une belle Entrée. Atlas prit ensuite trois autres Muses, Calliope,

Melpomene, & Erato, & les faisant chanter auprés du Globe, il en vit sortir l'Asie avec ses filles,[3] la Syrie, la Palestine, la Mesopotamie, la Chaldée, l'Assyrie, l'Arabie, & la Perse. Le Golfe de Bengala, la Mer Rouge, & la Mer Caspienne, avec le Tigre, l'Inde, le Gange, l'Euphrate, le Jourdain, & le Tanaïs, firent diverses Entrées. Les Pages des Princesses étoient vétus à la Moscovite, à la Tartare, à la Turque, à l'Indienne, à la Juifve, à l'Egyiptienne, à la Phrygienne, &c. Chacun avoit un flambeau allumé comme les precedens, & ils danserent leur avant Ballet.

Atlas avec les trois autres Muses fit sortie l'Afrique du Globe, en chantans ces Vers.[4]

Immediately, the part of the Globe, where the Map of Europe was painted, opened. Europa emerged, dressed as a Queen, with her five Daughters: France, Spain, Germany, Italy, & Greece; the Ocean & the Mediterranean Sea accompanied her with their five Rivers: the Loire, the Guadalquivir, the Rhine, the Tiber, & Achelous. Each Princess had three Pages: France, a Basque, a Lower Breton, & a Lorraine; Spain, a Portuguese, an Aragonese, & a Catalan; Germany, a Hungarian, a Bohemian, & a Dane; Italy, a Neapolitan, a Venetian, & a Bergamasque; Greece: a Turk, an Albanian, & a Bulgarian: each dressed in their traditional national garb, & carrying a torch, with which they danced the avant-ballet, after the custom of that time where one never failed, to introduce the Pages or Slaves who danced with the torches. After this avant-ballet, Princes emerged from the Globe, and danced a lovely entry dance with the Princesses.

Then Atlas took three other Muses, Calliope, Melpomene, & Erato, and making them sing near the Globe, he saw Asia emerge from it with her daughters, Syria, Palestine, Mesopotamia, Chaldea, Assyria, Arabia, & Persia. The Bay of Bengal, the Red Sea & the Caspian Sea, with the Tigris, Indus, Ganges, Euphrates, Jordan, & Tana, entered severally. The Pages of these Princesses were dressed as Muscovite, Tartar, Turk, Indian, Jewish, Egyptian, Phrygian, &c. Each one carried a flaming torch, as previously, and they danced their avant-ballet.

Atlas with the last three Muses bid Africa emerge from the Globe, singing these lines:

---

[2] See Color Plates 3 and 4.
[3] See Color Plates 5 and 7.
[4] See Color Plates 6 and 8.

Sortez Afrique monstrueuse
En erreurs plus qu'en animaux,
Et cherchez en cette Isle heureuse
Le repos tous vos travaux.
C'est icy que la Verité
Veut que son temple soit planté.

L'Afrique sortit aussitôt accompagnée de quatre Princesses, la Barbarie, la Numidie, la Lybie & l'Ethiopie. L'Ocean Atlantique & l'Ethiopique les escorroient avec le Nil, le Zambere, le Niger, & l'Agaise. Les Pages étoient du Bresul, de Madagascar, de la Guinée de Tunis, de Fez, d'Alger, de Moravie, & du Mozambique, vétus à la maniere de leurs Pays. Ce furent autant d'Entrées de Ballet à la maniere des precedentes, chaque Mer, & chaque fleuve apporta des presens à la Princesse.

Come forth, Africa, prodigious
In errors more than in animals,
And seek in this happy Isle
The repose for all your labors.
It is here that Truth
Wants her temple to be established.

Suddenly, Africa came forth, accompanied by four Princesses, Barbary, Numidia, Libya, and Ethiopia. The Atlantic & Ethiopian Oceans escorted them with the Nile, the Zambesi, the Niger, & the Zaire[?]. The pages were from Brazil, Madagascar, Guinea, Tunis, Fez, Algeria, Moravia, & Mozambique, dressed in the manner of their countries. There were just as many masque scenes as before; each Sea, and each river brought gifts to the Princess.

APPENDIX 2
Related Images

App 2.1 Indo Africano. Cesare Vecellio, *De gli Habiti Antichi, et Moderni* (Venice, 1590), p. 493. Courtesy of the Huntington Library.

App 2.2 *The Virgin and Child with a Monkey*, Engraving by Albrecht Dürer (Nuremberg, ca.1498), Cleveland Museum of Art, Dudley P. Allen Fund, 1964.29.

Bibliography

Akkerman, Nadine, ed., *The Correspondence of Elizabeth Stuart, Queen of Bohemia, Volume 1, 1603-1631*. Oxford: Oxford University Press, 2015, https://doi:10.1093/actrade/9780199551071.book.1.
Akkerman, Nadine. *Elizabeth Stuart, Queen of Hearts*. Oxford: Oxford University Press, 2022, https://doi.org/10.1093/oso/9780199668304.001.0001.
Ashbee, Andrew. *Records of English Court Music*. Vol. 4, 1603-25. Snodland: Author, 1991.
Ashbee, Andrew, and David Lasocki, eds. *A Biographical Dictionary of English Court Musicians, 1485-1714*. Aldershot: Ashgate, 1998.
Austern, Linda Phyllis. *Music in English Children's Drama*. Philadelphia: Gordon and Breach, 1992.
Austern, Linda Phyllis. "'For Musicke Is the Handmaid of the Lord': Women, Psalms, and Domestic Music-Making in Early Modern England." In *Psalms in the Early Modern World*, ed. Linda Phyllis Austern et al., 89-92. Farnham: Ashgate, 2013, https://doi.org/10.4324/9781315602783.
Baildon, W. P., ed., *The Records of the Honorable Society of Lincoln's Inn: The Black Books*. Vol. 2. London: Lincoln's Inn, 1898.
Bentley, Gerald Eades, ed. *A Book of Masques*. Cambridge: Cambridge University Press, 1967.
Berringer, Ralph W. "Thomas Campion's Share in *A Booke of Ayres*, *PMLA* 58 (1943): 938-48, https://doi:10.2307/458919.
Bevington, David, and Peter Holbrook, eds. *The Politics of the Stuart Court Masque*. Cambridge: Cambridge University Press, 1998.
Bowles, Edmund A. "Haut and Bas: The Grouping of Musical Instruments in the Middle Ages." *Musica Disciplina* 8 (1954): 115-40, https://www.jstor.org/stable/20531877.
Buch, David J. *Dance Music from the Ballets de Cour, 1575-1651: Historical Commentary, Source Study, and Transcriptions from the Philidor Manuscripts*. Stuyvesant: Pendragon Press, 1993.
Canova-Green, Marie-Claude. "'Particularitez des Resjoyssances Publiques et Cérémonyes du Mariage de la Princesse': An Ambassadorial Account of the Palatine Wedding." In *The Palatine Wedding of 1613: Protestant Alliance and Court Festival*, ed. Sara Smart and Mara R. Wade, 353-69. Wiesbaden: Harrassowitz, 2013.
Clive, H. P. "The Calvinist Attitude to Music, and Its Literary Aspects and Sources." *Bibliothèque d'Humanisme et Renaissance* 19 (1957): 80-102, https://www.jstor.org/stable/20673881.
Clive, H. P. "The Calvinists and the Question of Dancing in the 16th Century." *Bibliothèque d'Humanisme et Renaissance* 23 (1961): 296-323, https://www.jstor.org/stable/20674294.
Craven, Wesley Frank. *The Virginia Company of London, 1606-1624*. Williamsburg: Virginia 350th Anniversary Celebration, 1957.
Crouch, Patricia. "Patronage and Competing Visions of Virginia in George Chapman's 'The Memorable Masque' (1613)." *English Literary Renaissance* 40 (2010): 393-426, http://www.jstor.org/stable/43740814.
Curran, Kevin. "James I and Fictional Authority at the Palatine Wedding Celebrations." *Renaissance Studies* 20 (2006): 51-67, https://doi.org/10.1111/j.1477-4658.2006.00113.x.
Curran, Kevin. *Marriage, Performance, and Politics at the Jacobean Court*. Farnham: Ashgate, 2009.
Cutts, John P. "Robert Johnson and the Court Masque." *Music and Letters* 41 (1960): 111-26.

Dart, Thurston. "The Repertory of the Royal Wind Music." *Galpin Society Journal* 11 (1958): 70–77, https://doi.org/10.2307/842105.

Dart, Thurston. "Two English Musicians at Heidelberg in 1613." *Musical Times* 111 (1970): 29, 31–32, https://doi.org/10.2307/952296.

Davis, Walter R., ed. *The Works of Thomas Campion*. London: Faber and Faber, 1969.

Daye, Anne. "'Graced with Measures': Dance as an International Language in the Masques of 1613." In *The Palatine Wedding of 1613: Protestant Alliance and Court Festival*, ed. Sara Smart and Mara R. Wade, 289–318. Wiesbaden: Harrassowitz, 2013.

Daye, Anne. "Torchbearers in the English Masque." *Early Music* 26 (1998): 246–62, https://www.jstor.org/stable/3128624.

Dean, William. "Masques and like Devices in Chapman's Plays: Towards *The Memorable Maske*." *Parergon* 9 (1991): 31–43, https://doi.org/10.1353/pgn.1991.0042.

Doelman, Jim. "A Seventeenth-Century Publication of Three of Sir Philip Sidney's Psalms." *Notes and Queries* 38 (1991): 162–63, https://doi.org/10.1093/nq/38.2.162.

Downey, Peter. "Understanding the Italian Trumpeters' Method: The Trumpet Ensemble Contribution to Schütz's Psalm Settings." Forschungsportal Schola Cantorum Basiliensis, 2021, http://www.forschung.schola-cantorum-basiliensis.ch/de/forschung/improvisation-trompeten-ensemble/downey-italian-trumpeters-method.html.

Duffin, Ross W. "'Cornets & Sagbuts': Some Thoughts on Early Seventeenth-Century English Repertory for Brass." In *Perspectives in Brass Scholarship: Proceedings of the International Historic Brass Symposium, Amherst, 1995*, ed. Stewart Carter, 47–70. New York: Pendragon Press, 1997.

Duffin, Ross W. "Framing a Ditty for Elizabeth: Thoughts on Music for the 1602 Summer Progress." *Early Music History* 39 (2020), 115–48. https://doi.org/10.1017/S0261127920000066.

Duffin, Ross W. "Hidden Music in Early Elizabethan Tragedy." *Early Theatre* 24 (2021): 11–61, https://doi.org/10.12745/et.24.1.4162.

Duffin, Ross W. *Shakespeare's Songbook*. New York: W. W. Norton, 2004.

Duffin, Ross W. *Some Other Note: The Lost Songs of English Renaissance Comedy*. Oxford: Oxford University Press, 2018.

Duffin, Ross W. "Thomas Morley, Robert Johnson, and Songs for the Shakespearean Stage." In *The Oxford Handbook of Shakespeare and Music*, ed. Mervyn Cooke and Christopher R. Wilson, 356–86. Oxford: Oxford University Press, 2022, https://doi.org/10.1093/oxfordhb/9780190945145.013.12.

Dugan, Holly. "'To Bark with Judgment': Playing Baboon in Early Modern London." *Shakespeare Studies* 41 (2013): 77–93, https://hcommons.org/deposits/item/hc:19691.

Duncan-Jones, Katherine. *Sir Philip Sidney, Courtier Poet*. New Haven: Yale University Press, 1991.

Elliott, John R. Jr. "Invisible Evidence: Finding Musicians in the Archives of the Inns of Court, 1446–1642." *Royal Musical Association Research Chronicle* 26 (1993), 45–57. https://doi.org/10.1080/14723808.1993.10540961.

Evans, Blakemore. *The Plays of George Chapman*. Urbana: University of Illinois Press, 1970.

Field, Jemma. *Anna of Denmark: The Material and Visual Culture of the Stuart Courts, 1589–1619*. Manchester: Manchester University Press, 2020, https://doi.org/10.7765/9781526142504.

Forster, Leonard. "Two Drafts by Weckherlin of a Masque for the Queen of England." *German Life and Letters* 18 (1965): 258–63, https://doi.org/10.1111/j.1468-0483.1965.tb00078.x.

Garden, Greer, ed. *La Délivrance de Renaud: Ballet danced by Louis XIII*. Turnhout: Brepols, 2010.

Garside, Charles Jr. "Calvin's Preface to the Psalter: A Re-Appraisal." *Musical Quarterly* 37 (1951): 566–77, https://www.jstor.org/stable/739611.

Ginzel, Christof. *Poetry, Politics, and Promises of Empire*. Göttingen: V&R unipress, 2009.

Gordon, D. J. "Le 'Masque Mémorable' de Chapman." In *Les Fêtes de la Renaissance*. Vol. 1, ed. J. Jacquot, 305–17. Paris: C.N.R.S., 1956.

Gough, Melinda J. *Dancing Queen: Marie de Médicis' Ballets at the Court of Henri IV*. Toronto: University of Toronto Press, 2019, https://doi.org/10.1080/0268117X.2021.1991677.

Gough, Melinda J. "Marie de Medici's 1605 *ballet de la reine*: New Evidence and Analysis." *Early Theatre* 15 (2012): 109–44, https://www.jstor.org/stable/43499606.
Greer, David, ed. *Collected English Lutenist Partsongs*, Musica Britannica 53–54. London: Stainer and Bell, 1987–89.
Gutknecht, Dieter. "Vergleichende Betrachtung des Goudimel-Psalters mit dem Lobwasser-Psalter." *Jahrbuch für Liturgik und Hymnologie* 15 (1970): 132–45. https://www.jstor.org/stable/24193786.
Hamlin, Hannibal. "'The Highest Matter in the Noblest Forme': The Influence of the Sidney Psalms." *Sidney Journal* 23 (2005): 133–57.
Holbrook, Peter. "Jacobean Masques and the Jacobean Peace." In *The Politics of the Stuart Court Masque*, ed. David Bevington and Peter Holbrook, 67–87. Cambridge: Cambridge University Press, 1998.
Holman, Peter. "An Englishman Abroad: Thomas Simpson Revisited." *Viola da Gamba Society Journal* 18 (2024): 18–51.
Holman, Peter. *Four and Twenty Fiddlers: The Violin at the English Court, 1540–1690*. Oxford: Oxford University Press, 1993.
Holman, Peter. "*Terpsichore* at 400: Michael Praetorius as a Collector of Dance Music." *Viola da Gamba Society Journal* 6 (2012): 34–51.
Honigman E. A. J., and Susan Brock. *Playhouse Wills, 1558–1643*. Manchester: Manchester University Press, 1993.
Jackson, Clare. *Devil-Land: England under Siege, 1588–1688*. London: Allen Lane, 2021.
Jones, Pamela. "Spectacle in Milan: Cesare Negri's Torch Dances." *Early Music* 14 (1986): 182–96, https://doi.org/10.1093/earlyj/14.2.182.
Knowles, James. "'Can Ye Not Tell a Man from a Marmoset?': Apes and Others on the Early Modern Stage." In *Renaissance Beasts: Of Animals, Humans, and Other Wonderful Creatures*, ed. Erica Fudge, 138–63. Urbana, 2004.
Knowles, James. "The 'Running Masque' Recovered: A Masque for the Marquess of Buckingham (c.1619–20)." *English Manuscript Studies* 8 (2000): 79–135.
Limon, Jerzy. *The Masque of Stuart Culture*. Newark: University of Delaware Press, 1990.
Lindley, David, ed. *Court Masques: Jacobean and Caroline Entertainments, 1605–1640*. Oxford: Oxford University Press, 1995.
McGowan, Margaret. *L'Art du Ballet de Cour en France, 1581–1643*. Paris: C.N.R.S., 1963.
McManus, Clare. "When Is a Woman not a Woman? Or, Jacobean Fantasies of Female Performance (1606–1611)." *Modern Philology* 105 (2008): 437–74, https://doi.org/10.1086/591257.
McManus, Clare. *Women on the Renaissance Stage: Anna of Denmark and Female Masquing in the Stuart Court, 1590–1619*. Manchester: Manchester University Press, 2002.
Mulryne, J. R., Helen Watanabe-O'Kelly, and Margaret Shewring, eds. *Europa Triumphans: Court and Civic Festivals in Early Modern Europe*. Vol. 2. Aldershot: Ashgate, 2004.
Munro, Lucy. *Children of the Queen's Revels: A Jacobean Theatre Repertory*. Cambridge: Cambridge University Press, 2005.
Nelson, Alan H., and John R. Elliott, eds. *Records of Early English Drama: Inns of Court*. Vol. 1. Cambridge: D. S. Brewer, 2010.
Nevile, Jennifer. *Footprints of the Dance: An Early Seventeenth-Century Dance Master's Notebook*. Leiden: Brill, 2018.
Nichols, John. *Progresses, Processions, and Magnificent Festivities of King James the First*. Vol. 2. London: Author, 1828.
Norbrook, David. "'The Masque of Truth': Court Entertainments and International Protestant Politics in the Early Stuart Period." *Seventeenth Century* 1 (1986): 81–110, https://www.tandfonline.com/doi/abs/10.1080/0268117X.1986.10555252?journalCode=rsev20.
Norbrook, David. "Panegyric of the Monarch and Its Social Context under Elizabeth I and James I." D.Phil. diss., Oxford University, 1978, https://ora.ox.ac.uk/objects/uuid:514b9c61-be87-4832-a397-cdda040dcd06.

Norbrook, David. "The Reformation of the Masque." In *The Court Masque*, ed. David Lindley, 94–110. Manchester: Manchester University Press, 1984.

Orgel, Stephen, and Roy Strong. *Inigo Jones: The Theatre of the Stuart Court*. Vol. 1. Berkeley: University of California Press, 1973.

Pakes, Anna. "Reenactment, Dance Identity, and Historical Fictions." In *The Oxford Handbook of Dance and Reenactment*, ed. Mark Franko, 79–100. Oxford: Oxford University Press, 2017.

Parolin, Peter. "The Venetian Theater of Aletheia Talbot, Countess of Arundel." In *Women Players in England, 1500–1660: Beyond the All-Male Stage*, ed. Pamela Allen Brown and Peter Parolin, 219–40. Aldershot: Ashgate, 2005.

Patterson, W. B. "Pierre du Moulin's Quest for Protestant Unity, 1613–18." *Studies in Church History* 32 (1996): 235–50, https://doi.org/10.1017/S0424208400015436.

Pidoux, Pierre. *Le Psautier Huguenot*. Basel: Bärenreiter, 1962.

Quitslund, Beth. *The Reformation in Rhyme: Sternhold, Hopkins and the English Metrical Psalter, 1547–1603*. Aldershot: Ashgate, 2008.

Ravelhofer, Barbara. *The Early Stuart Masque: Dance, Costume, and Music*. Oxford: Oxford University Press, 2006.

Ravelhofer, Barbara. "Visual Effects in the Wedding Masques of 1613." In *Churfürstlicher Hochzeitlicher Heimführungs Triumph: Inszenierung und Wirkung der Hochzeit Kurfürst Friedrichs V. mit Elisabeth Stuart (1613)*, ed. Nichola Hayton, Hanns Hubach, and Marco Neumaier, 277–90. Ubstadt-Weiher: Verlag Regionalkultur, 2020.

Sabol, Andrew J., ed. *Four Hundred Songs and Dances from the Stuart Masque*. Hanover, NH: Brown University Press, 1982.

Sabol, Andrew J., ed. *A Score for The Lords' Masque by Thomas Campion*. Hanover, NH: Brown University Press, 1993.

Segerman, Ephraim. "The Lower-bout Back Fold on English Treble Viols." *Fellowship of Makers and Restorers of Historical Instruments Quarterly* 24 (1981): Communication 352, 16–17, 52.

Spohr, Arne. "English Masque Dances as Tournament Music?" In *The Palatine Wedding of 1613: Protestant Alliance and Court Festival*, ed. Sara Smart and Mara R. Wade, 546–65. Wiesbaden: Harrassowitz, 2013.

Spohr, Arne. "From 'Seiten-Kunst' to 'Fursten Gunst': The Careers of the Anglo-German Musicians William, Christian, and Steffen Brade in the Context of the Thirty Years War." *Journal of Seventeenth-Century Music* 26, no. 1 (2020): par. 2.1–10, https://sscm-jscm.org/jscm-issues/volume-26-no-1/spohr-anglo-german-musicians-brade/.

Stegman, André. "La Fête Parisienne à la Place Royale en Avril 1612." In *Les Fêtes de la Renaissance*. Vol. 3, ed. J. Jacquot and E. Konigson, 373–92. Paris: C.N.R.S., 1975.

Sternfeld, Frederick W. "A Song for Campion's Lord's Masque." *Journal of the Warburg and Courtauld Institutes* 20 (1957): 373–75, https://doi.org/10.2307/750790.

The Register of Admissions to Gray's Inn, 1521–1889, ed. Joseph Foster. London: Hansard, 1889.

Vivian, Percival, ed. *Poetical Works, in English, of Thomas Campion*. London: Routledge, 1907.

Walls, Peter. *Music in the English Courtly Masque, 1604–1640*. Oxford: Oxford University Press, 1996.

Ward, John M. "The Morris Tune." *Journal of the American Musicological Society* 39 (1986): 294–331, https://doi.org/10.2307/831532.

Ward, John M. "Newly Devis'd Measures for Jacobean Masques." *Acta Musicologica* 60 (1988): 111–42, https://doi.org/10.2307/932788.

White, Jason. *Militant Protestantism and British Identity, 1603–1642*. London: Pickering and Chatto, 2012, https://doi.org/10.4324/9781315656052.

Wiggins, Martin, and Catherine Richardson, *British Drama, 1533–1642: A Catalogue, Volume VI: 1609–1616*. Oxford: Oxford University Press, 2015.

Willetts, Pamela. "Sir Nicholas Le Strange's Collection of Masque Music." *British Museum Quarterly* 29 (1965): 79–81, https://doi.org/10.2307/4422895.

Williams, Deanne. *Shakespeare and the Performance of Girlhood*. Chapter 5, "A Dancing Princess," 127–48. New York: Palgrave Macmillan, 2014, https://link.springer.com/content/pdf/10.1057/9781137024763_6.pdf.

Wilson, Christopher R. "Some Musico-Poetic Aspects of Campion's Masques." In *The Well Enchanting Skill: Music, Poetry and Drama in the Culture of the Renaissance: Essays in Honour of F. W. Sternfeld*, ed. John Caldwell, Edward Olleson, and Susan Wollenberg, 91–105. Oxford: Oxford University Press, 1990.

Wilson, Christopher. *Words and Notes Coupled Lovingly Together: Thomas Campion, a Critical Study*. New York: Garland, 1989.

Winkler, Amanda Eubanks. "A Tale of *Twelfth Night*: Music Performance, and the Pursuit of Authenticity." *Shakespeare Bulletin* 36 (2018): 251–70, http://doi.org/10.1353/shb.2018.0023.

Index

For the benefit of digital users, indexed terms that span two pages (e.g., 52–53) may, on occasion, appear on only one of those pages.

Figures are indicated by an italic *f* following the page number.

Adson, John, 4–5, 14, 64
Airs de differents autheurs (Bataille), 166
Akkerman, Nadine, 162–63
Anne, Queen, 27
antimasques, 4–5, 14, 16, 63–64, 116
As by the streames of Babilon (Campion), 65–66
Aurelius, Abraham, 169
avant-ballet, 171–72, 210, 213, 214

baboons, 62, 63–64, 74–75, 86*f*, 116–17
ballad meter, 6–7, 15–16, 17–18, 68–69
ballet de cour, 20, 171
Bataille, Gabriel, 166
Beaumont, Francis. See *The Masque of the Inner Temple and Gray's Inn* (Beaumont)
Bèze, Théodore de, 165–66, 167, 208–10, 211–12, 213, 214–15
Bochan, Jacques (alias Cordier), 12–13
A Booke of Ayres (Campion, Rosseter), 119–20
Brade, William, 4–5, 115
branles, 22, 120–21
Bring away this sacred Tree (Lanier), 6–7

Calvinists, 176–77
Campion, Thomas. See also *The Lords' Masque* (Campion)
  A Booke of Ayres, 119–20
  A Description of a Maske, 13
  First Booke of Ayres, 18–19
  Mistris since you so much desire, 17–18, 119–20
  Second Booke of Ayres, 14–15, 117
  Somerset Masque, 5, 6–7, 12–13, 19
  As by the streames of Babilon, 65–66
  Third Booke of Ayres, 24–25, 118
  Where shee her sacred bowre adornes, 15
Carleton, Anne, 62–63, 115
Carleton, Dudley, 115–16
Chamberlain, John, 62–63, 115–16

Chapman, George. See *The Memorable Masque of the Middle Temple and Lincoln's Inn* (Chapman)
Comoedianten Tantz, 119
Confesse, Nicolas, 12–13
contrafacta, 6–9, 13–14, 62, 152
Coprario, John, 12–13, 114–15, 118
corantos, 22, 120–21, 146, 211
Corkine, William, 66, 69–70
Courtly Masquing Ayres (Adson), 14, 64
Cutting, Thomas, 61
Cutts, John P., 61

dance reconstruction, 8
d'Auvergne, Henri de la Tour, Duc de Bouillon, 169–70
Daye, Anne, 16
A Description of a Maske (Campion), 13
double consort, 12, 14, 27–28
Dowland, John, 15, 61, 64–65, 66–67, 119, 120–21
  First Booke of Songes or Ayres, 15, 120–21
  Now O now I needs must part, 66–67
  Wofull hart with griefe oppressed, 119
Du Moulin, Pierre, 169

Elizabeth, Princess. See Stuart, Elizabeth
Emeraud, Anthoine, 211

Ferrabosco, Alfonso, Jr., 12–13
First Booke of Ayres (Campion), 18–19
The First Booke of Songes & Ayres (Jones), 118–19
First Booke of Songes or Ayres (Dowland), 15, 120–21
Fitzwilliam Wind Manuscript, 118
Ford, Thomas, 65, 68
Foscarini, Antonio, 162–63

232 INDEX

Four Hundred Songs and Dances from the Stuart Masque (Sabol), 4–5, 7–8
Frederick, Count Palatine, 3–4, 159, 163, 169–70

galliards, 22, 120–21, 146
Giles, Thomas, 12
Ginzel, Christof, 169
Goudimel, Claude, 165–68
Grayes Inne Masque, 121

Henry, Prince, 3–4, 12–13, 61, 162–65, 168–70, 174–75
Herne, Jerome, 12
Holman, Peter, 8–9

James I, King, 3–4, 159, 169
Jocquet, D. See *The Masque of Truth* (Jocquet)
Johnson, Robert, 12–13, 61–62
Jones, Inigo, 12, 61, 67
Jones, Robert, 22–24, 61, 118–19, 121–22
   The First Booke of Songes & Ayres, 22, 118–19
   A Musicall Dreame, or the Fourth Booke of Ayres, 23–24
   She whose matchles beauty stayneth, 22
   Ultimum Vale, 121–22
Jonson, Ben, 12–13, 16–17, 62
   Love Freed from Ignorance and Folly, 12–13, 62
   Masque of Beauty, 16–17
   Masque of Blackness, 16–17
   Oberon, the Faery Prince, ix, 61

Lanier, Nicholas, 6–7
Le Jeune, Claude, 167–68
Les Cent Cinquante Pseaumes de David (Le Jeune), 167–68
Les pseavmes mis en rime françoise (Goudimel), 167–68
Lobwasser, Ambrosius, 165–66
The Lords' Masque (Campion)
   Aduance your Chorall motions now, 15, 17–18, 35*f*, 36–37
   Antimasque— Fantasticks, 30*f*, 32–33
   Antimasque— Torchbearers, 37*f*, 37–40
   Breath[e] you now, while Io Hymen, 46*f*, 47
   Cease, cease you Reuels, rest a space, 50*f*, 50–51
   Come away; bring thy golden theft, 14–15, 33*f*, 34–35
   Come triumphing, come with state, 51*f*, 51–53
   Dance, dance and visit now the shadowes of our ioy, 54*f*, 54–56

Entry— Orpheus, 28*f*, 29–30
first line index, 155–56
index to song sources, 153–55
introduction to, 3–10, 11*f*, 12–25
No longer wrong the night, 57*f*, 57
payment for, 12–13
Powerfull Joue, that of bright starres, 18–19, 42*f*, 42–43
Second Measure: *The second of the Lords,* 48*f*, 49
summary of, 152–53
Svpported now by Clouds descend, 16–18, 40*f*, 40–42
Table of Musical Contents, 26–59
Third Measure: *The third of the Lords,* 58*f*, 58
Wooe her and win her, 19*f*–20*f*, 19–20, 43*f*–45*f*, 43–44, 45–46
Love Freed from Ignorance and Folly (Jonson), 12–13, 62
Lupo, Thomas, 12–13

Marot, Clément, 165–66
Masque of Beauty (Jonson), 16–17
Masque of Blackness (Jonson), 16–17
The Masque of the Inner Temple and Gray's Inn (Beaumont)
   On blessed youthes, for Joue doth pause, 141–43, 141*f*
   at the entrance of the King, 127–36
   First Antimasque concludes, 132*f*, 132–33
   First Antimasque-Nymphs, 116, 129*f*, 130–31
   first line index, 155–56
   index to song sources, 153–55
   introduction to, 3–10, 113*f*, 114–22
   knights attire, 136–37
   Maine Masque, 136
   More pleasing were these sweet delights, 144*f*, 144–46
   payment for, 114
   priests habits, 137
   Second Antimasque— May-Dance, 133*f*, 135
   Shake off your heauy traunce, 137–39, 137*f*
   summary of, 152–53
   Table of Musical Contents, 123–49
   Ye should stay longer if we durst, 146–49, 146*f*
The Masque of Truth (Jocquet)
   authorship, 168–70
   Ballet CCLIX, 199*f*
   Ballet CCLXVIII, 188*f*
   Ballet des Amazones CCLXX, 198*f*
   Ballet des Anglois CCLXXI, 203*f*
   Ballet des feus CCLXXIX, 193*f*–94*f*

Ballet des Princesses CCLXXVII, 206f
Bransle de la Torche XV, 185f–86f
dances, 170–72
Dramatis Personae, 173–75
introduction to, 159–77
Le Monde te vient faire hommage, 181f
lyrics, 164–68
metrical psalms, 165–68, 176, 211–12
notes on music, 208–16
origins, 162–64
performance, 175–77
Que ceux, à qui la Repentance, 205f
Quittez vos anciennes querelles, 200f
resources, 172–75
Sortez AFFRIQVE monstrueuse, 196f
Sortez EVROPE la premiere, 183f
Sortez Reyne, de qui les yeux, 190f–91f
Table of Musical Contents, 178
transcription of, 179
masquers, 16, 20, 22, 25, 64, 67–68, 115–16, 118–19, 120–21, 172–73
The Memorable Masque of the Middle Temple and Lincoln's Inn (Chapman)
Antemasque— Torchbearers, 99f, 100
Antimasque— Baboons, 85, 86f
Antimasque— Loud Music, 89f, 89
Bright Panthaea borne to Pan, 68, 103f, 104–5
Descend (faire Sun) and sweetly rest, 65, 93–94, 93f
first line index, 155–56
First Measure: *The first of the Temple*, 100f
index to song sources, 153–55
introduction to, 3–10, 60f, 61–71
Now sleepe, binde fast, the flood of Ayre, 68–69, 105f–7f, 106, 108
Ope Earth thy womb of golde, 64, 91f, 91–92
payment for, 61–62
Second Measure: *The second of the Temple*, 101f, 103
Singe, Singe a Rapture to all Nuptial eares, 110f, 110–12
singing of first lyric, 16–17
summary of, 152–53
Table of Musical Contents, 72–112
Third Measure: *The third of the Temple*, 108f, 109
Menestrier, Claude-François, 163
metrical psalms, 165–63, 176, 211–12

Mistris since you so much desire (Campion), 17–18, 119–20
A Musicall Dreame, or the Fourth Booke of Ayres (Jones), 23–24
Musicke of Sundrie Kindes (Ford), 68–69

Newe Ausserlesene liebliche Branden, Intraden, Mascharaden, Balletten (Brade), 4–5, 20
Norbrook, David, 159, 161, 164, 172
Now O now I needs must part (Dowland), 66–67

Oberon, the Faery Prince (Jonson), ix, 61

Pakes, Anna, 8
Praetorius, Michael, 170–72

revels, 22, 49, 67–69, 103, 119–21, 146, 152
Rosseter, Philip, 61, 119–20
Des Rothschencken Tantz, 118

Sabol, Andrew, 4–5, 7–8, 9, 13, 152
Schede, Paul, 165–66
Second Booke of Ayres (Campion), 14–15, 117
The Second Booke of Ayres (Corkine), 69–70
She whose matchles beauty stayneth (Jones), 22
social dances, 67–68, 211
Somerset Masque (Campion), 5, 6–7, 12–13, 19
Standish, John, 165–66
Stuart, Elizabeth, 3–4, 69–70, 73–74, 121–22, 124–25, 159–60, 162–64, 168–70, 176–77, 210
Sylvester, Josuah (Joshua), 168–69

Terpsichore (Praetorius), 170
Third Booke of Ayres (Campion), 24–25, 118
torchbearers, 16, 37f, 62–63, 67–68, 99f, 171–72, 210–14

Ultimum Vale (Jones), 121–22

Walls, Peter, 8–9
Webbe, George, 159–60
Weckherlin, Georg Rudolf, 162–63, 168
Where shee her sacred bowre adornes (Campion), 15
Wofull hart with griefe oppressed (Dowland), 119